100 THINGS
TEXAS A&M FANS
SHOULD KNOW & DO
BEFORE THEY DIE

100 THINGS
TEXAS A&M FANS
SHOULD KNOW & DO
BEFORE THEY DIE

Rusty Burson

TRIUMPH
B O O K S

Library of Congress Cataloging-in-Publication Data

This book is available in quantity at special discounts for your group or organization. For further information, contact:
 Triumph Books LLC
 814 North Franklin Street
 Chicago, Illinois 60610
 (312) 337-0747
 www.triumphbooks.com

Printed in U.S.A.
ISBN: 978-1-60078-839-0
Design by Patricia Frey
Photos courtesy of the author unless otherwise indicated

To one of my all-time best friends and one of the greatest Aggie fans ever, Sandy Heidtke. In June 2012, doctors informed her she had 20+ tumors from her brain down to her legs. They estimated she had six months to live. They were wrong. So wrong. Sandy inspired all of us who love and admire her with her resolute faith in Jesus Christ, her toughness in battling cancer, and her remarkable attitude of gratitude. She overcame more odds in 2012 than even her beloved Aggies in their first year in the SEC.

Contents

Foreword *by Dat Nguyen* xi

Acknowledgments. xiii

Introduction. xv

1 Salute Gen. James Earl Rudder for the Best Decision Ever 1

2 Wear a Bow Tie in Honor of Dr. Loftin 5

3 Give to the 12ᵗʰ Man Foundation 8

4 2012 Heisman Winner Johnny Manziel 13

5 Dat Nguyen. 17

6 Von Miller. 22

7 The Bonfire Game of 1999 24

8 The 1939 Aggies 28

9 The Financial Reward of Winning It All. 31

10 The 1998 Big 12 Championship Game. 33

11 The 2012 Upset of Alabama 36

12 TexAgs.com. 39

13 Stopping Bo in the Cotton Bowl. 44

14 1957 Heisman Winner John David Crow. 46

15 R.C. Slocum 49

16 The Best Loss Ever in 2011. 52

17 A November to Remember in 1985 55

18 John Kimbrough 58

19 Kevin Murray 61

20 Bucky Richardson 64

21 Jackie Sherrill. 67

22 Red, White, and Blue Out 71

23 Dana Bible 74

24 E. King Gill. 78

25 The 1986 Comeback Against Baylor. 81

26 Junction 83

27 Kevin Smith 87

28 Homer Norton 90

29 The 1940 Loss to Texas 92

30 Kiddie Corps. 95

31 Ray Childress. 98

32 Kevin Sumlin 101

33 Emory Bellard 104

34 Edd Hargett 107

35 Luke Joeckel 109

36 The 1956 Texas Game 113

37 The 1975 Texas Game 115

38 Ed Simonini 117

39 The 1967 Texas Game 120

40 Bear Bryant. 123

41 The 1998 Nebraska Game. 125

42 The 1967 Texas Tech Comeback 129

43 Quentin Coryatt and The Hit. 131

44 Chet Brooks and the Wrecking Crew 135

45 The Rise and Fall of the '57 Aggies. 137

46 The 2012 Ole Miss Game. 140

47 The 1990 Holiday Bowl 144

48 The 1975 Loss to Arkansas 147

49 Joe Routt. 149

50 Ryan Swope. 151

51 Lester Hayes 154

52 Darren Lewis. 156

53 Greg Hill. 161

54 Terrence Murphy 163

55 The Texas Special 166

56 Jack Pardee 168

57 Johnny Holland. 172

58 Stay in the Stands for the Fightin' Texas Aggie Band 175

59 12th Man Kickoff Team. 178

60 The 2010 Nebraska Game 180

61 Attend Yell Practice. 182

62 Shane Lechler 185

63 The Rice Comeback in 1955. 189

64 Aaron Wallace. 191

65 Tony Franklin. 194

66 Jacob Green. 196

67 Ryan Tannehill 199

68 Billy Liucci 201

69 Bob Smith. 205

70 The 1968 Cotton Bowl. 207

71 Jake Matthews and His Brothers 209

72 Dave Elmendorf 213

73 Curtis Dickey 215

74 Sam Adams. 217

75 Dave South 219

76 Gene Stallings 222

77 Joe Boyd 224

78 Pat Thomas. 227

79 Ray Mickens 230

80 Aaron Glenn 232

81 Larry Jackson. 235

82 Alan Cannon. 238

83 Homer Jacobs 242

84 Gabe Bock. 245

85 Randy Bullock. 248

86 Forget the Fran Era. 251

87 Beating No. 1 Oklahoma in 2002. 255

88 Brent Zwerneman 257

89 Antonio Armstrong. 259

90 Dan Campbell. 262

91 The McKinney Brothers 265

92 Ty Warren. 267

93 John Roper 270

94 Jerrod Johnson 273

95 Corey Pullig 276

96 Charlie Moran. 278

97 Stealing Tim Brown's Towel. 282

98 Reveille 284

99 The Hurricane Game of 1956. 288

100 Billy Pickard 290

Sources 293

About the Author. 295

Foreword

In the midst of an extremely frustrating, discouraging, and embarrassing redshirt season at Texas A&M in 1994, I seriously contemplated quitting the football team, leaving College Station, and going back home to Rockport. I wasn't exactly sure what I would do next, but at least for a short time, I thought often about writing off my decision to attend A&M as a big mistake, regrouping for a while in my hometown, and possibly transferring to another school to start all over again.

Maybe I still would have wound up with a good degree and a solid football career if I had followed through with those thoughts so long ago and transferred somewhere else. But I have thanked God continuously through the years for guiding me to stick it out through the tough times and stay at A&M.

Looking back on it now, it was one of the best decisions of my life. I met my wife and the mother of my three children at Texas A&M; I had some of the greatest times of my life and earned a degree from A&M; I was part of 35 victories, three bowl games, two South Division titles, and one Big 12 championship as a player at A&M; I was part of one Big 12 South Division tri-championship and two bowl games as an assistant coach at A&M; and I met some of the best friends and most important connections in my life at Texas A&M, including the author of this book.

I feel uniquely qualified to endorse this book for a variety of reasons. First and foremost, I love Texas A&M football, and I am very proud to have played a part in the history of a prominent and prestigious collegiate program. Secondly, I am intrigued by all the personalities in this book, from recent players like Von Miller and Johnny Manziel to some of the early legends of Aggieland like Joe Routt and Joe Boyd. I also love exploring the history of the program back when coaches like Dana Bible, Homer Norton, and Bear Bryant recruited to an all-male military institution. And finally, I have a pretty close relationship with the author, who has been a friend ever since he wrote the first story about me back in 1995.

After writing that first story in '95, Rusty Burson wrote many other articles about me during my collegiate days, and he also wrote a book with me that was first published in 2005 and was recently released again in paperback. We had a great time crisscrossing the state while doing interviews for the book, as I taught him an appreciation for sushi, and he taught me a few things about sentence structure and punctuation. (At least I let him think he taught me something.)

In all sincerity, Rusty and I have been friends a long time, and I was honored that he asked me to write this foreword. I am sure you will enjoy this stroll down Aggie Memory Lane, which includes more than 100 years of Aggie football moments and memories. I am sure you will disagree with where some items are ranked, why some things have been left out, and why other items were included. Just remember that if you have any complaints or serious disagreements, address them with Rusty, not me. I just handled the foreword. The rest was his responsibility.

Gig 'em and God Bless.

—Dat Nguyen

Acknowledgments

Thanks Dr. R. Bowen Loftin for having the courage to make some extremely difficult decisions on Texas A&M's behalf in 2010 and 2011. It would have been easy to tag along with the Longhorns' westward-bound, Pac-16 mass exodus plans in the summer of 2010. It also would have been easier to merely shake your head in disgust at the audacity of Texas' desire to televise high school games on the Longhorn Network and to manipulate the Big 12's TV policies in Texas' favor in '11. Instead, Loftin took a bold stand and led Texas A&M to the premier football conference in America. He also made another extremely difficult decision to fire former head football coach Mike Sherman after the 2011 season instead of giving him one more year to coach for his life in the SEC. This book wouldn't have happened without the Aggies moving to the SEC or if Sherman had been allowed to coach in it.

Thanks to Kevin Sumlin for bringing a new swagger and "no excuses" mentality to Aggieland. Sumlin's swashbuckling edge gave the 2012 Aggies a confident and courageous advantage that hadn't been evident at Kyle Field—at least by the home team—since the heydays of the Wrecking Crew. Sumlin also hired a remarkable staff, including my old buddy Larry Jackson, who is the best, most effective, and most physically imposing strength and conditioning coach in all of college football. Just look at the difference between the 2011 Aggies, who blew double-digit, second-half leads in five games, and the 2012 Aggies, who finished foes by owning the fourth quarter. No publisher would have approached me about writing this book without Sumlin, Jackson, and the rest of the coaching staff who made 2012 so memorable.

Thanks also to Johnny Manziel, who produced in 2012 the most amazing individual season in the history of Aggie football. Manziel

At The College Football Awards Show. (Photo courtesy of Rusty Burson)

also allowed this longtime Aggie observer to do some things—like fly to New York in December to cover the Heisman Trophy ceremony—that I never imagined I would be able to do. This book definitely wouldn't have been published without the Johnny Football craze that engulfed Aggieland and swept the nation in 2012.

Obviously, this book covers the history of Aggie football and the traditions that make Texas A&M so unique. But nine of the 100 main items involve people, events, or games that happened/played in 2011 and/or '12. These really are historic, celebratory times at Texas A&M, and hopefully, what transpired in 2012 is just the beginning.

If things continue to go as well for A&M in the immediate future as they did in the first year of the SEC, many more A&M football-related books will be written soon. And just to make it public record right here in print: yes, my longtime friend and colleague at the 12th Man Foundation, Homer Jacobs, and I are interested in soon writing the definitive Johnny Manziel book. And the Kevin Sumlin book. And the national title book. And the Larry Jackson workout book…

Until then, enjoy this one. And enjoy these memorable times at Texas A&M.

Introduction

I wrote this book in about three months. At least that's the time frame that passed from when I actually started writing until the day I finished. But realistically, this book is more than 20 years in the making, and it took me writing eight other books before I was fully prepared to write this one.

In 1991, I covered my first Texas A&M football game in College Station as a reporter for the *Galveston Daily News*. One year later, I covered my second one and met my future wife and the mother of my three children at the Dixie Chicken after that last-second A&M win over Texas Tech at Kyle Field.

Texas A&M football has essentially been one of the focal points of my life ever since. That woman I met in 1992, the former Vannessa Blasingame, started really giving me a chance to win her heart after I introduced her to star running back Greg Hill in a College Station Jack in the Box. We planned our wedding in 1993 around football season and sang the "War Hymn" as part of the reception. We later scheduled the births of our three kids—Payton, Kyleigh (named after Kyle Field), and Summer—around football season.

Most of the significant vacations in our married lives have involved Aggie away games (the Sugar Bowl, Notre Dame, Pittsburgh, Utah, the Holiday Bowl, etc.) or 12th Man Foundation summer board meetings. Most of our free time today is spent at Aggie athletic events, whether they are being played at Kyle Field, Olsen Field at Blue Bell Park, Reed Arena, or some other venue. And many of our friends are former A&M athletes, current A&M athletic department employees, or former A&M students.

On top of all that, I have spent the last 22 years writing A&M stories for publications such as the *Galveston Daily News*, *Fort Worth Star-Telegram*, *Aggies Illustrated*, and *12th Man Magazine*. By

March 2013, I had also written eight A&M-related books about Aggie players, coaches, games, facilities, or historical events.

Most people would think—and I certainly thought—that all of the aforementioned experiences and qualifiers would make this a really easy book to write. And honestly, it wasn't too difficult to write. But it was agonizing, excruciating, and next-to-impossible for me to conclusively rank the items and to eliminate so many people, events, traditions, and so forth that did not make the final cut.

Quite frankly, I initially stressed over the rankings so much that I finally threw up my hands and simply began writing as fast as I could without worrying about who wasn't on the list and where people, events, and games were positioned. But then I began shuffling the rankings as I went along. Over and over and over again. If I didn't shave my head already, I would have pulled out my hair.

What you have in your hands now are my final rankings. Thank God I can't change them anymore. But I am still not sure I ranked them accurately or appropriately. And I don't expect you to agree with how they are ranked, either. You could argue that Marshall Robnett, Jack Little, Tommy Maxwell, Steve O'Neal, Dennis Goehring, Maurice Moorman, Garth Ten Naple, Doug Williams, Mike Arthur, and Marcus Buckley—who were each named to All-American teams—should have been on the list or at least mentioned in the sidebars. Trust me, I considered them all and would have definitely included them all if there had not been a word-count limit.

But what I tried to do in my rankings was to take an all-encompassing look at Aggie football that included more than merely the games, players, and coaches. I also attempted to include some key administrators, behind-the-scenes personnel, and even media members who shape the perception of the Aggies, which added more possibilities for inclusion in the book and more anguish for me.

The funny thing is that I actually thought that writing this book would be so much easier than the *100 Things Rangers Fans Should Know & Do Before They Die* book I wrote in 2012. But the Rangers' history in Texas only dates back to 1972. The Aggies were playing football for 78 years before that, which opens up so many other possibilities to include here.

Ultimately, I stopped agonizing about the rankings on the day I finally sent it to the publisher, March 25, 2013. But I'd love for you to stir up all those anguishing memories after you read through the book. Let me know your comments, suggestions, and even your complaints by following me on Twitter (@12thManRusty). I'd love to hear what you think…especially since it is finally too late for me to change it.

Enjoy the journey, and let the debate begin.

1 Salute Gen. James Earl Rudder for the Best Decision Ever

If World War II had never taken place, it's conceivable that James Earl Rudder could have been hired as the head football coach at Texas A&M. After all, Rudder, a 1930 graduate of A&M, had already earned his first collegiate head coaching job at John Tarleton Agricultural College (now Tarleton State) by the time he was 28 in 1938.

Perhaps Rudder could have succeeded Homer Norton as head coach in Aggieland in 1948 instead of Harry Stiteler, who "led" A&M to its only winless season in school history and lasted only three years in College Station. Perhaps Rudder could have prevented A&M from falling upon such unfortunate football times, as the Aggies were just 28–56–7 from 1946–54.

Maybe Rudder, with his legendary leadership skills, would have been so successful at his alma mater that the Aggies would have never needed to lure Paul "Bear" Bryant from Kentucky.

We'll never know, as World War II did occur, and Rudder became one of the most revered military heroes of the D-Day invasion. As commander and trainer of the Second Ranger Battalion, Rudder's Rangers stormed the beach at Pointe du Hoc and, under constant enemy fire, scaled 100' cliffs to reach and destroy German gun batteries. The perilous mission resulted in a higher than 50 percent casualty rate, and Rudder was wounded twice during the fighting.

He later became Texas Land Commissioner and served as the 16th president of Texas A&M from 1959 until his death in March 1970.

Sul Ross: The Man Who First Saved A&MC

When the Agricultural and Mechanical College of Texas opened its doors on October 4, 1876, as the first public institution of higher learning in Texas, there was a little town north of campus called Bryan, which had been established in 1859 and incorporated in 1871. College Station didn't officially exist until 1877 when the Postal Service named it a railway stop. So it would be fair—and accurate—to say A&M was built in the middle of nowhere.

The location for A&M was chosen primarily because the school would be situated roughly in the middle of Dallas, Houston, and Austin. But lawmakers in Austin were not necessarily looking out for A&M's best interests.

Even though A&M opened its doors a few years before the University of Texas, A&M was considered—by design of lawmakers—as an annex to UT. All along, lawmakers planned for the school in Austin to feature a diverse and broad-based academic curriculum, while A&M would be limited to only agricultural and mechanical studies.

By the time UT was officially founded in 1883, A&M was a fledgling school. Rumors swirled across the state that the school was on the verge of being shut down because of poor management and other issues. It was not until 1891, when a former two-term governor of Texas named Lawrence Sullivan Ross arrived as the school's president, that A&M found its niche.

Ross declared that, in order to survive, A&M's central mission would be military training. Classes soon took somewhat of a backseat to military training, and A&M began to establish its legacy as the all-male, all-military outpost that welcomed brave, common men of meager means without reservation. In those earliest days, students went to the University of Texas to focus on their core classes; young men went to Texas A&M to become part of the Corps of Cadets.

Everything at A&M became centered around military tradition and training. With no female companions on campus to distract them and little else in the immediate community, the cadets stayed on campus, marched together, drilled together, trained together, attended classes together, and ate together. Many of A&M's traditions started during Ross' time as president, and from the time he assumed control of the university in 1891 until he died on January 3, 1898, at the age of 59, the university experienced tremendous growth in its enrollment and its facilities.

He saved A&M from extinction and, perhaps most significantly for the sake of this book, the Aggies began playing football in 1894—during Sul Ross' tenure as president.

Ross is still having an impact in the community. Students place pennies at the feet of the "Sully" statue of Ross in the academic plaza, hoping for good luck on exams. The tradition stems from the story of when Ross was president of A&M and was always willing to help students with anything, even tutoring for class. When the students offered to pay him, all he would accept was a penny.

According to a 2009 article in *The Battalion*, the pennies are collected every weekend by the Texas A&M chapter of Circle K International, a community-service and leadership-development organization. The pennies are then donated to the local Boys and Girls Club of America.

So put a penny on Sully for good luck...or to support the Boys and Girls Club.

He never officially coached a game for A&M. But he certainly deserves the top spot in any book that documents, celebrates, or pays homage to the evolution of Aggie football. For that matter, Texas A&M wouldn't be Texas A&M as we know it today without Rudder's ground-breaking influence and leadership.

During Rudder's administration, the university doubled its enrollment, expanded its research programs, and improved academic and faculty standards. And one extremely controversial Rudder decision laid the groundwork for future growth and—among other things—athletic success, as Rudder transformed the university by making the military requirement optional and opening admission to women.

Until Rudder's landmark decision in the mid-1960s, A&M was all male, all military, and all but forgotten in the minds of most prospective students and student-athletes in Texas. By 1962, for example, A&M's enrollment barely topped 8,000, as high school students throughout the region chose instead to seek admission to coeducational state universities such as Texas, Texas Tech, and Houston.

Rudder could envision an increasingly bleak future for the university, and instead of allowing his alma mater to dwindle into obscurity, he forced radical changes during the recess of an Association of Former Students (AFS) board meeting on January 25, 1964. According to Homer Jacobs' book, *The Pride of Aggieland*, it was on that day that Rudder approached John Lindsey, president of the AFS board, and handed him a torn piece of paper with a handwritten note that essentially stated, "Admit women on a full-scale basis."

Although the wives of students and daughters of A&M faculty had been allowed to take courses since the college's earliest days, the idea of a full-fledged coeducational institution had been fought vigorously by students and former students for generations. Lindsey knew the note Rudder had handed him would likely whip the attendees into a volatile frenzy. Nevertheless, Lindsey made his announcement.

"Gen. Rudder gave me a resolution to admit women all the way," Lindsey said to the group following the recess. "He wants it and needs it. Gentlemen, this is the best thing for our university—and now I'm going to call on a vote."

Lindsey later described the scene to Homer Jacobs: "I said, 'Those in favor say aye,' and there were some ayes. I then said, 'All opposed say no,' and there were a lot of them. But I said, 'The ayes have it,' and that was that. Many of the men were yelling for another voice vote or ballot vote, but I refused."

With that "vote," Rudder had all he needed for the board of directors to provide the green light to admitting women. At first, the growth of the female student population was extremely slow, but by 1974–75, one-fourth of the student body was made up of women.

Not coincidentally, the 1974 and '75 football teams at A&M finished in the Top 20 of the final Associated Press rankings for the first time since Bear Bryant had departed the school in the late 1950s. Recruiting the top male athletes to A&M suddenly became much easier with female students on campus. Quite frankly, women made winning on a consistent basis a possibility at A&M.

2 Wear a Bow Tie in Honor of Dr. Loftin

On January 18, 2013, Texas A&M officials announced that the historic end of the Aggies' 2012 football season—the school's first in the SEC and one that culminated in Johnny Manziel winning the Heisman Trophy and A&M trouncing Oklahoma in the Cotton Bowl—translated into $37 million in media exposure for the university. That figure, based on research conducted by Joyce Julius & Associates, covered a two-month stretch that began on November 10, 2012, the day of the Aggies' road victory over eventual national champion Alabama, and concluded on January 6, 2013, two days after the Cotton Bowl.

One week later, an in-house study was released, revealing that the Texas A&M University System generated an estimated $4.3 billion for the Bryan–College Station community in 2012. That was a $540 million increase over 2011 and a $2.2 billion increase since 2002. University and city officials concluded that much of the increase in the contribution to the local economy was linked to A&M's move to the SEC, as attendance at athletic events increased by about 98,000 in 2012 from the previous year.

In other words, the move to the SEC has already been financially beneficial, and it has generated an unprecedented amount of national media attention, praise, and positive publicity for a university that in previous years and decades was often in desperate need of a marketing and public relations shot in the arm. And the best news from A&M's standpoint is that those financial figures and media impressions are merely the tip of the iceberg. The Aggies' future in their new league—which will include increasing brand value, licensing and sponsorship opportunities, the SEC Network income, and so much more—is as bright as the summertime sun in Central Texas.

The bold transition from the Big 12 to the SEC may ultimately prove to be the second-best decision in the university's history in terms of its positive effect on the long-term future of A&M, and the forward-thinking man most responsible for pulling the trigger on that much-debated move is Dr. R. Bowen Loftin, the 24th president of Texas A&M and the visionary with the trademark bowtie.

Loftin, who first served as interim president beginning on June 15, 2009, is a 1970 physics graduate of A&M who holds an M.A. and Ph.D. from Rice. He's an articulate, personable, unassuming, and highly intelligent man who has the rare ability to relate to regents, professors, and today's students with a distinctive flair that is both professional and amiable. Most significantly—at least in terms of how it relates to this book—Loftin understands and embraces the far-reaching power of a strong athletics department that serves as the university's public relations front porch.

He also possesses the self-confidence—in himself and the increasingly powerful university brand he represents—to take a stand against moves that might not be in A&M's best interest. That was obvious in the summer of 2010 when Loftin and university Board of Regents member Jim Wilson, among others, tapped the breaks on the Pac-10 expansion train that was being driven by University of Texas president Bill Powers, Longhorns AD DeLoss Dodds, and Pac-10 commissioner Larry Scott. Behind closed doors, Texas officials had essentially arranged for Texas A&M, Texas Tech, Oklahoma, Oklahoma State, and Colorado to be included with the Longhorns in a landscape-altering move that would have created the Pac-16.

Instead of merely latching on to the Longhorns' coattails—as the rest of the aforementioned schools seemed more than willing to do—Loftin, Wilson, and other A&M officials tossed a wrench in the fast-moving "Powers play," announcing that the Aggies would first explore all options, including a possible move to the SEC, before blindly hitching one of the most proudly conservative universities in the country with left-coast/left-wing schools like Cal-Berkeley, UCLA, and so forth.

As it explored SEC membership, A&M temporarily saved the Big 12 and derailed the Longhorns' initial plans.

The following summer, as Texas celebrated the Longhorn Network and distanced itself financially from the rest of the Big 12, Loftin re-engaged SEC commissioner Mike Slive and laid the groundwork for what Loftin coined as a "100-year decision." After Loftin navigated the school through legal hurdles in the summer, A&M officially became the 13th member of the SEC in September 2011.

Thanks to an aggressive marketing and brand-awareness plan that was crafted and guided by Jason Cook, the vice president for marketing and communications and one of Loftin's best hires, A&M capitalized on the move to the SEC by winning public relations battles in the media, strategically shaping its own messages, and taking the university brand to new heights.

Loftin punched all the right buttons and made the necessary calls throughout the transition to the SEC, and he ultimately paved the way for the incredible success of the Aggies' first football season in the SEC when he made the extremely difficult final call on firing former head coach Mike Sherman after A&M finished at 6–6 in the 2011 regular season.

If Sherman had not been fired, Kevin Sumlin would have likely left the University of Houston to fill the opening at Arizona State, and Manziel may have played receiver at A&M or possibly served as the backup quarterback to Jameill Showers, who was more of a pure dropback pocket passer that Sherman liked for his traditional offense. There would have been no Heisman, and there likely would not have been the success that the Aggies enjoyed in 2012.

Nor would there be quite as much optimism regarding A&M's future. So when you are planning your wardrobe for the next big SEC game day in College Station, consider wearing a bowtie in honor of the president who has made it all possible.

3 Give to the 12ᵗʰ Man Foundation

One of the primary reasons Kyle Field has received national acclaim for its phenomenal atmosphere on game days is that Aggies do not merely come to a game to watch the action; they attend a game hoping to impact it with their passionate support.

Since the mid-1890s when football first began at A&M, Aggies have often viewed their game-day role in the stands more seriously than fans from other schools. That's why they attend yell practice the night before a game; that's why they do not boo their own team; and that's why students still stand symbolically throughout the game, united, as the 12ᵗʰ Man. Each Aggie is trained to do his/her part at Kyle Field.

If those fans would take the same approach to their financial support of athletics, however, the Aggies would likely have many more championships to celebrate.

But the reality is that only a small percentage of A&M former students give back financially to support athletics. According to various sources, there are more than 350,000 living former A&M students. As of March 2013, however, the 12th Man Foundation, the fundraising organization of A&M athletics, registered only 17,617 active donors (excluding first-year graduates who receive a one-year free membership). In other words, more than 330,000 living A&M graduates do not annually provide financial support to athletics through the 12th Man Foundation.

"Former students and fans of Texas A&M are known nationally for their rabid support of Aggie athletics on the competition fields and courts," said Mark Riordan, the 12th Man Foundation's vice president of marketing and brand management. "While this form of support is essential to the Aggie experience, we also need Aggies everywhere to step up and support athletics financially. Your financial support is necessary for A&M athletics to be competitive in the SEC and nationally, now and for years to come. There's a perception that you need to give major, six- or seven-figure donations to make any kind of a difference, but former students and fans could collectively make a huge difference by simply donating at the minimum of $150 per year."

Since its inception on April 2, 1950, the 12th Man Foundation has evolved into one of the most respected fundraising organizations in collegiate athletics. In 1950, the 12th Man Foundation—then known as The Aggie Club—raised $16,182 in annual funds. In 2001, the Foundation topped $10 million in annual giving for the first time, and in 2011–12, the organization raised nearly $23 million in annual funds. The donor base has also grown significantly in recent decades. In 1990, the 12th Man Foundation had only 5,000 donors.

While the increases in total donors and dollars raised are impressive, consider how much more could be raised annually to

Miles Marks: Implementing "Major" Changes at the 12th Man Foundation

Miles Marks grew up in an Aggie family in Beaumont, dreaming about one day making an impact at Texas A&M. And Marks eventually fulfilled his childhood dreams by graduating from A&M with a degree in accounting in 1979 and earning his MBA in '82.

Marks also met and married the former Molly Wehner, who has deep family ties to A&M. Marks left a positive impression on Aggieland as a student. But it wasn't until many years later that he truly left a legacy.

After working in the banking industry in Houston for 15 years, Marks became the president and CEO of the 12th Man Foundation on the first day of 1998. He inherited a small, 12-person full-time staff that was split into two small offices and focused entirely on annual fundraising.

Shortly thereafter, Marks expanded the organization's staff and vision, hiring a major gifts fundraiser and embarking on a capital campaign to begin reshaping A&M's athletic facilities. On February 14, 2000, the 12th Man Foundation staff moved into its far more expansive offices inside The Bernard C. Richardson Zone, and just more than a month later, the Championship Vision capital campaign was unveiled.

Since then, the 12th Man Foundation has grown significantly in the size of its staff, adding an entire ticketing department to handle all A&M athletic events and numerous other staff members. And the athletic facilities landscape has been completely altered thanks to the generosity of numerous donors through various phases of capital campaigns. Marks resigned in the fall of 2012 as president and CEO after 15 years with the 12th Man Foundation. But his legacy remains forever intact.

"I am proud that I was able to use my prior experience both in business and as a donor to impact the organization at the right time for A&M," Marks said. "As a prior donor, I felt like the only time I ever heard from the 12th Man Foundation was when money was due. We changed that with better communication, recognition, and events. We grew the involvement of donors to athletics by making them feel like they are part of a family working together to a common goal. I see the quality of the directors I worked to identify and recruit to be on our board, and it's clear we attracted the best and brightest to serve.

"I was also able to hire an incredibly talented staff that is the envy of the athletic fundraising industry. When I introduced the concept of major gift fundraising, it appeared to our board at the time to be a radical expansion of our mission of annual fundraising for scholarships. Today, it is gratifying to see the huge advances in athletic facilities we were able to fund with hundreds of millions of donor gift dollars."

In March 2013, the 12th Man Foundation announced that Irven E. "Skip" Wagner had been named president and CEO and would lead the organization's efforts while embarking on the redevelopment of Kyle Field.

fund athletics if additional former students chose to give annually at the $150 minimum. If 20 percent of the 330,000 former students who do not currently give annually made a minimum donation, it would add 66,000 donors and $9.9 million in annual funds.

Donations are vital to the health of A&M athletics, which are completely self-supporting and cannot receive state money or public tax dollars. Through its donors, the 12th Man Foundation funds scholarships, programs, and facilities in support of championship athletics. In return, the organization offers its donors a variety of benefits, including priority ticket options for football and basketball games and one of the finest sports magazines in the country, *12th Man Magazine*.

While the 12th Man Foundation could certainly use more donors to positively affect the future of A&M athletics, the organization's donors have already dramatically changed Aggie athletics through capital campaigns and major gifts.

The Championship Vision capital campaign was unveiled in 2000 with an original goal of raising $35 million for facility improvements. In a span of 10 years, more than 2,500 families contributed roughly $125 million to fund facilities such as the

Bright Football Complex; the Cox-McFerrin Center for Aggie Basketball; the Alice and Erle Nye Academic Center; the McFerrin (Indoor) Athletic Center; the Rhonda & Frosty Gilliam Indoor Track Stadium; the Carolyn and Jack Little west campus facilities for track and field, cross country, soccer, and softball; the Paul Wahlberg Aggie Golf Learning Center; the Coolidge Grass Practice Fields; Olsen Field at Blue Bell Park; and so much more.

More recently, the 12th Man Foundation's Major Gifts Department has funded the Becky and Monty Davis Aggie Football Player Development Center, the R.C. Slocum Great Hall/Nutrition Center, and the expansion of the Lohman Center at the front of the Bright Complex through the Campaign for Aggie Football. From March 2000 to March 2013, the 12th Man Foundation raised almost $200 million in major gifts donations, and that's just the beginning.

In February 2013, the 12th Man Foundation began the initial fundraising fazes of a proposed $450 million renovation and complete overhaul of Kyle Field, the largest expansion and renovation project in the history of college athletics, to date.

"It is going to require a shared vision that in order to be great in the Southeastern Conference, we need to enhance the intimidation factor of Kyle Field," said Sam Torn, the Chair Elect of the 12th Man Foundation's Board of Trustees. "The design allows us to do that. And everyone needs to understand that we are all going to need to make sacrifices. We all need to commit to doing what Aggies do best—coming together in support of a larger goal. This is something that everyone will be proud of. It's something that everybody will benefit from, and it's something that we all need to contribute to in order to make it happen."

In other words, it's time for many more Aggies to answer the call financially with the same fervor and commitment that has long been a trademark of game days at Kyle Field.

2012 Heisman Winner Johnny Manziel

Prior to the start of Texas A&M's spring practices in 2013, national sports media members began speculating on whether Johnny Manziel would enter the NFL draft following his sophomore season in '13 or perhaps wait until his junior year in '14.

Others pondered in print and on broadcasts whether he'd win one more Heisman Trophy or more, while also opening the debate on the pros and cons of him taking online classes at A&M as opposed to actually sitting in classrooms.

Meanwhile, his legions of Twitter followers, along with the paparazzi, gossip columnists, and supermarket tabloid types, debated the authenticity of his tattoos, the sex appeal of his girl-friend compared to A.J. McCarron's, which high-profile location or major sporting event he might be seen at next, what costume he'd wear next Halloween, and what celebrity he would pose with at his next outing.

With each passing day and every new photograph or news story that featured him on the Internet, it became more and more obvious that Manziel is already the most iconic, captivating, polar-izing, identifiable, and fascinating personality in the history of Texas A&M football. And he essentially became all of that in a span of about five months.

Part of Manziel's transcendent celebrity appeal is that his meteoric rise to fame was so utterly unlikely and involves an out-of-nowhere element that seems more like a Hollywood script than a nonfiction documentary. By the end of the 2012 season, Manziel became a national household name and the first freshman to ever win the Heisman Trophy.

2012 Heisman Trophy winner Johnny Manziel. (Photo by Rusty Burson)

Four months earlier, he was barely known outside the A&M locker room.

Following 2012 spring practices under first-year head coach Kevin Sumlin, sophomore Jameill Showers—Ryan Tannehill's backup under Mike Sherman—appeared to be the leading candidate to be the starting signal caller for the opening of the season. Manziel, a redshirt freshman, had been impressive at times during the spring, but he was often careless with the football.

After streamlining his throwing mechanics under the tutelage of quarterbacks guru George Whitfield, Manziel won the starting position in the summer. Although his tremendous athleticism was obvious and he'd reduced his turnover totals, former offensive coordinator Kliff Kingsbury admitted that the coaches didn't know what kind of weapon they possessed in Manziel.

"[Not tackling him in practice] was a huge part of not knowing what we had," Kingsbury said at the Heisman ceremony in New York. "After the loss to Florida in the opening game of the year, I felt like we could have done a lot more with his legs with quarterback runs. All spring, Coach Sumlin would blow the whistle when the defense would get close. Johnny would come over pissed off, spike the ball, and say, 'They wouldn't have got me.' I said [condescendingly], 'Sure, Johnny, they wouldn't have got you.' But come to find out, they wouldn't have gotten him. He has that type of elusiveness and athleticism."

Manziel's athleticism allowed him to produce huge numbers and jaw-dropping plays in wins over SMU, South Carolina State, Arkansas, Ole Miss, Louisiana Tech, Auburn, and Mississippi State. He played fairly well and produced big plays in losses to Florida and LSU, but his statistics were often viewed skeptically by national media types until November 10.

That's the day everything changed. In front of a sellout crowd at Bryant-Denny Stadium as well as the college football world and a national television audience, Manziel put on a magical performance, producing 345 total yards, two touchdowns, and plenty of gutsy plays in the 29–24 win over Alabama. Manziel maneuvered through the Tide defense like a New York City cab driver, placing the pedal to the metal, weaving in and out of traffic, and passing in tight situations.

After that victory, *Sports Illustrated*'s Andy Staples, in his Week 11 Heisman Watch video, said he'd seen the biggest Heisman moment of the year and that the unwritten rule that prevented freshmen from winning the award needed to be forgotten. He also looked into the camera and addressed fellow Heisman voters, saying that if they were not thinking of voting for Manziel, they were not following the instructions on the ballot.

That video, as well as many others, soon went viral and probably had a major role in focusing Heisman attention on Manziel.

The national scrutiny increased significantly after Manziel won the Heisman and went on a lengthy celebrity appearance tour that included appearances on *Late Show with David Letterman, Fox & Friends, Good Morning America*, and many other television shows.

Skeptics wondered if he'd be ready for the Cotton Bowl after all the fanfare. He quickly put those concerns to rest, as Manziel accounted for 516 rushing and passing yards in leading the Aggies to a 41–13 thrashing of Oklahoma.

"Johnny Manziel is everything he was billed to be, expected him to be," Oklahoma coach Bob Stoops said afterward.

There's no reason to believe that Manziel won't handle future challenges just as spectacularly as he handled growing expectations throughout the 2012 season. But no matter what happens in the future, Johnny Football has already permanently carved his place into Texas A&M's athletic Mount Rushmore among the greatest athletes to ever wear a Maroon and White uniform.

Even if Manziel never played another down after the 2013 Cotton Bowl, a strong case could be made that he was already the most impactful player in A&M history…and quite possibly the best ever. One other Aggie has won the Heisman Trophy, but no player in school history has ever brought more positive publicity to the program, the A&M brand, and the national image than Manziel. Likewise, no Aggie has ever transcended the game quite like Johnny Football.

And his mesmerizing story is just at its beginning.

Dat Nguyen

Before Johnny Manziel came out of nowhere to win the Heisman Trophy in 2012, perhaps the most captivating national story regarding an Aggie football player belonged to linebacker Dat Nguyen, who was born in a Vietnamese refugee camp in Arkansas and went on to live the American dream to its fullest, earning All-American honors at A&M and even playing for "America's Team" in the NFL.

Many Aggies know at least something about the Nguyen family's miraculous journey from Southeast Asia to south Texas and Nguyen's Aggieland transformation from "Fat Dat" to Wrecking Crew legend. But here's a nugget that may have gone unnoticed after Nguyen returned as an assistant coach on Mike Sherman's staff in 2010–11.

Nguyen also played a role—albeit a small one—in luring Manziel to College Station. Nguyen and former A&M quarterbacks coach Tom Rossley scouted the Kerrville Tivy–San Antonio Madison game after Manziel had committed to Oregon. Rossley was already completely sold on Manziel's multiple skills, and after Nguyen witnessed Manziel in person, he also told Sherman that Manziel was such a sensational playmaker that the Aggies needed

Dat Nguyen is the all-time leading tackler in A&M history.
(Photo courtesy of 12ᵗʰ Man Magazine)

to do everything possible to persuade him not to leave the Lone Star State.

Manziel wasn't the tall prototypical pocket passer that Sherman coveted, but…"The guy was just a playmaker and a phenomenal football player," Nguyen recalled. "Coach Rossley was the lead guy on that recruiting trail, and I was just the guy tagging along with him and confirming everything Tom told Mike. Manziel may have been undersized as a quarterback in the estimation of some, but he clearly had a great presence on the field. He made things happen and was absolutely the best player on the field."

That exact description was also applicable during the playing days of the 5'11" Nguyen, who exceeded everyone's expectations at virtually every level. The guy was just a playmaker and a phenomenal football player. Period.

Unfortunately for Nguyen, his second tenure as part of the A&M football program did not ultimately turn out as he had hoped. As an assistant coach, he played a major role in the Aggies' defensive revival in 2010, and former inside linebacker Michael Hodges credited Nguyen for his tremendous development as a senior. But after the 6–6 regular season in 2011, Sherman was fired and Kevin Sumlin brought in an entirely new staff.

As a result, Nguyen's return to Aggieland, which began with a memorable introduction at an A&M-Texas basketball game and a standing ovation from the maroon masses at Reed Arena, ended unceremoniously. But that didn't diminish his legendary status at his alma mater. Because of how he played the game and how he represented A&M as a player, Nguyen is probably still the most popular defender in A&M history.

He is certainly the most prominent tackler in the A&M record books, as Nguyen shattered the school records with 517 career stops from 1995–98. He made 51 consecutive starts at A&M, earned SWC Defensive Newcomer of the Year honors in 1995,

Read *Dat: Tackling Life and the NFL*

According to a long list of New York publishers who rejected the book proposal, Dat Nguyen simply didn't possess a big enough name nationally at the time (2003–04) to warrant a book.

Fortunately, Texas A&M University Press was willing to take a chance on publishing *Dat: Tackling Life and the NFL*, and the book immediately became one of the all-time best sellers that the campus-based publishing house had ever produced.

While the book, originally released in 2005 and now available in paperback, certainly has a football focus, it's so much more than that. Nguyen recounts his father's decision to flee Vietnam; the boat trip that took his family to freedom; and their eventual settling in Rockport, Texas, where a community of Vietnamese shrimpers established an economic livelihood using skills brought from the old country. He describes the racism his family encountered while he was growing up and how the friendship of one young Caucasian boy and his family overcame prejudice through an invitation to participate in sports. He also describes his humorous courting of his wife, Becky, during his college days.

The *San Antonio Express-News* described the book this way in its review: "It is a compelling story of survival, both on and off the football field. For fans of stories in which the human spirit and a deep religious faith triumph over obstacles and adversity, the book is an inspiration. It takes you behind the locker room door into the workings of the [Dallas Cowboys'] franchise."

was a three-time All-Big 12 performer, and helped lead the Aggies to the 1998 Big 12 championship, the same year he won the Lombardi and Chuck Bednarik Awards.

Not bad for a kid who was extremely lucky to have even made it to America.

Nguyen's family, which once lived happily in a South Vietnam village called Ben Da, narrowly escaped the mortar fire, land-mines, and machine guns of the North Vietnamese Army on April 28, 1975. His mother, pregnant with Dat at the time, along his brothers, sisters, and about 25 other refugees, made it to Thailand some 30 days later. Another 30-day wait followed in a Thailand port before a Catholic church in the U.S. sponsored his family's move to America. Nguyen was born in an Arkansas refugee camp, and his family eventually settled on the Texas coastline in Rockport.

At Rockport-Fulton High, Nguyen helped to unite a racially divided community by starring on the football field and earning a scholarship to A&M. But before his rise to prominence in Aggieland, he almost quit the team.

In 1994, Nguyen was one of five linebackers the Aggies signed. Of those five, he was the least known, the most out of shape, and the only one who did not play as a true freshman. He seriously considered transferring or quitting, but he eventually resolved to reshape his body and refocus his mind. Because of an injury to Trent Driver days before the 1995 season opener, Nguyen was inserted as the Aggies' starting inside linebacker against LSU.

He started every game from that point forward, leading the team in stops in each of his four seasons as a starter. Despite concerns about his size, Nguyen was selected in the third round of the NFL draft by the Dallas Cowboys.

"My career at A&M was just such a blessing," said Nguyen, who met his wife, Becky, while playing at A&M. "I played with so many great guys and met so many tremendous people. I'll always be grateful for the opportunity I had at A&M, and it obviously shaped my future."

Nguyen became the first player of Vietnamese descent to play in the NFL, and he spent seven seasons with the Cowboys, leading the team in tackles in three of his final five years. Then in 2007, he joined the Dallas staff as an assistant linebackers coach and defensive quality control representative before returning to Aggieland with his wife and three daughters.

After Sherman was fired, Nguyen considered several career options, including a possible return to the Cowboys. Instead he chose to begin a career as a sports-talk radio co-host with ESPN Radio in San Antonio.

6 Von Miller

Following the 2009 season—a year in which he led the nation in sacks with 17—Texas A&M defensive end/outside linebacker Von Miller seriously considered leaving school early to enter the NFL draft, where he likely would have been a second- or third-round selection. But after consultation and carefully considering all of his options, Miller ultimately decided to return for his senior year in hopes of improving his draft status.

He did so much more than that.

Miller's sack productivity actually went down as a senior in 2010, as he dealt with an ankle injury. Also, opponents consistently used double- and triple-team blocking schemes against the ultra-athletic Miller, who earned the nickname "The Matrix" because of his ability to twist and contort his body to avoid blockers.

Despite the added attention from opponents and the high ankle sprain, Miller still managed 10.5 sacks and 17.5 tackles for losses as a senior. Beyond that, he became the bespectacled face of the Aggies' defensive revival that helped A&M end the 2010 season on a six-game winning streak and earn a share of the Big 12 South title. Miller was so outspoken in his love for A&M and his appreciation of Aggies' fans that he became probably the most popular player to wear the Maroon and White since Dat Nguyen last suited up in the 1999 Sugar Bowl.

Miller, a consensus All-American and the first A&M recipient of the Butkus Award in 2010, was probably the Aggies' first social-media/multimedia rock star, which was evident by the thousands of A&M fans who wore replica Von Miller glasses to the 2011 Cotton Bowl.

Even after playing his final game for the Aggies, Miller continually promoted Aggieland as his draft stock skyrocketed following sensational performances at the Senior Bowl and the NFL Combine. Miller ended virtually every interview with every media outlet with his trademark phrase: "Thanks and gig 'em."

In April 2011, Miller was the second overall pick in the first round, joining Quentin Coryatt (1992), John David Crow (1958), and John Kimbrough (1941) as the highest draft selections in A&M history. Later that year, Miller went from regional rock star to national sensation by bursting onto the scene during his rookie season with the Denver Broncos.

Through the first 10 games of the 2011 season—prior to a thumb injury requiring surgery forced him to miss a game and reduced his maneuverability—Miller produced 9.5 sacks, which put him on pace to break Jevon Kearse's NFL rookie sack record set in 1999.

"It's time we forgot talk of best rookie and started to think in terms of Pro-Bowl, All-Pro, maybe even Defensive Player of the Year," wrote Sam Monson of ProFootballFocus.com after Miller's sensational start.

Unfortunately, the injury to Miller's right thumb also forced him to wear a huge cast for the remaining four regular season games and two playoff games. The injury dramatically reduced Miller's dominance the rest of the way, but he was still selected as the NFL's Defensive Rookie of the Year, and he was also chosen to play in the Pro Bowl as a rookie.

Miller vowed during the 2012 off-season to work harder and be even better during his second season, and he once again delivered in grand style. He finished the 2012 season with 18.5 sacks, six forced fumbles, and his first career touchdown on an interception return. He was a first-team All-Pro selection and was chosen as a Pro Bowl starter. And in a glowing mid-January 2013 feature in *Sports Illustrated*, fellow Denver linebacker D.J. Williams said that he had pulled Miller aside as a rookie and told him, "'If you can play off-the-ball linebacker as well as you rush the passer, within three years you'll be the best defensive player in the league, hands-down.' [In 2012] he applied himself to being a true linebacker. He's definitely on his way to being the hands-down guy.'"

Throughout his meteoric rise to national stardom, Miller has continued to proudly use his pedestal to promote Texas A&M to football fans across the country. Don't expect that to change anytime soon.

"It's not a chore for me [to promote A&M]," Miller told *12th Man Magazine*. "I don't have to be conscientious about talking about A&M. It's just who I am. It just happens. I don't think, 'Man, I need to talk about A&M.' I have been saying 'gig 'em' so long that it just flows out of my mouth. It's just a part of who I am. But I certainly want to represent A&M whenever I can in the brightest light."

7 The Bonfire Game of 1999

At 2:42 in the morning on November 18, 1999, Texas A&M was forever changed. Since 1909, when Aggies first gathered around a burning trash heap, bonfire had served as a symbolic reminder that A&M possessed a spirit like no other rival. As the decades passed, bonfire grew from a garbage pile to a grandiose, six-tiered stack of some 6,000 logs.

But no matter its size, bonfire was always primarily about bonding. Each year, roughly 5,000 students dedicated approximately 125,000 man hours to erect the monstrous structure that would burn prior to the annual Texas game in front of 50,000 to 70,000 students, former students, and fans.

Bonfire started as an emblematic campfire of sorts, symbolizing A&M's burning desire to beat the hell outta Texas. But it became so much more than that. From the camaraderie of "the cut" to the final frantic days of "push," building bonfire became an annual rite of passage.

In the wee hours of the morning on November 18, 1999, as Push Week—a time when students worked six-hour shifts, 24 hours a day—the stack was again taking shape, climbing 40 feet into the crisp fall air. The site was buzzing with activity as 50 or more students straddled swings, climbed logs, and barked commands like generations of Aggie students had done before.

But this would not be another ordinary November morning in Aggieland. It would be a day of mourning like never before.

Shortly after 2:30 AM, the stack began to shift. The grinding and cracking of monstrous logs pierced the air. Bonfire was coming down in a massive, morbid heap. The majority of the students on the stack survived the harrowing crash, riding the logs to the ground like surfers. Others were thrown from the stack, breaking limbs as they hit the ground beyond the perimeter.

They were the lucky ones. By the afternoon of November 18, exhausted rescue workers had pulled 11 dead Aggies from the twisted, mangled stack. A 12th victim, Tim Kerlee, was removed from the stack alive, but after battling severe internal injuries for 48 hours, the 17-year-old was pronounced dead.

The university mourned; the community grieved; and Aggies around the world dropped to their knees as national newscasters delivered shocking reports. Football practice was canceled that afternoon as A&M players joined rescue workers and other students to remove logs. One blood drive in Houston collected 228 units of blood in a few hours. At a memorial service that night, more than 12,000 Aggies and some Longhorns gathered inside Reed Arena to pray and pay tribute to the injured and deceased.

In the days following the tragic collapse, there was some discussion about not playing the November 26 game against the Longhorns. "But very quickly, we decided that at some point we had to move forward and let the healing process begin," said former A&M head coach R.C. Slocum. "In hindsight, we made the right decision. But in all my years of coaching, I've never been a part of an atmosphere quite like that. The emotions of that day were the most unique I've ever experienced."

One of the most surreal events happened the night before the game, when bonfire had been scheduled to burn. Roughly 50,000 people gathered at the accident site for a candlelight vigil. Both the future and former presidents from the Bush family joined the tribute as candles flickered in the breeze in perhaps the most memorable tribute ever in Aggieland.

Game day, however, was even more memorable. The pregame ceremonies included tributes such as Air Force jets, piloted by A&M former students, flying over Kyle Field in the "missing man" formation. Twelve doves were released in honor of the 12 victims, and a moment of silence was observed.

A record-setting crowd of 86,128 had spent much of the previous eight days choking back tears. They needed a reason to smile; they needed a release; they needed a reason to cheer. The Aggies provided that and more. On a day charged with emotion and filled with meaning, A&M fell behind early and trailed 16–6 at the half. But as the game wore on, Ja'Mar Toombs and D'Andre Hardeman began to wear down Texas' outstanding defensive front.

Toombs brought the Aggies to within 16–13 on a 9-yard run late in the third quarter, and the Aggie defense shut down the No. 7–ranked Longhorns throughout the second half, setting up a

Visit the Bonfire Memorial

While visiting the Bonfire Memorial on the Texas A&M campus will likely elicit tears and tragic memories, it's a must for Aggies who remember bonfire and all those who are too young to recall what a spectacular event it was on campus for so long.

The memorial embodies many layers of meaning associated with the Aggie Spirit—a deep sense of belonging, a strong spirit of teamwork and leadership, and an enduring sense of tradition that unites thousands. The Bonfire Memorial celebrates the tradition, history, and spirit of A&M, and the dedication of those involved in the tragic collapse of the 1999 bonfire.

The Tradition Plaza marks the entrance to the memorial and reflects on activities that bring Aggies together, while the History Walk portrays the 90 years of bonfire preceding the 1999 collapse. The granite timeline is comprised of 89 stones arranged in a north-south line and begins with 1909, the first year bonfire was built on campus. A break in the timeline in 1963 signifies the year John F. Kennedy was assassinated and the only year that bonfire did not burn.

Finally, the Spirit Ring surrounds the site of the 1999 bonfire, and the 12 portals are oriented toward the hometowns of those who died. Twenty-seven stones with bronze inlays represent the injured students in '99 and connect the portals to complete the circle.

memorable fourth-quarter drive that Randy McCown engineered. With 5:02 left in the game, McCown hit his close friend, Matt Bumgardner, for a 14-yard touchdown pass that gave the Aggies a 20–16 lead.

"The ball came up and went right through the sun," Bumgardner said. "I lost it for a second. It's weird to say you were thinking about something at that moment because it happened so fast. But I recall thinking, 'I don't know where this thing is. I sure hope it doesn't hit me in the face mask and bounce off.' I just had my arms in a basket, and I was hoping it came out in the right place. Luckily, it fell right in. That whole game was surreal. In between whistles, it was still just football. But you could tell that even the Texas players were a little subdued because they felt bad about what happened. But we needed to win that game, and to catch the game-winning touchdown was very special."

The special victory was not sealed until the closing seconds. Texas inserted quarterback Major Applewhite in the final minutes, and the Longhorns began mounting a drive that had Aggie fans holding their collective breath. Texas was near midfield when A&M defensive back Jay Brooks came on a blitz, stripping Applewhite of the ball. At the bottom of a pile, freshman linebacker Brian Gamble came up with the loose ball. Gamble dropped to his knees, holding his arms up toward the heavens to commemorate what is likely the most emotionally meaningful win in A&M history.

"Even at that moment, I knew that recovering that fumble and winning that game would be one of the most unforgettable moments of my life," Gamble said. "We never had a doubt that we would win that game; we always believed something would happen in our favor to help us win it. We had endured plenty of disappointments throughout that season, and Texas was probably a much better team—at least on paper. But we knew that was more than a game; we knew we had to win it."

The 1939 Aggies

From 1940 through the end of the 2012 season, Texas A&M has had several teams in prime position to make a run at the national championship late in the year (1940, '57, and '75, for example). A&M also produced two teams (1956 and '94) that finished the year with an unbeaten record, although each team had a tie and was ineligible for a bowl game because of NCAA probation.

The Aggies have also fielded a couple of teams in recent history that were playing so well at the end of the season (1985 and 2012) that they could have won a national championship playoff...if one had existed at the time.

But entering the 2013 season, no A&M football team had replicated what the 1939 squad achieved. At the time of this writing, it is still the only team in school history to go undefeated in the regular season, win a bowl game, and finish atop the Associated Press final national rankings. At that time, however, most of the players on the team had no idea that they had achieved something so significant.

"We didn't know there was such a thing as playing for No. 1," said Tommie Vaughn, the center of the '39 team, prior to his death. "When you look back at what we did, it's very impressive. But it wasn't even a big deal back then. What we had going for us was the fact that we were tough as an old boot."

Like an old boot, the Aggies did some serious kicking. A&M outscored its first four opponents—Oklahoma A&M, Centenary, Santa Clara, and Villanova—by a combined score of 86–10. But the players didn't realize they were anything special until they traveled to Fort Worth for the first Southwest Conference game of the season against defending national champion TCU. The Frogs had beaten A&M 34–6 the previous year.

"We traveled to TCU and kicked their purple-clad butts 20–6 at Amon Carter Stadium," Roy Bucek wrote in his 2012 book, *Roy Story*. "That's when I realized we were really good, and we continued on our roll by beating Baylor 20–0 and Arkansas 27–0. As the season went along, we just kept getting better, as did John Kimbrough. He was really something, and he definitely led us by how hard he played and ran."

After the Arkansas game, the largest crowd (30,000) ever to see a game at Kyle Field poured into the stadium on November 11 to see the Aggies face SMU on a miserably dreary day. With

A&M leading 6–0 in the fourth quarter, SMU drove deep into Aggie territory, and the Mustangs lofted a pass toward the end zone. It was caught, but the conditions were so miserable and the players' uniforms were so muddied that it was initially difficult to determine who came up with the ball. A&M's Derace Moser made the interception, but he then tried to lateral the ball forward. The Aggies were penalized and took possession at their own 5-yard line with a few minutes left in the game.

SMU then stopped the Aggies and blocked Bill Conatser's punt in the end zone. Scrambling through ankle-deep water, Conatser beat several SMU players to the ball to recover it for a safety instead of a Mustangs touchdown. The perfect season was preserved by the narrowest of margins as A&M held on for a 6–2 win.

Following a victory at Rice the next week, a standing-room-only crowd in excess of 38,000 packed into Kyle Field on Thanksgiving Day to watch the Aggies dominate the Longhorns, 20–0.

The closest game all year came in the Sugar Bowl against Tulane on January 1, 1940. Kimbrough's one-yard touchdown run in the first quarter gave the Aggies a 7–0 advantage, but the Green Wave scored the next two touchdowns to take a 13–7 lead in the fourth quarter. A&M then began a 70-yard scoring drive capped by Kimbrough's second scoring run of the day. The ensuing extra point by Cotton Price gave A&M a 14–13 victory and a perfect 11–0 record.

The 1939 team still holds an NCAA record for total team defense, allowing 76.3 yards per game. The Aggies also finished first in the country in rushing defense (41.5 yards per game) and scoring defense (2.8 points allowed per game). Thanks to Kimbrough's running and the dominating defense that registered six shutouts, A&M won eight of 10 regular season games by at least 14 points.

The Financial Reward of Winning It All

Nowadays, college football is a huge business. Winning a national championship can be a financial gold mine for an institution, which explains why Alabama delivered Nick Saban a contract extension in March 2012 that provided a total compensation of nearly $5.5 million.

For that matter, even playing for the national title can result in a financial windfall. *Forbes* magazine estimated that Notre Dame generated $69 million in revenue during its perfect 2012 regular season. And as previously noted, the final two-month stretch of the '12 season for Texas A&M translated into $37 million in media exposure for the university.

While today's financial figures can be mindboggling, the reality is that winning big has always been vital to a program's bottom line. In fact, the Aggies' last national championship did much more for the school's financial foundation than it did for the program's football reputation.

After suffering through bleak seasons under the direction of head coach Madison Bell (1929–33), some of the more frustrated former students at A&M College were in favor of dropping the football program prior to the 1934 season instead of spending the funds to hire a new coach.

But cooler heads prevailed, and a contingent of A&M officials offered the head coaching job to Homer Norton in January 1934. He took it, although he may not have done so if he had known the difficult circumstances he would inherit.

While A&M featured a concrete, 38,000-seat stadium called Kyle Field, Norton did not realize until after he'd taken the job that the stadium's bonded debt was $210,000. Times had been so tough in 1933 that the athletic department had only managed to pay the interest on its debt. Tickets had been slashed to $1.50 apiece, but in the midst of economic uncertainty, filling those seats was a significant problem.

A&M did not even have money for scholarships, and the university could not supply enough jobs—mess hall waiters, uniform pressers, candy salesmen, etc.—to attract potential student-athletes with supplemental funding. Football players were already forced to live four to a room in "project houses" near the south end of the stadium.

"I remember we were practicing prior to the start of the 1939 season, and we had a water break underneath the west side grandstands of Kyle Field," recalled Roy Bucek, a member of the '39 Aggies. "During the break, the stadium's namesake, Edwin Jackson Kyle, Class of 1899, visited with us. Kyle, who at one time or another served as professor of horticulture and president of A&M's General Athletics Association, told us, 'You fellas have a big burden on your backs. We haven't made a principal payment on this stadium in three years. If we don't make a principal payment on the stadium this year, the bank is going to foreclose on us. You understand what that means?'

"We all nodded, as we didn't want to appear like fools, but truthfully, none of us knew what the hell Kyle was talking about. Most of us didn't know what a principal payment was in the first place, and we had only a vague understanding of what might happen if the bank 'foreclosed' on us. I, for one, thought that maybe they'd take the stadium away from us if we didn't put more people in the stands and make money. I'd seen homes and farms that had been foreclosed, and other people moved into them. I wondered if some other football team might move into our stadium."

Fortunately, Bucek and the rest of the '39 team never had to worry about that. A&M averaged an attendance of only 5,000 people in 1938, but the '39 Aggies were 5–0 and ranked fifth nationally by the time A&M played its first SWC home game against Baylor.

That game drew a big crowd, despite an increase in the price of tickets to $2.50 apiece. And despite rainy conditions for the next home game against SMU on November 11, more than 30,000 fans packed Kyle Field on that day. The regular season finale against Texas on November 30 drew a standing-room-only crowd.

"A&M College also received a big paycheck for winning the Sugar Bowl, and that check—along with all the ticket revenues from earlier in the season—helped A&M finally emerge from its huge debt problems," Bucek said. "We had won the title and saved the football program. All the coaches and administrators patted us on the backs and congratulated us when we returned from New Orleans."

The 1998 Big 12 Championship Game

After the breakup of the Southwest Conference following the 1995–96 school year, Texas A&M spent the next 16 years as a member of the Big 12. It certainly isn't difficult to pick one football moment from that era that stands out above all the rest.

In 16 years as a member of the Big 12, the Aggies claimed only one league championship. But that one championship game victory was so shocking, so memorable, and so exhilarating that members of that team are still often reminded about it by former students and fans.

"That was definitely one of my favorite memories from college," former A&M All-Big 12 safety Rich Coady recalled. "I played in St. Louis [with the Rams] with a guy from Kansas State, Jerametrius

Matt Bumgardner makes a leaping catch in the 1998 comeback win over Kansas State. (Photo courtesy of Texas A&M SID)

Butler. We were friends, and he was a good guy, but I never let him forget that game. It is still a great memory for [Aggies], and people still talk to me about it. But it probably gets a lot more credit than it deserves [in A&M circles] because A&M wasn't in that position again throughout the Big 12."

What made the win so unforgettable for so many Aggie fans was the unexpected nature of it. The Wildcats were unbeaten and ranked No. 1 nationally in one poll entering the game against the 10–2 Aggies. To play for the 1998 national championship, K-State needed only two things to happen on December 5: Miami needed to beat UCLA, and the Wildcats needed to beat the Aggies.

The first part of that equation happened. The second part seemed to be unfolding in K-State's favor as the Wildcats built a 27–12 lead in the fourth quarter. However, after the public address announcer inside the Trans World Dome informed the crowd and the K-State players that Miami had beaten UCLA, the Wildcats tightened up.

And one of the most unlikely heroes in A&M history—back-up quarterback Branndon Stewart—led one of the most improbable comebacks for the Aggies. Stewart, who was playing because Randy McCown had been injured the week before in a loss at Texas, delivered a fourth-quarter performance for the ages, tossing darts at A&M's receivers and daggers into K-State's heart.

Stewart, who completed just four passes in the first three quarters of the game, caught fire late. He dissected the nation's No. 2 defense for 324 passing yards, three touchdowns, and 452 yards of total offense. He made it look easy.

"I hate to say it, but it was like [the Wildcats] were leaving guys open on purpose," said Stewart many years later. "It just happened to be the guys I was looking at most of the time. I guess I was in a zone. It seemed like they were going, 'Okay Branndon, we're just going to leave [tight end] Derrick [Spiller] open on this one, so you might want to send him for 20 yards.' It was that easy."

As A&M battled back into contention, Stewart said he could read the frustration in the eyes of the K-State players. Then when A&M pulled to within a touchdown and two-point conversion of the lead, Stewart noticed that the Wildcats' frustration was turning into panic.

"They wanted to get it over with," Stewart said. "It's kind of like the last test you have to take on a Friday before spring break. You have to pass the test, so you can go skiing or hit the beach. But when you finally get into that test, it ends up being a lot more than you expected."

A&M continued to turn up the heat and forced the game into overtime thanks to some key defensive plays and Stewart's pinpoint passing. A&M tied it at 27–27 with 1:05 left in the fourth on a nine-yard pass from Stewart to Sirr Parker and a two-point conversion pass, also to Parker.

Once the Aggies forced it to overtime, it was over for K-State.

"When we got it into overtime, we had all the momentum," Stewart said. "They were so frustrated and didn't know what was going on. I think they lost a little confidence at that point. People were smiling, having a good time on our sidelines. We all knew that they were down on themselves."

Despite the wave of confidence on the A&M side of the field, the Aggies still appeared to be in trouble in the second overtime. A&M trailed 33–30 and faced a third-and-17 from the 32. When the play call came in from the sidelines, Stewart assumed the Aggies were setting up a field-goal attempt.

"We wanted to hit Sirr on the slant, because that's a high-percentage pass and you don't want to go for a bomb and miss it and have a super long field goal," Stewart said. "That's what I was trying to do—trying to get us to a position to be able to kick the football with a good throw and a good read."

The short pass, however, turned into an unforgettable 32-yard jaunt when Parker avoided a tackler and dove into the end zone to give the Aggies a dramatic 36–33 win and the school's only Big 12 title.

11 The 2012 Upset of Alabama

In the end, Texas A&M's stunning upset of No. 1 Alabama on November 10, 2012, didn't lead the Aggies to a conference championship or a BCS Bowl. Nor did it prevent the Tide from winning its third national championship in a span of four seasons.

But perhaps no other regular season game in the history of Texas A&M football ever did more for the Aggies' positive national perception than the spine-tingling, tension-filled triumph in Tuscaloosa.

It was the signature victory of a sensational 11-win season. The national television broadcast on CBS and the ensuing multimedia frenzy that followed the Aggies for weeks after the upset captivated the college football world and catapulted A&M into the national consciousness.

The game represented the "Heisman moment" for the first freshman ever to win the premier award in American sports. And it officially served notice to the skeptics, who had chastised the Aggies for leaving the presumably safer confines of the Big 12 for the SEC, that Texas A&M was not intimidated by any foe in college football's most dominant conference.

Not even big, bad Bama.

A&M took it to the Tide early, building a 20–0 lead at the end of the first quarter, and then the Aggies answered every Alabama challenge late in the game to register A&M's first road victory over a No. 1–ranked team in 117 years of football. The victory vaulted A&M from No. 15 to No. 9 in the AP polls, but it did more for the Aggies' image than anything else. The national media raved on and on about "Johnny and the Giant Killers."

For example, "A team that was thought to be outmanned and overmatched with its move from the Big 12 to the SEC made the doubters look very silly," wrote ESPN.com's Edward Aschoff. "And this wasn't a letdown loss for the Tide following an emotional win over LSU (on November 3). The Aggies dominated Alabama for four quarters. The Tide were supposed to wear down A&M, but the players in the crimson tops were the ones huffing, puffing, and panting deep into the fourth quarter, as the Aggies' up-tempo offense left Alabama's defense dazed, confused, and susceptible to a handful of big plays."

"This was Texas A&M, the new kid on the block with its new-fangled offense and its phenom freshman quarterback, beating the defending national champs and the SEC's reigning juggernaut on their own field," *Sports Illustrated's* Stewart Mandel wrote. "And in doing so…A&M raced to a 20–0 first-quarter lead against a defense that had not allowed 20 points in a game for nearly a year."

The Aggies outgained Alabama 172–26 on offense, while Johnny Manziel completed 10 of his 11 pass attempts for 76 yards and rushed for another 74 yards in the fascinating first quarter. The defining play of the quarter—and maybe Manziel's race to the Heisman—came on A&M's second drive. On third-and-goal from the 10, Manziel took the snap, bumped into his own offensive lineman, bobbled the ball 2' in the air, spun around with his back to the defense, sprinted out of the pocket, squared his shoulders, and threw across his body to a wide-open Ryan Swope in the back of the end zone.

Alabama eventually closed the gap to 23–17, and with 101,821 fans howling inside Bryant-Denny Stadium, Manziel hooked up with Swope again for a 42-yard pass between two Bama defenders. Swope paid a price for catching the pass, but one play later, Manziel hooked up with Malcome Kennedy for a 24-yard, over-the-shoulder TD pass that put the Aggies up, 29–17.

The A&M defense did the rest, although the Tide did cut the lead to 29–24 with just more than six minutes left in the game. Bama looked to be in position to pull off a dramatic comeback victory when A.J. McCarron connected with Kenny Bell for a 54-yard pass to the A&M 6 late in the fourth quarter. One week earlier, McCarron had rallied Alabama to a 21–17 win over No. 5 LSU with a game-winning drive that covered 72 yards in five plays in just 43 seconds.

But on first-and-goal from the A&M 6, Kirby Ennis and Sean Porter stopped McCarron for no gain. Ennis, coming up big in the clutch, then stopped Eddie Lacy for a one-yard gain on second down. And Dustin Harris made a great solo stop at the A&M 2 when McCarron scrambled out of the pocket.

On fourth-and-goal from the 2, Alabama attempted to flood the right flat with receivers and run a pick play. But sophomore cornerback Deshazor Everett stepped in front of the receiver for the interception that helped seal the magical upset. It was the third turnover of the game that the Aggies had forced that along with A&M's tremendous start, was the key to victory. The A&M offense did not turn over the ball against Alabama.

TexAgs.com

Perhaps one of the greatest examples of the passion Texas A&M fans possess for Aggie athletics is TexAgs.com, which in a relatively short time frame has grown exponentially to become one of the most influential, informative, and innovative online sites in college athletics.

TexAgs is the place where Aggies go online to discuss, debate, and dispute the latest games, recruiting rumors, trends, or news items. It's where A&M fans start their morning, browse during breaks in their work day, or conclude a long evening. It's a source of entertainment and enlightenment. It can be incredibly thought-provoking or momentously mind-numbing. It's a place where both reverent prayers and risqué photos are shared. It's the reason Aggies win most Internet polls, it's constantly evolving as changes occur in technology, and it's the beast of all college-athletics-related websites.

If TexAgs was a college football program, it would be Alabama. If it was an intersection, it would be Broadway and 7th Avenue

Jason Cook: Applying the Perfect Marketing Message

Not so long ago, Texas A&M University, as well as the school's athletic department, was often its own worst enemy in terms of its lack of marketing savvy, its external communications shortcomings, and its lack of big-picture brand imaging. As one longtime athletics department employee said for many years, "Our idea of marketing is opening the ticket windows."

Then Jason Cook was hired and, almost overnight, everything changed.

Cook, who was first Texas A&M's vice president for marketing and communications and is now in a similar role in athletics, is a forward-thinking, sharp, innovative, proactive, message-shaping marketing machine. He was vital in shaping A&M's brand management as the Aggies entered the SEC in 2012–13, and he was invaluable in maximizing A&M's exposure regionally and nationally after the highly successful first football team's season in the SEC and Johnny Manziel's Heisman.

It was Cook who led efforts to have Manziel's image placed on an electronic billboard in the heart of Times Square after he won the Heisman in early December, and it was Cook who led a well-planned campaign to place Manziel's image in national publications such as *USA Today* and *Sports Illustrated* right after the ceremony in New York.

For all of those efforts—and many more—Cook was named the 2012 International Brand Master by the Educational Marketing Group (EMG), a Colorado-based international brand-managing firm.

"Jason Cook has managed to reinvent and reinvigorate the Texas A&M brand while staying consistent and paying homage to the traditions that make the university such a unique institution," noted EMG in a statement announcing that Cook won the award for a variety of accomplishments in 2012, including the university's move to the SEC. "Perhaps the most telling demonstration of Jason's talent is his work unifying both Texas A&M's academics and athletics brands, an effort that has presented a united front during a time when the university has had more national exposure than ever before."

And perhaps the best is yet to come as Cook is just starting his wide-sweeping marketing efforts to maximize A&M's brand exposure in his new role in athletics.

in the heart of Times Square. And if it was a sports television network—and it's not that far off—it would be ESPN.

"It's amazing to see how much we've grown over the years, especially in recent years," said Brandon Jones, TexAgs president and CEO. "We've certainly evolved and added components to how we cover A&M as times and technology have changed. But the sheer power of our numbers is a testament to the passion of A&M fans."

Here's a sampling of some of the staggering numbers TexAgs can mention when distinguishing itself among other college websites or when making a sales pitch to advertisers:

- On September 7, 2011, in the midst of the SEC news cycle, TexAgs generated 4.22 million page views.
- The average number of postings a day by users hovers around the 15,000 mark.

Those numbers are even more phenomenal considering its humble beginnings. In the website startup days in 1996, computer-savvy fans of Big 12 schools could intermingle on GoBig12.com. But soon there were rumors that the website would be incorporated into a Longhorn-heavy site sponsored by Austin 360 and its parent company, the *Austin American-Statesman.*

Texas A&M graduate Peter Kuo heard rumblings from A&M users on GoBig12, and he thought a maroon-focused home for Aggies would work well. "The Aggies were wondering where they could go," Kuo told *12th Man Magazine*'s Homer Jacobs. "There was no Facebook. If they were to shut down that site, nobody would have known how to get a hold of each other. I said, 'Well, I guess it's a good time to learn how to install forum software.' I picked up [the book] *Html For Dummies*, and I started teaching myself how to design, write code, and upload it. I played with it and got it to work. Obviously, it would be a bad forum now."

Needing a name for the new site, Kuo looked no further than his vehicle's back bumper. His Tennessee license plate proudly displayed, "Tex Ags." Early in 1997, the traffic on TexAgs began to double weekly. It was exciting and frightening for Kuo, who was living in Nashville and dumping money into the website with no real return on investment.

"I sold T-shirts to raise money, and then there were some people who sent me $100 or $200 to keep it running," he recalled. "This is before ads and before the site was monetized. When the site hit half a million views, I signed on with 24/7 Real Media out of New York, and I put banner ads up. As soon as I recovered my money, and it was starting to profit, I wrote checks to people for what they gave me and I either doubled their money or gave them a 50 percent return."

As the site grew, Kuo resisted buyout overtures from larger websites like Rivals.com and Fox Sports. But in January 1999, Brandon Jones logged on to a TexAgs chat room, eagerly awaiting the recruiting musings of Billy Liucci. While running a software company and designing Internet sites for pharmaceutical companies, Jones initially looked at TexAgs from a fan's perspective. Then his business acumen took over. Jones and his brother met with Kuo at a Fort Worth Mexican food restaurant, and Jones ultimately bought 49 percent of TexAgs and took over as president of the company in December 1999.

Jones survived the Internet crash of 2000, although finances became extremely tight. In a last-ditch effort to keep the site alive at one point, Jones and his software company partner, Josh Oelze, partnered with Billy Liucci and former A&M football standout Hunter Goodwin, who owned the Maroon & White Report.

Liucci essentially rented space on the website so that he could sell his premium content. He attracted subscribers and revenues, which appealed to advertisers. After developing the premium subscription model in 2002, TexAgs slowly moved into the black using Liucci's recruiting content as its money driver. From then on, it has often been a storybook tale of success.

While premium memberships, advertisers, and users grew through the years, however, numbers were often dependent on the success of A&M football. Following the 4–8 season in 2008, for example, memberships declined dramatically. "In May of 2009, I met payroll by $10," Jones said. "There was $10 left in the bank, and that was after letting an employee go."

While TexAgs became one of the largest independent collegiate websites in the country in 2009 and '10, nothing generated growth and long-term stability like the SEC saga of 2011.

"During the SEC stuff for two months in 2011, we were averaging a 30-day snapshot of 14 to 15 million page views on our mobile product," Jones said. "When you add the main site with that, it was about 60 million page views for 30 days. It was an enormous amount of traffic."

Subscribers and advertisers have flocked to TexAgs ever since the summer of 2011 when Liucci became a national media name for his reports and minute-to-minute updates on A&M's move to the SEC.

"In the summer of 2011, the perfect storm came together that legitimized TexAgs nationally and regionally," said Liucci, who now owns 25 percent of TexAgs. "It has gone way beyond anything any of us could have ever anticipated, and yet I am not totally surprised because we have good people providing really good content on a great format. I am very proud of what we have achieved and even more excited about what is in store for us in the future."

13 Stopping Bo in the Cotton Bowl

It's a moment that has been immortalized by one of the most famous football photos in Texas A&M history…a photo that has been framed and displayed in board rooms, game rooms, and bedrooms of A&M fans for decades.

The photo, which once occupied prime wall space in the A&M football offices, is from the 1986 Cotton Bowl, and it features Auburn Heisman Trophy winner Bo Jackson being stuffed and driven backward by a swarm of Aggie defenders led by John Roper and Rod Saddler. It was one of the game-altering plays in an outcome-defining defensive stand.

But the Wrecking Crew's signature moment on that sun-splashed New Year's Day in Dallas lasted much longer than one play or one series. The Aggies' dominating defense earned nationwide recognition before an overflow crowd in Fair Park and a national television audience because of its ability to shut down the game's greatest running back whenever the Aggies needed it most.

"To me, the [performance against Jackson] was the epitome of what the Wrecking Crew was all about," said R.C. Slocum, A&M's defensive coordinator in the mid-1980s. "The defense just rose to the occasion and did the job that had to be done. It was an incredible thing to witness and a very special moment for me as defensive coordinator. And it wasn't one guy. It was different guys all working together to stop a great opponent. The way our defense played, especially in the fourth quarter, gave our team a lift.

"It was a huge win for the program, and it really gave the Wrecking Crew some national recognition. And I think because of that, it subsequently helped our recruiting."

The Aggies didn't completely stifle Jackson, as he accounted for 129 rushing yards on 31 carries. He staked Auburn to an early 7–0 lead on a five-yard run in the first quarter and put the Tigers back on top in the second quarter by turning a short pass into a 73-yard touchdown reception. But with the game on the line in the second half, the Aggies were able to continually stop the most heralded Tiger in his tracks.

After rushing for 1,786 yards and an average of 6.4 yards per carry during the 1985 season, Jackson was considered one of the greatest college runners of all time. And with the Tigers trailing 21–16 early in the fourth quarter, Auburn drove 93 yards inside the A&M 10 and turned to Jackson to do the rest.

Four straight times, head coach Pat Dye gave the ball to Jackson. He never did reach the end zone. On fourth-and-goal from the 1, A&M freshman linebacker Basil Jackson caught the Heisman winner two yards behind the line of scrimmage.

"If he scores right there, I imagine they would have won the game," Basil Jackson said afterward.

But Bo Jackson didn't score then, and the Aggies would once again turn away Jackson later in the fourth quarter. With A&M still clinging to a 21–16 lead with a little more than five minutes remaining, Auburn faced fourth-and-2 at the A&M 27. The Tigers handed the ball again to Jackson, who was stopped by Larry Kelm and Wayne Asberry for no gain.

"The key was our inability to convert those fourth-down plays and their ability to come up with some great plays," Dye said. "A&M is probably the strongest team we have faced all year."

During those two key fourth-quarter drives, Jackson was stopped five times in a row for either no gain or a loss of a yard.

Following the second fourth-down stop, the Aggies put away the game with a touchdown that was set up when Kevin Murray completed a 37-yard pass to tight end Rod Bernstine. Murray then connected with running back Keith Woodside for a nine-yard TD.

In the closing seconds of the game, Anthony Toney scored on a one-yard run off left tackle for a meaningless touchdown that left Auburn questioning Jackie Sherrill as a sportsman.

"After that, I'm surprised they didn't go for a two-point conversion," a bitter Auburn staffer, who asked not to be identified, told the *Dallas Morning News.*

14 1957 Heisman Winner John David Crow

In early December 1957, Texas A&M senior John David Crow received a phone call from his mother, informing him that the president of Texas A&M University had called her.

His heart immediately began racing, his stomach churned, and Crow instantly retraced his steps in his mind. Had he failed a test? Had he done something else wrong? Was he in trouble?

"I was relieved to find out that I was not in trouble," Crow recalled. "Quite the opposite, in fact. The president of the Downtown Athletic Club in New York called the president of A&M and then he called my mother to let her know I had won the Heisman Trophy. My mom said it must be a big award because they were flying her, Dad, and my wife, Carolyn, to New York. I didn't know much about the Heisman, but I sure was glad I wasn't in trouble.

"That trip was the highlight of my mother's life at the time. The funniest story about that trip is that they asked me if I wanted to ship the trophy home. I said, 'No, I will take it with me on the plane.' It's a huge trophy, and I laugh at the thought of someone trying to carry that trophy onto a plane today. But even when I brought it back to College Station, I didn't realize it was that big of a deal."

In the ensuing years, Crow began to realize that the Heisman was, indeed, a really big deal, which is why Crow was beaming with maroon pride when he watched Johnny Manziel accept the 2012 Heisman Trophy 55 years after he had won it.

Crow was absolutely ecstatic about welcoming another Aggie into the Heisman fraternity, especially since he has spent so much of his life promoting, publicizing, and praising A&M. Crow, who arrived at A&M in 1954 from Springhill, Louisiana, is the consummate Aggie in every sense.

He was a two-way star for Bear Bryant in the mid-1950s, earning All-SWC honors in 1956 and '57. Crow rushed for 562 yards as a senior, but he may have been even more impressive on defense where he intercepted five passes during his senior year. The hard-nosed, gutsy Crow was also one of Bryant's all-time favorite players, and the legendary coach told anyone who would listen that Crow was the best player in America in 1957.

"I owe Coach Bryant so much for so many things," Crow said. "I certainly owe him for me winning the 1957 Heisman Trophy. He'd mentioned to a bunch of sportswriters earlier in the year that if I didn't win the Heisman they should stop giving it. I had a good senior year, but I truly believe that he is the reason I won the Heisman."

After his stellar collegiate career, Crow was selected by the Chicago Cardinals in the first round of the 1958 NFL Draft. He played 11 seasons in the NFL, and when his playing career was complete, he was hired as a running backs coach at Alabama under Bryant. He later worked as an assistant with the Cleveland Browns and San Diego Chargers before he was given the opportunity to return to his home state to become the head coach and athletic director at Northeast Louisiana.

In addition to all those roles, the hard-working, multitalented Crow had his real estate license and insurance license in Arkansas and Texas. But he was especially proud in 1983 when Jackie

1957 Heisman Trophy winner John David Crow was a two-way star for Bear Bryant. (Photo courtesy of Texas A&M SID)

Sherrill offered him an opportunity to return to A&M as an assistant athletic director. When Sherrill left in 1988, Crow became the athletic director and was able to hire R.C. Slocum, who would become the winningest football coach in A&M history.

"To this day, I take great pride in that decision and many other positive developments that took place at A&M when I was within the athletic department," said Crow, who retired in College Station and still lives in the area. "Not because those things reflect positively on me, but rather because they reflected positively on a place I have grown to love and cherish—Aggieland. Through the years, I've run into many Aggies who still begrudge Coach Bryant for leaving A&M. But I totally understand why he left. To Coach Bryant, leaving A&M meant going home to Alabama. There is something magical about going home. I know. I was able to come home to Aggieland, and I've been here ever since 1983."

And Crow is still one of the Aggies' greatest ambassadors.

R.C. Slocum

As he prepared to leave for New York City in early December 2012, where he was inducted on December 4 into the National Football Foundation's College Football Hall of Fame, former Texas A&M head coach R.C. Slocum could hardly contain his burgeoning excitement.

The expansive, charismatic smile on his face, however, had little to do with the induction ceremony at the Waldorf-Astoria Hotel, where Slocum joined 13 others with A&M connections in the Hall of Fame. The engaging and personable Slocum was most excited about the possibility of basking in the Maroon and White glow of Johnny Manziel's Big Apple spotlight, as Manziel became the second Aggie ever to win the Heisman Trophy on December 8.

Slocum, the winningest coach in Texas A&M history, still beams with Maroon and White pride, and he possesses a reflective, long-term perspective of Texas A&M football that is essentially unmatched.

Slocum was raised in Orange, played collegiately at McNeese State, and began his college coaching career as an assistant at Kansas State in 1970. He returned to the Lone Star State in 1972, practically pleading with new A&M head coach Emory Bellard for a position on his staff. Bellard made Slocum a receivers coach at A&M in 1972, and he has essentially been representing A&M—except for a one-year trip to USC in 1981—in one capacity or another ever since.

Slocum was a revered defensive coordinator from 1982–88 for the Aggies during the birth of the Wrecking Crew, and he became the A&M head coach in 1989. A&M appeared to be on the verge of severe NCAA punishment—perhaps even the death penalty—at the end of 1988, so Slocum's primary assignment from the A&M administration was to prevent recruiting violations and to clean up the program's soiled reputation.

He did so much more than that, and it didn't take years for Slocum to restore the football team's swagger. It took about 15 seconds. In the 1989 opener against LSU, A&M's Larry Horton took the opening kickoff 92 yards for a touchdown as Kyle Field was whipped into a frenzy.

"After Larry took that opening kickoff back for a TD, I looked around the sideline and told my assistants, 'This head coaching stuff is easier than I thought,'" the personable Slocum joked. "I was kidding, of course. But it was a heckuva way to start your career as a head coach."

It was also a sign of things to come...in the game and the entire Slocum era. If Jackie Sherrill awakened the sleeping giant at A&M, then Slocum stirred it, nurtured it, and transformed it into a menacing monster. While Slocum was hired primarily to clean up the program, his teams often cleaned opponents' clocks.

A one-point loss to Arkansas in 1989 and a one-point loss to Texas in 1990 prevented the Aggies from winning conference championships in Slocum's first two seasons as head coach. Nevertheless, the Aggies ruled the SWC in its final years. A&M won three straight conference championships from 1991–93 and would have won it again in '94 if not for being on probation (as

*Texas A&M coach R.C. Slocum (right) talks with Kansas State's Bill Snyder
(left) before the 1998 Big 12 Championship Game.*
(Photo courtesy of 12th Man Magazine)

a result of a summer jobs scandal that had nothing to do with the
coaching staff).

The Aggies compiled amazing numbers under Slocum, winning
31 consecutive games at home from 1990–95 and going 29 straight
conference games without a loss (1991–94). A&M often dominated with defense, and Slocum made his coaching name with
ball-hawking, blitzing, blood-thirsty speedsters who often seemed
to engulf opposing quarterbacks like an angry bed of fire ants.

The Aggies failed to live up to lofty expectations in 1995 and
endured a 6–6 season in 1996, the first year of the Big 12. But

Slocum led the Aggies to the 1997 Big 12 South title, and A&M won it all in 1998 after shocking Kansas State in the league title game. It was the only Big 12 championship for A&M in its 16-year affiliation with the conference.

Slocum, who compiled an overall record of 123–47–2 in his 14 years as the head coach at A&M, was fired following a 6–6 season in 2002. But one of the coaches on his staff in that season was Kevin Sumlin, whom Slocum had hired in 2001 and had identified years earlier as a young coach on the rise.

Sumlin's success in 2012 at A&M added to the overall enjoyment of the season, said Slocum, who has served most recently as a special assistant to A&M President Dr. R. Bowen Loftin.

"From when I first started as an assistant on Emory Bellard's staff in 1972 until now, I've been associated with Texas A&M for four decades and have been privileged to be involved with some memorable and truly special teams," Slocum said. "But in 40 years of being associated with Texas A&M, this [2012 squad] is the most exciting, fun team I've ever seen. I can't say enough about the job Kevin Sumlin has done.... I can't say I expected him to be this successful in his first year in the SEC and in his first year as a head coach at A&M, but I knew he'd be successful here. He's a winner."

Just like the coach who first hired him at A&M.

16 The Best Loss Ever in 2011

Prior to the 2011 Texas A&M–Texas game at Kyle Field, *12th Man Magazine* surveyed numerous former A&M players about their feelings toward Texas, their favorite memories of games they played against the Longhorns, and their advice to the '11 Aggies as they prepared to face Texas in the last scheduled game between the two rivals for the foreseeable future.

The most memorable responses the magazine received were the passionate pleas directed toward the 2011 team.

"I've always *hated* that school," former A&M linebacker Ed Simonini wrote in an email. "Not their players, as I respect them as worthy opponents, but the school they represent, the orange puke school. Use any and every tool, skill, and/or play to kick their butts. The final of this game will follow you *forever*." "[My advice to the current team is] don't lose or we all will suffer for life," wrote former defensive back Pat Thomas.

Added former A&M safety Rich Coady, "When you're in the locker room getting dressed, remember that you are playing for everyone who has ever put on an Aggie uniform and for the hundreds of thousands of Aggies who wish they could be out there. This is more than just a game. It is the end of one of the greatest rivalries in sports. The score of the game and the style in which you play the game will be talked about and remembered forever."

The 2011 Aggies failed to follow the advice of those former players—and many others, dating back to the late 1930s—and played as apathetically as they had all year long. In Mike Sherman's final game as head coach at A&M, the Aggies cratered in the clutch again, blowing another double-digit lead by turning over the ball and making just enough blunders to allow a mediocre Texas team to win on the final play of the game.

It was a fitting finish to a furiously frustrating season for the Aggies. A&M built a 13–0 lead in the second quarter and led 16–7 at the half. But just like they had blown big leads in losses against Oklahoma State, Arkansas, Missouri, and Kansas State, the Aggies exhibited no killer instinct. They couldn't execute down the stretch and couldn't finish.

A&M muffed a punt in the first half, allowed an 81-yard punt return in the third quarter, and tossed three interceptions, including one that was returned for a TD. In spite of all that, the Aggies still rallied to take the lead at 25–24 late in the fourth quarter.

But Texas' Justin Tucker kicked a 40-yard field goal as time expired to give the Longhorns a 27–25 victory that sucked the air out of Kyle Field and ended—at least temporarily—the 118-year rivalry. Texas' final drive was aided by a bogus 15-yard personal foul penalty against A&M defensive back Trent Hunter.

"They played their hearts out tonight," Tucker said about the Aggies after hitting the game-winning field goal. "But sending them off to the SEC with a sour taste in their mouth feels pretty good."

It obviously hurt all Aggies at the time. But now—in hindsight—it may have been one of the biggest blessings in disguise in the history of Texas A&M football.

Think about it. What if Tucker had missed? What if Hunter had not been flagged? What if Ryan Tannehill had not tossed three interceptions?

If the Aggies had won that game, it would have undoubtedly resulted in a great party in College Station on the night of November 24, 2011. But long-term, it likely would have generated far more frustration, mediocrity, and misery in Aggieland.

If A&M had beaten Texas and finished the regular season at 7–5 instead of 6–6, Sherman probably would have kept his job. If that had been the case, here's the domino effect: Kevin Sumlin would have taken the vacant head coaching job at Arizona State (or somewhere else); Jameill Showers would have begun the 2012 season as A&M's starting quarterback; Larry Jackson would have never infused the A&M football program with a new strength and conditioning mentality (and consequently the Aggies would have been just as bad in the second half of games as they had been in 2011); and Johnny Manziel probably would have earned a few snaps at wide receiver or defensive back while backing up Showers.

There would have been no dynamic new head coach, no transcendent Heisman Trophy–winning quarterback, no signature victory at No. 1 Alabama, no sticking it to the Big 12 in a blowout victory in the Cotton Bowl, and no real end in sight to the decade-long stretch of mostly underachieving and uninspiring A&M football teams under Dennis Franchione and Mike Sherman.

So hey, Justin Tucker, thanks a million. That sour taste seems pretty sweet now.

17 A November to Remember in 1985

In 1984, the United States Supreme Court ruled in *NCAA v. Board of Regents of University of Oklahoma* that individual schools could negotiate their own television rights. That decision opened the door for ESPN to begin broadcasting live, regular season college football games during the 1984 season, beginning with the BYU-Pittsburgh game.

The popularity of those early games on the relatively new cable network—it had launched in September 1979—was moderate at best. And ESPN certainly couldn't compare to the traditional afternoon broadcasts on ABC or established regional networks.

But one year later, the network found the right partner, the ideal situation, and the perfect storm to turn college football on the network from a novelty to a must-see event. Texas A&M made history in November 1985 by finishing the year with four impressive wins to earn the school's first outright Southwest Conference championship and first Cotton Bowl bid in 18 years.

Three of those games were at home against fellow contenders SMU, Arkansas, and Texas. All three were at night. All three were broadcast on ESPN. And all three were memorable for their atmosphere and drama.

The November to remember began on November 2 as SMU, fresh off a 44–14 win over Texas, came to Kyle Field looking to extend a five-game winning streak over the 5–2 Aggies. On a drizzly 55-degree night, the Mustangs rallied to take a 17–16 lead with 4:46 left in the game on a four-yard TD run by Jeff Atkins. A&M then began its most important drive of the season—at least at that point—at its own 19. Kevin Murray moved A&M to the SMU 31 but the drive stalled, setting up a 48-yard field-goal attempt by Eric Franklin.

Franklin's kick hovered in the wind as the Aggies' championship hopes hung in the balance. Fatefully, the ball fell just over the crossbar to give the Aggies a 19–17 lead. Kip Corrington then intercepted an SMU pass on the ensuing drive to secure the win.

One hurdle down. Many more to go.

"The Eric Franklin field goal, if you don't make that, you don't win the game," said R.C. Slocum, the Aggies' defensive coordinator at the time. "Then it doesn't set you up for the next game."

The next game brought the 8–1 Arkansas Razorbacks to Kyle Field on November 16. In a defensive struggle, the Aggies finally appeared to take control of the contest midway through the third quarter when Murray hit Roger Vick on an 18-yard TD pass to give the Aggies a 10–0 lead.

But midway through the fourth quarter, Arkansas moved to the A&M 19 and had a golden opportunity to close the gap. But on fourth-and-2 from the 19, Corrington, the 170-pound defensive back from College Station, stopped Arkansas fullback Bobby Joe Edmonds in his tracks.

The Hogs eventually scored in the closing minutes to make the final 10–6, but it was too little, too late.

After back-to-back nail-biters, the Aggies traveled to TCU on November 23 and received just what they needed: an easy victory. A&M rolled over the hapless Frogs 53–6 to improve to 8–2 overall

Grab a Beer or Burger at the Dixie Chicken

Like any other college community in the country, Aggieland is filled with plenty of bars, pubs, or holes-in-the-wall where beers are cold and burgers are thick and juicy. But perhaps the most authentic and well-known watering hole in the community is the Dixie Chicken.

The Chicken, located along University Drive in the heart of the Northgate district, has been an Aggie tradition and the place to grab a longneck and double cheeseburger basket since Don Anz and Don Ganter founded it in 1974. The Chicken has essentially remained the same through the years, as generations of Aggies have walked through the same swinging doors to grab a beer, meet friends, carve their names into tables, peer at the live snake behind the Plexiglas, play dominoes, dunk their rings, or simply people-watch on the back porch.

Open seven days a week, the Dixie Chicken claims to serve the most beer per square foot of any bar in the United States, which certainly seems possible considering how crowded the bar can be on football game weekends.

and set up a Thanksgiving Night showdown at Kyle Field against 8–2 Texas for the right to go to the Cotton Bowl.

A then-record crowd of 77,607 fans shoehorned into Kyle Field on a 46-degree overcast night, and the Aggies gave those fans a memory they will never forget. A&M led only 7–0 at the half, but the Aggies exploded for 21 third-quarter points, the most dramatic of which came on a Murray scramble and pass. The 12th Man was more than appreciative and played a part in the win.

With A&M leading 21–0 and Texas backed up to its own 15-yard line, Texas quarterback Bret Stafford refused to snap the ball because the crowd was so deafening. Stafford hoped the din would subside if he waited long enough, but it didn't. In fact, it grew louder.

When Stafford finally snapped the ball, he was smothered by Alex Morris and Domingo Bryant for a 10-yard sack. The rout was officially on. A&M eventually won the game 42–10 as cotton balls showered down from the second and third decks of Kyle Field. All hurdles cleared. All documented on ESPN.

18 John Kimbrough

William Augustus Kimbrough moved from Alabama to Haskell, Texas—some 55 miles north of Abilene—in 1907 to serve as the rural town's first doctor. Kimbrough was particularly outspoken about two things—his love for medicine and disdain for football. His hatred for the sport grew stronger when a boy who played for Texas Tech died following a head injury.

Kimbrough happened to be the doctor for the dead boy's family, and he vowed to keep his sons away from the sport. He made one of his boys quit playing in high school, and he forbade another son from ever playing.

"As a young boy, I figured I was going to be a doctor," John Kimbrough recalled in a 1996 interview with *12th Man Magazine*. "But my father died when I was in the seventh grade, and there wasn't $500 cash from Fort Worth to El Paso in this part of the country. So that was the end of my hopes to become a doctor. I played football because I wanted to go to college, and that was a way I could get to college. If my father had lived, there was no way I would have played."

If Kimbrough had not played, A&M's football history would have been much different and far less glorious.

Kimbrough was truly the first celebrity in Aggie football, a rugged, hard-nosed, and relentless workhorse on the gridiron whose toughness and high-knee running style carried the 1939 team to the national championship. Kimbrough, the runner-up to Michigan's Tom Harmon for the 1940 Heisman Trophy, also possessed Hollywood heartthrob good looks that helped him star in two movies, made him a cover boy on national magazines, and earned him appearances on billboards across the country.

The Liggett & Myers Tobacco Company, for example, paid him $15,000 to use his picture on the Chesterfield cigarette advertisements.

"I was a rich man with that money," said Kimbrough, a two-time All-American in 1939 and '40. "I was also probably the most popular guy in College Station because every week a full case of cigarettes was sent to me. I didn't smoke, so I'd give them to all the guys who smoked. The only problem with me not smoking is that they had to paint a cigarette in my mouth [for the ad]. If you don't smoke, you don't know how to hold a cigarette."

While Kimbrough didn't smoke, he lit a fire under the Aggies after his arrival in College Station. He originally earned a scholarship to Tulane, but once he was in New Orleans, the Tulane coaching staff converted the 6'2", 210-lb. Kimbrough into a tackle.

It was a disastrous move for Kimbrough, who was cut from the team almost immediately. When his scholarship was taken away, Kimbrough began searching for a school and a football team that would take him.

He ended up at A&M despite the fact the Aggies had already brought in 100 freshmen in 1937. The future Aggie legend actually began his football career at A&M as a 10th-team running back.

It was only because Kimbrough was so far down on the depth chart that he ever received his opportunity. In the opening SWC game of the 1938 season, No. 1-ranked TCU was so thoroughly dominating A&M that head coach Homer Norton pulled his starters and inserted the scrubs in the third quarter. But Kimbrough, a sophomore at the time, was so impressive in limited action against the Frogs that he started every game during the rest of his A&M career.

Kimbrough, who became known as "Jarrin' John," led the Aggies to an unbeaten record in '39 and scored both touchdowns in the 14–13 victory over his former team, Tulane, in the 1940 Sugar Bowl.

Following his stellar collegiate career, he was the No. 1 draft pick in 1941 of the NFL's Chicago Cardinals, who offered Kimbrough $1,000 a game. The American Football League's New York Americans countered by signing Kimbrough to $1,500 per game, which made him the highest paid player in pro football.

In 1942, Kimbrough left the game and joined the U.S. Army, serving in the Allied Forces World War II efforts. Then in 1946, Kimbrough returned to play professionally with the Los Angeles Dons of the All-America Football Conference until 1948 when, as a 30-year-old, he suffered the first of three heart attacks. Doctors said Kimbrough had three to five years to live. Obviously, they underestimated the toughness of a man who once played a full game with two broken ribs.

The hero of the Aggies' 1939 national championship team didn't die until May 8, 2006, following a battle with pneumonia. He was 87, and it was his time to go. Toward the end of his life, Kimbrough had been stricken with a variety of health problems. The cruelest was probably the loss of his recollection of his heroic achievements.

19 Kevin Murray

Throughout Texas A&M's history, Aggie fans have taken great pride in the fact that they do not boo their own team. But that doesn't mean they don't occasionally grumble.

As a sophomore in 1984, quarterback Kevin Murray was aware of the grumbling going on at Kyle Field as he stepped into the huddle in the third quarter of the Arkansas State game—the third game of the '84 season.

A&M's heralded coach, Jackie Sherrill, had guided the Aggies to records of 5–6 in 1982 and 5–5–1 in '83. The maroon masses wanted to see much more in '84, and they were not at all happy when Arkansas State led A&M in the third quarter.

Murray sensed the mounting pressure on Sherrill, and he desperately wanted to do something dramatic for the coach's sake. Murray and Sherrill shared a special bond—Murray chose A&M over Oklahoma and his hometown team, SMU, specifically because of Sherrill.

"I took a chance on Jackie and knowing his history—that he'd coached Dan Marino at Pittsburgh, and Marino was always my favorite quarterback," Murray recalled. "When Coach Sherrill came to A&M, the program was totally unstable, but I wanted to throw the football and play a key role in turning things around. I was willing to do whatever it took to win."

Murray proved that time and again at A&M, including in the Arkansas State game on September 29, 1984, at Kyle Field. While engineering a comeback 22–21 win, Murray scrambled at the end of the third quarter and came down awkwardly on his right ankle, which shattered on Kyle Field's artificial turf.

It was a gruesome, career-threatening injury to the fleet-footed, strong-armed product from North Dallas High School. Murray missed the rest of the year, and skeptics wondered if he would ever return. Others predicted that even if he did return, he'd never be as effective as he had once been.

Those folks obviously underestimated the resolve and determination of one of the great leaders in the history of Texas A&M football. Murray returned in the spring of '85 and hobbled on one leg through practices. The ankle noticeably bothered him in the 1985 season-opening loss at Alabama, but the resilient signal caller made an indelible impression on Aggieland for the rest of his career with his sheer toughness and natural leadership qualities.

In leading A&M to back-to-back SWC titles in 1985 and '86, Murray was often remarkable, and in terms of the complete quarterback package—leadership, poise, pocket presence, arm strength, toughness—he still ranks as one of the greatest quarterbacks in A&M history. In fact, Murray even hosted another great quarterback in A&M history, Bucky Richardson, on his recruiting trip to College Station at the end of 1986, helping to lure Richardson to Aggieland.

If not for the severity of his 1984 ankle injury—and the resulting failed physicals when he pursued his professional dreams—Murray may have been the first Aggie quarterback to be selected in the first round of the NFL draft a couple of decades before Ryan Tannehill achieved that feat in 2012.

But Murray, who now trains aspiring youngsters at his Air 14 Quarterback Academy in the Dallas area, has no regrets about how things worked out at the next level. He chooses instead to focus on how well things worked out at A&M, especially after the injury.

In recent years, Murray has been honored numerous times for his accomplishments at A&M. He was inducted into the Texas A&M Lettermen's Hall of Fame in 1999, and in the spring of

2012 he was inducted into the Cotton Bowl Hall of Fame, which was especially meaningful to him because he'd grown up in Dallas going to the game with his father and had dreamt of playing in the bowl game.

Murray's father, Charles, died on November 15, 2011. Roughly a month later, Murray received notification from the Cotton Bowl that he was being inducted into the 2012 Hall of Fame class.

The headliner entering the 50th Cotton Bowl Classic on New Year's Day in 1986 was Heisman Trophy winner Bo Jackson of Auburn. But Murray took center stage against the Tigers, setting a Cotton Bowl record with 292 yards through the air. With A&M holding a 21–16 lead late in the game, "Murray the Magician" marched the Aggies 72 yards in nine plays for the game-clinching touchdown.

Murray added to those totals the following year in the Aggies' 28–12 loss to Ohio State, but it was the win over Auburn that remains one of the greatest moments in A&M's bowl history. Due to a variety of reasons, Murray says that the Auburn win may be his most personally rewarding memory from any game he played while at A&M.

"This is not just about me," Murray said of the Cotton Bowl honor. "This was a recognition of my teammates and coaches. I was representing my guys. On the 50th anniversary of this historical game, we were able to pull one off. It was magical to bring closure to an outstanding season. And I felt like that win and that season propelled Texas A&M over the next 20 years. It was great to be part of that."

And great to prove again that Murray was willing to do whatever it took to lead the Aggies to victory.

20 Bucky Richardson

Growing up in Baton Rouge, Louisiana, John Powell Richardson's resolve and remarkable competitive drive were first evident on a Little League baseball diamond. Richardson was a gifted baseball player who would eventually become a two-time All-State pitcher at Broadmoor High School in the mid-1980s.

But it was his tenacity—more than his raw talent—that made such a strong initial impression on his youth coaches. He loved to compete, and he cherished the opportunity to be in the spotlight when the game was on the line. He was such a "gamer" that one of his coaches began calling him "Bucky" in reference to the Yankees' shortstop in the late 1970s and early '80s, Bucky Dent.

In a 1978 AL East division playoff game at Fenway Park, Dent delivered a three-run homer that propelled the Yankees to a 5–4 win. Dent later hit .417 in the 1978 World Series, earning MVP honors. With his boyish good looks, he developed a huge fan following...except in Boston, where he was absolutely detested for adding to the Red Sox's misery.

So the comparison to Dent was a tremendous compliment to Richardson, and he ultimately embraced the nickname, which was fitting in so many ways. Richardson was such a big-time gamer on the football field and so sensational in the clutch in Aggieland that he is still beloved by adoring, appreciative A&M fans. And he is probably still loathed in Austin for adding to the Longhorns' misery as well as in Baton Rouge for not playing for the hometown LSU Tigers.

"I just played with passion," said Richardson, who played quarterback with a linebacker's tenacity. "I loved representing our fans, and I tried to embody the spirit and passion of the 12th Man in the way I played."

He did those things exceptionally well. Richardson was part of a monster 1987 recruiting class, and he made an immediate impact in College Station. While Craig Stump was viewed as A&M's primary passing quarterback, Richardson started five games and eventually earned SWC Offensive Newcomer of the Year honors. He rushed for 102 yards, including an 82-yard run, in the first game he ever played against Southern Miss, and he went for 137 rushing yards against Rice.

"My favorite memories from that first season involve the final two games," Richardson recalled. "I didn't start the Texas game at Kyle Field, and when I first got into the game, it was pretty frustrating because the Longhorns' defenders kept pulling off my shoe after they'd tackle me. I finally had to have our equipment manager, Billy Pickard, tape my shoes to my calves.

"Late in the game, with the score tied at 13–13, the SWC title on the line, and our fans whipped into a feverish pitch, I kept on a speed option play and scored on a seven-yard run that helped us to secure a 20–13 win. It was A&M's fourth win in a row over Texas, and it gave us a third consecutive conference title. It also sent us to the Cotton Bowl where we faced Heisman Trophy winner Tim Brown and Notre Dame. On a chilly afternoon in Dallas, we thoroughly whipped Notre Dame, 35–10."

At the end of a disappointing 1988 season, Richardson blew out his knee in the Texas game, as A&M went 7–5. He missed the entire 1989 season to rehabilitate from major knee surgery.

By the end of the 1990 season, however, he was back in prime form, finishing up the season with a magnificent performance in the 1990 Holiday Bowl. Richardson rushed for his first touchdown early in the second quarter, caught a touchdown pass from Darren Lewis later in the second quarter, and threw his first touchdown

Bucky Richardson played quarterback with a linebacker's mentality.
(Photo courtesy of Texas A&M SID)

pass just before halftime. When it was finally over, Richardson had led the Aggies to a 65–14 win.

In 1991, Richardson led the Aggies back to another SWC title, just as he did as a freshman. After that season, he was drafted by the Oilers in the eighth round and spent the next three years playing in Houston. He then had short stints with the Patriots, Cowboys, and Chiefs.

"After football, I entered private business, and that's when I really began to understand the power of the Aggie network," Richardson said. "When I was a sophomore at A&M, Coach

[Jackie] Sherrill had introduced me to Charlie Milstead, who had been a quarterback for the Aggies in the late 1950s. During school, I became good friends with Mr. Milstead's son, Lyle, who was also a student at A&M.

"When I left football for good following the 1996 training camp, I asked Mr. Milstead to introduce me to some business people in Houston. Soon thereafter, Mr. Milstead offered me a sales job with his company, Environmental Improvements, Inc., a company that works with cities throughout Texas and Oklahoma on installing and integrating new water treatment and waste treatment systems."

He's been with the company ever since, becoming a partner with Lyle Milstead and former A&M linebacker Larry Kelm.

"With each passing year, the power, reach, and sincerity of the Aggie network never ceases to amaze me," said Richardson, the father of three. "Other than my decision to ask the love of my life, the former Tracey Turner, to marry me in 1997, my decision to choose Texas A&M is probably the best one I have ever made."

Aggie fans still feel the same way about Richardson.

Jackie Sherrill

Following Emory Bellard's resignation/forced firing midway through the 1978 season, Texas A&M promoted Tom Wilson as head coach. Wilson went 4–2 in the second half of '78 and then went a combined 10–12 in 1979–80.

That was enough to stir the anxious A&M faithful into action. Despite a decent season in 1981 (the Aggies went 7–5 and beat Oklahoma State in the Independence Bowl), Wilson was fired at the end of the year.

Watch Games (And Eat) at Wings 'N' More or Sully's

Following a Texas A&M win in an afternoon game at Kyle Field, perhaps there is nothing better than settling in at a restaurant for dinner where the food is good, the atmosphere is great, and college football is readily available to watch wherever you look.

Two places in College Station where the food, atmosphere, and availability of games is hard to beat are Wings 'N' More and Sully's. Both restaurants are great places to unwind after a game at Kyle Field or watch the Aggies when they are on the road...in any sport.

Sully's, located directly across from the A&M campus on Texas Avenue and formerly known as Fowl Digits, features wall-to-wall, flat-screen, high-definition televisions everywhere you look. The owners have expanded the menu from its original chicken-only selections, and it was voted in 2013 as the best new restaurant in the Brazos Valley. It features the typical sports bar cuisine, but the food is so much better—especially the chicken and waffles—than the typical greasy burger and fries. And the sports-bar atmosphere couldn't be better.

While Sully's, named in honor of Ol' Sul Ross, is a relatively new addition to Aggieland, Wings 'N' More is a staple. The food is exceptional, and so is the atmosphere, which is a credit to the

With Wilson gone, H.R. "Bum" Bright, a wealthy Dallas businessman and the chairman of the A&M Board of Regents in 1981, decided to seek expert opinions in the search for the next head coach. Bright contacted four legendary figures in college football: Texas' Darrell Royal, Oklahoma's Bud Wilkinson, Alabama's Bear Bryant, and Dallas Cowboys' scouting director Gil Brandt. He asked each of them to list the five best coaches in college football.

When Bright compiled all the names on the lists, three clear targets appeared as potential candidates: Michigan's Bo Schembechler, Florida State's Bobby Bowden, and Pittsburgh's Jackie Sherrill. Bright contacted Schembechler, who said he would owner and former A&M football standout Mark Dennard, an offensive lineman for the Aggies from 1974–77.

During Dennard's tenure in Aggieland, the Aggies went 36–11 and played in four bowl games. Dennard, a first team All-SWC selection in 1977, was chosen by Miami in the 10th round of the 1978 NFL Draft. While playing for the Dolphins, Dennard and other Miami players were introduced to postgame parking lot parties that featured incredibly tasty buffalo wings. The wings were basted in various sauces—as opposed to merely deep-fried—and practically melted in Dennard's mouth.

"I had never heard of buffalo wings previously, but I became a big fan," Dennard said. "My wife was reluctant to try them, but once she did, she was hooked. My children soon followed. [After my NFL career], I opened my first Wings 'N' More in Houston on Highway 290 in 1986. The first College Station restaurant opened across from the A&M campus in 1988. We opened a second College Station location in Southwood Valley in 1994.

"We now have our largest restaurant on University Drive, which replaced the location across from campus. I'm so thankful to the people of Bryan–College Station, along with the current and former students of Texas A&M, who have helped make Wings 'N' More a permanent part of Aggieland."

need a 10-year contract to even consider a move. He also contacted Bowden, who had no interest. But Sherrill was intrigued enough to talk.

Bright sent A&M regents William McKenzie and John Blocker to Pittsburgh to interview the 38-year-old Sherrill. They convinced him to come to the A&M campus, where Sherrill discovered a sleeping giant.

He vowed to awaken Aggieland from its slumber, and A&M certainly made national news when it hired Sherrill as head football coach and athletic director on January 20, 1982. A&M awarded Sherrill a six-year contract worth $282,000 per year—an outlandish amount of money, according to a scathing *Sports Illustrated* commentary that was written shortly after the hire. Sherrill's deal also included television and radio fees, an automobile, and a housing allowance.

Unfortunately, the Aggies did not produce big results under Sherrill right away. In his first two seasons (1982–83), A&M went 10–11–1, and after the first nine games in '84, A&M was just 4–5. The natives were restless, wondering aloud if Jackie was the latest Aggie joke. All the Aggies' fears about Sherrill began to subside at the conclusion of the '84 season, as A&M defeated nationally ranked TCU and Texas.

A&M used that momentum, along with the impressive recruits Sherrill had been accumulating, to win the next three SWC championships. From 1985–87, Sherrill's bunch went 29–7, won three straight SWC titles, won two Cotton Bowls, and placed Texas A&M's name prominently among college football's premier programs.

Sherrill instilled supreme confidence in his players and filled the entire campus with contagious enthusiasm.

"We would have run through a brick wall for Coach Sherrill," said former quarterback Kevin Murray, who became known in A&M circles as Murray the Magician. "He was our leader, and we knew he'd always fight for us. Jackie was a lot of things to a lot of different people, but he was one hell of a motivator. He knew how to motivate our team and our whole campus."

The campus evolved during Sherrill's time at A&M. Enrollment continued to grow in College Station—likely a direct result of the national exposure the football program received under Sherrill's direction.

Unfortunately for A&M, all the national attention on Sherrill did not remain positive. A&M was placed on NCAA probation prior to the start of the '88 season for alleged recruiting violations. The Aggies' championship run and Sherrill's stay in College Station ended later that year.

22 Red, White, and Blue Out

In the early 1900s, Texas A&M's official school colors were red and white. The school colors did not change until almost 30 years later, when an order for football jerseys was placed and the supplier mistakenly returned maroon jerseys. Instead of returning the jerseys, athletic department officials decided to keep them.

Throughout its history, however, perhaps A&M's truest colors have been patriotic ones—red, white, and blue. Ever since Lawrence Sullivan Ross arrived as school president in 1891, A&M has prided itself on producing military leaders and serving the United States. Almost 20,000 Aggies fought in World War II, and A&M has produced soldiers and officers who have fought for freedom in virtually every battle the U.S. has waged since the 1890s.

Today, mandatory military training is a distant part of A&M's past. Although the university has undergone immense changes since World War II, patriotism is still a tremendous source of pride on the A&M campus. That was never more evident than in the aftermath of the 9/11 terrorist attacks.

On the day after hijacked planes slammed into the World Trade Center, the Pentagon, and a Pennsylvania field, Texas A&M junior Eric Bethea visited TexAgs.com, one of the most widely used independent college athletic sites in the country. Typically, the banter on TexAgs.com involves dissecting A&M players, coaches, and calls as well as recounting recruiting successes or near-misses.

But on September 12, 2001, TexAgs.com served as an emotional outpouring of therapeutic messages for a community in mourning. It was on that day that Bethea called for a "Red, White, and Blue Out" game at Kyle Field. Three years earlier, the "Maroon

A&M fans at their patriotic best in the aftermath of the September 11, 2001, terrorist attacks. (Photo courtesy of Texas A&M SID)

Out" tradition had been born prior to the 1998 A&M-Nebraska game. But Bethea's idea would be much more difficult to pull off, as it would involve a remarkable amount of coordination and cooperation in a tiny window of time.

Despite the overwhelming odds of turning his idea into a real-life tribute, Bethea, along with four other primary student organizers (Cole Robertson, Nick Luton, Josh Rosinski, and Courtney Rogers), decided that the September 22 home game against Oklahoma State would be the right time to show the nation A&M's true colors.

While the idea had picked up momentum on TexAgs.com, the first organizational meeting for the event—held on a Sunday afternoon, six days before the OSU game—did not produce many volunteers. Nevertheless, the student leaders were undaunted, and through the power of the Internet and the generosity of a local T-shirt printing shop—C.C. Creations—the idea began to pick up more steam.

Kenny Lawson, the president of C.C. Creations, placed an initial order of 15,000 red, white, and blue T-shirts, and on Monday morning, the sales began. The shirts were sold for $5 each, and by mid-week, T-shirt vendors from across the state of Texas began offering their services to accommodate the demand for the T-shirts, which were emblazoned with the words, "In Memory of 9–11–01, Standing for America, Aggieland, USA," across the front.

By 7:00 AM on Saturday—roughly four hours before the 11:30 kickoff between the Aggies and Cowboys—fans began lining up to buy T-shirts to match their seats—red on the third decks, white on the second decks and blue on the first decks. Even the A&M coaching staff dressed in red, white, and blue T-shirts to support the effort, and many Oklahoma State fans purchased blue T-shirts, slipping them over their orange attire to be part of the tribute.

By game time, roughly 70,000 T-shirts had been produced, delivered, and sold in the space of a week, including 30,000 on game day. The sales and the students' efforts produced a stunning and spectacular exhibition of patriotism that was unmatched anywhere in the country. The color-coordinated crowd of 82,601 was the fourth largest at that time in Kyle Field history.

"There's not another place in the country where that would happen," said former A&M quarterback Mark Farris, who guided the Aggies to a 21–7 win over OSU. "People can say, 'Oh, we could have done it.' No, they could not have. That's just a fact. It made you really proud to be an American and an Aggie."

The game was not particularly memorable, but the tribute will never be forgotten by those who witnessed it and took part in it. And it did not end when the crowd left the stadium.

The Red, White, and Blue Out organizers raised $180,000 in T-shirt sales, and its organizers hand-delivered the money to New York Fire Department and Police Department relief funds. Longtime A&M donor and former student David Evans, the president of the Baytown A&M Club at the time, helped to organize the trip for the five students by contacting Continental Airlines and a Hilton Hotel in New York City. The airlines and the hotel were both so impressed with the students' efforts that they donated airfare and rooms for the organizers.

Dana Bible

In September 1916, Texas A&M hired a diminutive young man named D.X. Bible as its freshman coach. The 5'8" Bible, who'd grown up in Tennessee, immediately did so well that his freshman team regularly beat the Aggies' varsity in preseason practices. Midway through the '16 season, LSU contacted A&M officials about hiring Bible as its head coach.

Technically, the Aggies agreed to "loan" Bible to LSU, but by the conclusion of the 1916 season, both the Tigers and Aggies were strong Bible believers. Three things lured Bible back to A&M: An impressive salary that topped LSU's offer, the memory of the stellar freshman team he coached at A&M, and a sense of loyalty.

"I felt a moral obligation to A&M," Bible recounted to Kern Tips in the 1964 book, *Football Texas Style*. "They had consented to let me go help LSU. Now they wanted me back. I was delighted and honored to return."

The Aggies were delighted, too. Long before the Wrecking Crew became synonymous with Aggie football, Bible brought a

The Legend of Joel Hunt

Perhaps the greatest A&M player to ever suit up for Dana Bible's Aggies was Joel Hunt, who earned the starting quarterback job midway through the 1925 season and guided the Aggies to a 7–1–1 record and the Southwest Conference championship.

Two years later as a senior, Hunt was absolutely remarkable in leading A&M to an 8–0–1 record and the national championship, according to one ratings system. Hunt scored 19 touchdowns and 128 points in '27, which was an SWC scoring record for 62 years. In one spectacular 39–13 victory at SMU, Hunt scored four touchdowns, intercepted four passes, and punted eight times for a 43-yard average.

After graduating, Hunt signed a pro contract with the baseball St. Louis Cardinals before going into coaching, first as an assistant at A&M and later as the head coach at LSU and Georgia.

dominating defense to A&M. Beginning with his first game as head coach at A&M in 1917 and concluding with the final game of the 1920 season, Bible's A&M teams went 25 consecutive games without surrendering a single point.

During that span, the Aggies outscored opponents 771–0. Obviously, the game was much different than it is today. But 25 consecutive shutouts is remarkable in any era.

Only World War I dented A&M's defensive armor at that time. After leading the Aggies to a perfect 8–0 season and the 1917 SWC title in his first year as head coach, the 26-year-old Bible was called to France as a pursuit pilot overseas and missed the 1918 season.

A&M was coached by D.V. "Tubby" Graves in Bible's absence. Graves led A&M to a 6–1 record, but the Aggies lost to Texas near the end of the 1918 season, giving the Longhorns the SWC title. Graves' porous defense also allowed 19 points in seven games.

In November 1918, however, an armistice with Germany was signed, creating a ceasefire and essentially ending World War

Dana Bible's A&M teams went 25 games without allowing a single point. (Photo courtesy Texas A&M SID)

I. When Bible returned to the United States, he continued his assault on the Southwest Conference, compiling a 10–0 record and outscoring opponents 275–0 in 1919. Although Harvard (9–0–1) was crowned by the Helms Athletic Foundation and several other sources as the 1919 national champions, the 2008 NCAA Championship Book listed A&M as No. 1 according to the Billingsley Report and the National Championship Foundation.

A&M appeared to be on its way to back-to-back national titles in 1920, as the Aggies went 6–0–1 in the first seven games. As Aggies traveled to Texas for the conclusion of the 1920 season, A&M had played 100 consecutive quarters under Bible without surrendering a single point. On the morning of the showdown between A&M and Texas, the *Austin American-Statesman* called the matchup "the greatest athletic contest ever played in Texas."

Unfortunately for A&M, the Aggies lost 7–3 as the Longhorns ended the most remarkable scoreless streak in A&M history.

Bible's early A&M teams were a tough act to follow, and the Aggies took steps backward in 1922 and '23, winning only five games in each of those seasons. But Bible produced an SWC championship team in 1925 and another team in 1927 that earned national championship honors (according to the Sagarin Ratings) after going 8–0–1.

After 11 memorable seasons at A&M, Bible received a call from Nebraska following the 1928 season. The Cornhuskers had gone after Knute Rockne, the mastermind of Notre Dame's dominant teams of the 1920s, but Rockne had turned down Nebraska with the following recommendation: "I am recommending a man you probably know little about. He is Dana X. Bible at Texas A&M, and I consider him the finest young coach in America. If you can get him, he is your man."

The Huskers landed him, and Bible led NU to six Big Six championships in eight seasons. He then moved to Texas, where he played quite a memorable role on the other side of the Aggies-Longhorns rivalry.

When Bible finally retired after 29 seasons at A&M, Nebraska, Texas, Mississippi College, and LSU, he had won 14 championships and compiled an overall record of 198–72–23. Only Amos Alonzo Stagg and Pop Warner had more wins at the time of Bible's retirement in 1946.

24 E. King Gill

By Dana Bible's standards, the 1921 team was easily the worst of his first four at A&M. The Aggies lost early in the season and finished the year by tying Rice and Texas. During the course of the eight-game regular season, A&M had also surrendered 43 points—36 more than A&M had allowed in the previous 26 games under Bible.

Nevertheless, the Aggies claimed a third SWC crown in a span of five years and earned an invitation to the Dixie Classic in Dallas' Fair Park, the predecessor to the Cotton Bowl. The offer to play in Dallas was extended by Joe Utay, who had played at A&M from 1905–07 and helped to organize the Lettermen's Association in 1907.

Utay then was an assistant coach at A&M under Charley Moran in 1912, while also serving as the school's athletic director. He also played an instrumental role in A&M joining the SWC.

As the enterprising promoter of the Dixie Classic with deep ties to A&M and Moran, Utay was delighted with the matchup he arranged for January 2, 1922, in Dallas: Bible's Aggies vs. the Centre College Praying Colonels, coached by Charley Moran. The Colonels, based in Danville, Kentucky, were the glamour team of college football, bringing an unblemished record to Dallas after upsetting previously unbeaten Harvard.

Moran was thrilled to bring his nationally recognized team to Texas for numerous reasons. First, it offered him a shot at vindication—a chance to shove it in the faces of A&M officials who had chosen to dismiss him after so much success. It was also a homecoming for many Centre players. When Moran took the job at Centre, his prime recruiting area had been Texas.

Bible, on the other hand, wasn't excited regarding the additional game. The Aggies were banged up by season's end, and he left the decision of whether or not to accept the invitation up to the players.

"[After the season] Coach told us, 'We've been invited to play in a postseason game, and I'll leave the decision up to you,'" said Sam Houston Sanders, an All-SWC halfback in '21. "'I'm not going to advise you what to do, but if you choose to play, we're going to limit the squad to as few members as we need. Remember this—you're going to miss the Christmas holidays, and some of you will be late starting other sports.'"

If Bible was trying to talk the Aggies out of playing, he should have been more succinct. Despite the coach's indifferent tone, the players leapt at the chance to face the Colonels. Eighteen players practiced and made the trip.

As the game began on January 2, 1922, injuries quickly mounted for the already depleted Aggies. Fullback Harry Pinson had broken his leg in the finale against Texas, and fellow fullback Floyd Buckner had seriously injured his leg in the pre-Dixie Classic practices. Captain Heine Weir, who missed much of the season with a broken leg, played against Centre...until he reinjured the leg on the third play. Sanders and Bugs Morris were also injured early in the game.

As injuries mounted, Bible looked around the sidelines. He surmised that he might not have enough bodies to finish the game. Then a thought struck him. One of his former players, E. King Gill, was working in the press box, serving as a spotter for Jinx Tucker of the *Waco News-Tribune*. Gill was quite an athlete, a multi-sport letterman who had been released at the end of the regular season to pursue basketball, his favorite sport.

With Centre out to an early 7–3 lead and the Aggies in increasingly dire physical conditions, Bible called A&M head yell leader Harry "Red" Thompson to the bench. He then sent Thompson to the press box to retrieve Gill. Once Gill made it to the sideline, Bible asked him to dress in the uniform of an injured player.

With no locker rooms at that time, Heine Weir and Gill went beneath the stands and switched clothes.

"I'll never forget what Coach Bible said to me," Gill recalled years later. "He said, 'Boy, it looks like we may not have enough players to finish the game. You may have to go in and stand around for a while.' I don't guess A&M has ever played more inspired ball. All of our remaining players managed to survive from that point forward."

Not only did they survive, they thrived. In the third quarter, A&M's Puny Wilson connected with A.J. Evans on an end-around pass play to put the Aggies on top. Wilson scored later on a five-yard run, and Ted Winn intercepted a pass and returned it 45 yards for a score. It was enough to give the Aggies a stunning 22–14 victory.

Gill never played. For that matter, he never made much ado about his willingness to play. He had, after all, been on the team prior to the end of the regular season. But Thompson, the yell leader, was so excited about the victory and so impressed by Gill's willingness to answer the Aggies' call that he scheduled a yell practice on the steps of the YMCA as soon as the team and students returned to campus.

At that yell practice, Thompson first used the words, "12th Man" in reference to Gill. Ever since, Texas A&M has been known nationally as "the home of the 12th Man." From one generation to the next, students at A&M have stood throughout games as a symbol of their willingness to follow Gill's lead and answer the Aggies' call, if necessary.

The 1986 Comeback Against Baylor

Many years after he'd departed Texas A&M as the school's all-time leading passer, Kevin Murray leaned against a golf cart at a San Antonio–area resort and told several 12th Man Foundation donors that he never really hated the University of Texas during his playing days.

"I'm not saying that I liked Texas, but I didn't hate them because we owned them when I was playing," Murray said as he waited to tee off. "But I absolutely hated Baylor. That was our big rivalry, and that's who I wanted to beat the most."

That made October 18, 1986, an especially memorable game for Murray. It was probably his most glorious performance in an A&M uniform, and it was probably the greatest comeback in A&M history. It also broke the hearts of all Baylor fans, which has never caused Murray to shed any tears.

From 1978 to 1985, the little private school on the banks of the Brazos River had its way with A&M, tormenting the much larger state school at virtually every meeting.

During that time span, Baylor held a 6–1–1 advantage over the Aggies, including a 20–15 win over A&M in 1985 that saw Murray toss three interceptions in Waco. To add insult to injury, Murray was replaced in the fourth quarter of the 1985 game, giving way to Craig Stump.

"I can remember [former A&M teammate] Todd Howard coming up to me in the summer of '86, telling me that he had spent some time with [former Baylor All-American safety] Thomas Everett and some of those other trash-talking Baylor guys," Murray said. "Todd told me they were mocking me, saying they were the 'Murray Busters.' That didn't set too well with me. I thought about it all the way leading up to our Baylor game in 1986, and we know what happened there. That was a game that so many Aggies still love to talk about."

In the 1990 edition of Dave Campbell's *Texas Football*, the magazine labeled the '86 A&M-Baylor showdown as the Game of the Decade in the Southwest Conference. And until the 1998 Big 12 Championship Game victory over Kansas State, most Aggies—at least those born from the 1960s on—proclaimed it as the most unforgettable comeback in A&M history.

"We had [74,739] fans packed into Kyle Field that day," said Johnny Holland, the defensive leader of the 1986 Aggies. "But there are probably 150,000 or more Aggies who claim they were there that day. It was an amazing game, an amazing finish."

Baylor entered the contest at 4–2 overall and 2–1 in SWC play, having just lost to SMU 27–21 a week earlier. Because SMU was out of the title hunt due to NCAA probation, the battle between the defending conference champion Aggies (4–1, 2–0) and the Bears would go a long way toward determining who would be in Dallas on New Year's Day 1987.

It certainly didn't start off in splendid fashion for the home team. Led by Cody Carlson on offense and Everett on defense, the Bears stormed to a 17–0 lead by the end of the first quarter. The Aggies were fortunate it was that close. The Bears had a chance to completely bury A&M in the opening quarter, but Howard stopped Baylor's Matt Clark a foot short of the end zone on a key fourth-and-goal play late in the quarter.

"At the start of the second quarter, I remember saying to the guys in the huddle, 'Let's go.' Then I can vividly remember one of [the Baylor defenders] knocking me across the head, and somehow I managed to stay on my feet and make a big play scrambling," Murray said. "That was essentially the start of something. Then it was boom, boom, boom, three plays later, we were in the end zone. The very next series, we shoved it right down their throats again to make it 17–14. Then it was a game. By the start of the fourth quarter, they had regrouped a little and were leading 27–17, but we still knew we had 15 minutes left. We hadn't played worth a crap the first 15 minutes, but that final 15 minutes [we] were going to make some magic happen."

That's just what the Aggies did. Murray hit Keith Woodside in the back of the end zone early in the fourth quarter to cut the deficit to 27–24, and Baylor added a field goal to up the lead to 30–24. That's when A&M began one of its most memorable drives in school history, converting two third-down situations before facing another crucial third down at the BU 4.

"I expected an all-out blitz, and that's exactly what I got," Murray said. "Their linebacker, Robert Watters, came barreling down on me. I had to keep the focus upfield, knowing this guy was coming with the hammer. I stepped a yard or two off the left hash to buy time, delivered the ball with this guy wrapped around me, put the ball where it needed to be, and Tony Thompson juggled it and then caught it. I was on my back, but I heard the crowd erupt. It was magic."

The Aggies used the 31–30 victory over Baylor as a springboard to their second straight SWC title. Afterward, Baylor head coach Grant Teaff stated the obvious in summing up the hero of the day. "Spell it M-u-r-r-a-y," Teaff said. "That's all you can say. Murray did the miracle things to win."

Junction

Behind the divorce of Marilyn Monroe and Joe DiMaggio, one of the biggest divorces of 1954 was Paul "Bear" Bryant's split with

Kentucky. In eight years, he'd transformed UK from a basketball school into a football powerhouse. Bryant compiled a 60–23–5 record at UK, winning a Sugar Bowl and a Cotton Bowl and finishing in the Top 25 three times.

But the chain-smoking, leather-necked Bryant hated Kentucky for one reason—he was in the shadow of basketball baron Adolph Rupp. So Bryant quit following the 1953 season.

Don't Bother Reading *The Junction Boys*

Author Jim Dent wrote an extremely entertaining book, *The Junction Boys*, that was released in 1999 and became a movie in 2002. It is an intriguing, sometimes riveting book that many college football fans would find difficult to put down, and it was certainly based on a true story. It's just not a history lesson. At least, not an altogether accurate one.

By and large, the publication takes readers into a gray area that is filled with half-truths, tall tales, and the author's vivid imagination. That's what many of the most prominent characters in the book told *12th Man Magazine* in 1999.

"There's a lot of truth in there, and [Dent] was right on with some of the things," said former A&M associate athletic director/facilities Billy Pickard. "But there's an awful lot of fiction, too."

"I can't believe [Dent's] written some of those things," said Dennis Goehring, one of the book's most documented characters and an All-American lineman in 1956. "I'm so exasperated with him about some of those things. There are some blatant things that he just had to make up. He's taken all of the old stories about Junction and romanced them and editorialized them and pieced them together to form a Hollywood script."

A rugged, tough football player and a sometimes mischievous prankster, Goehring readily admits that he was no angel in the mid-1950s.

"I did some things, some fighting and such, back then that I wish I could take back," Goehring said. "But I was never in that whore house. I think [Dent] must have based about a quarter of that book on the Broadway play, *The Best Little Whorehouse in Texas*. It's ridiculous, and it just ain't true."

His wife, Mary Harmon, cried, while Bryant accepted an invitation from Texas A&M chancellor Marion Thomas Harrington to meet him and other university officials at the Fairmont Hotel in Dallas. A&M officials believed—rightfully so—that a key to luring Bryant to Aggieland was to avoid letting him see campus until after he'd signed a contract.

Harrington offered Bryant a $15,000 base salary per year. W.T. Doherty, an independently wealthy man and a member of A&M's board of directors, said he'd pay an additional $10,000 annually from his personal account. Jack Finney, another member of the board of directors, said he'd arrange for a beautiful house in College Station, two Cadillacs for the family, and would work on securing a couple of oil wells for Bryant.

Bryant agreed to a contract, and he arrived in College Station on February 8, 1954. He was startled by the colorless, womanless bleakness of the campus in the dead of winter. Even the cadets who loved the place referred to it as "Sing Sing on the Brazos."

"At first glance, Texas A&M looked like a penitentiary," Bryant wrote in his 1974 autobiography. "No girls. No glamour. A lifeless community. A&M is a great educational institution, but at that time, it was the toughest place in the world to recruit to because nobody wanted to go there."

Nevertheless, Bryant immediately began beating the streets and the odds, signing what would become the senior class of '57. The impressive class featured names such as John David Crow, Charlie Krueger, Bobby Joe Conrad, Roddy Osborne, Jimmy Wright, and many others who helped reshape A&M's image.

"All I remember about that class was that they kept telling us that we had a bunch of great freshman," said Gene Stallings, who had been recruited the previous year by Ray George. "To be perfectly honest, I didn't know what to make of them initially. But after a while, it didn't take a genius to figure out guys like Crow, Krueger, and Conrad were darned good football players."

Before those freshmen ever participated in a practice for A&M, Bryant took his first varsity team on the well-documented, 10-day preseason journey to Junction in 1954. Hardly anyone outside of the 2,400 citizens who lived in Junction had ever heard of it in 1954. According to Mickey Herskowitz, the former legendary Houston columnist and author of *The Legend of Bear Bryant*, Bryant's decision to take his team to Junction was made after he observed his weak squad in the spring of '54. The alums were excited about the arrival of Bryant, and they often showed up on campus—far too often for Bryant's liking—to watch practice. So Bryant figured it would be best to take a trip.

"One of his coaches, Willie Zapalac, remembered A&M had acquired an old army base at Junction," Herskowitz wrote. "The housing was a cluster of Quonset huts with cement floors, plywood walls no thicker than a partition, tin roofs, and screens for doors and windows. In 1954, Junction was just a dust bowl 300 miles from the Aggie campus. All of the Hill Country and most of West Texas was in the grip of a seven-year drought, the worst of the century. There was little or no grass on the grounds. Bryant had the rocks cleared from the most level patch of earth he could find and had it marked off for a practice field."

On that setting, Bryant led the most famous field trip in college football history. He took approximately 115 players to Junction, but he returned with only 35 survivors. The rest of them quit because they were so exhausted and so beaten down—physically and mentally. Two busses went, one returned.

The depleted Aggies endured a miserable 1–9 season in '54, which would turn out to be the only losing season in Bryant's 38 years as a head coach.

The following year, however, the hardened survivors of Junction and the super sophomore class began to turn things around. The '55 Aggies went 7–2–1, losing only the first and final games of the season.

Then in '56, the Aggies went undefeated (9–0–1) for the first time since the national championship season of 1939. A&M beat Texas for the first time ever at Memorial Stadium, won the SWC title for the first time since 1941, and finished fifth nationally. Several key senior members of that '56 championship team—Gene Stallings, Dennis Goehring, Lloyd Hale, Jack Pardee, and Don Watson, among others—had been sophomore survivors of Junction.

"I went into Junction as a fifth-team sophomore fullback and linebacker," Pardee recalled. "After playing about eight different positions and losing more than 10 pounds during the camp, I returned as one of the Aggies' key players. There was one heat stroke, and we were real fortunate no one died. But Coach Bryant believed one of the keys to winning was to be in better condition than your opponents and to be tougher than they were. Those of us who came back from Junction were certainly toughened."

Indeed, they were tough enough to become champions.

27 Kevin Smith

The first time Kevin Smith walked into the Netum A. Steed Physiology Research and Conditioning Lab at Texas A&M, assistant strength coach Allen Kinley took one look at the diminutive youngster from Orange and guessed that he was a recruit's younger brother. Smith was too frail, too skinny, and too baby-faced to actually be a recruit, Kinley figured.

"I can hardly blame Coach Kinley for thinking that about me," Smith said many years later, following a remarkable career at A&M and in the NFL. "Even when I flip through the pages of some of the old media guides, I am amazed at how young I look. I was part of the same recruiting class as Quentin Coryatt, Robert Wilson, John Ellisor, and many others. But those guys looked like young men in their freshmen pictures, while I was looking quite boyish."

That boy became perhaps the greatest player to ever "man" the secondary in Aggieland. A&M has been blessed throughout its football history with a long line of great defensive backs, but Smith may be the best of the best. He was a lockdown cornerback who established school and Southwest Conference career records with 20 interceptions from 1988–91.

He was also a consensus All-American in 1991 for the Aggies and a first-round draft pick of the Dallas Cowboys in '92.

"Kevin was not just a cornerback; he was a difference-maker who shut down one whole side of the field," said Smith's former A&M teammate, quarterback Bucky Richardson. "I would watch him bait quarterbacks at times and just thank God I didn't have to challenge him."

When he arrived at A&M in the summer of 1988, Smith's goal was to find a way to earn playing time. He did much more than that, breaking up five passes and intercepting two, including one he returned 52 yards against Baylor.

While he played pretty well as a freshman, his sophomore season—R.C. Slocum's first as head coach in 1989—was the real breakout year for Smith. In the '89 season opener against LSU, Tigers' quarterback Tommy Hodson tried to make something big happen late in the game. Instead, Smith intercepted Hodson's pass and took it back 40 yards for a TD. It was a sign of things to come.

Throughout the rest of the year, opposing quarterbacks kept challenging Smith, and he kept intercepting passes. Smith intercepted at least one pass in every home game the Aggies played, finishing the year with nine picks.

In 1990, he added seven more interceptions, and in 1991, opposing coaches and quarterbacks finally decided to quit trying to pick on the 5'11" Smith, although he still intercepted two passes in '91 to finish his collegiate career with a total of 20.

Smith made 38 consecutive starts in college and was an All-SWC selection for three straight years.

He was the No. 1 draft pick of the Dallas Cowboys in 1992, and he was the youngest player on the Cowboys' roster when Dallas won Super Bowl XXVII. Overall, he was part of three Super Bowl titles in his eight-year NFL career.

"To play high school football in Texas, then to go to A&M, and then to be drafted by the Cowboys and to win three Super Bowls was a dream come true for me," Smith said. "Playing my entire career—all three levels—in Texas was really an unbelievably positive experience. I didn't escape without my share of bumps and bruises, however. I tore my Achilles in 1995 against the New York Giants, jeopardizing my career. But one of my proudest professional accomplishments is that I was able to come back from the injury and once again perform at a top level."

Smith believes one of his best years as a pro was the year after the Achilles tear. Back problems forced him to miss eight games in 1999, and although he was in training camp in 2000, Smith never returned to the playing field again.

Two years later, however, he did return to A&M to serve as the color analyst of the Aggie Radio Network's broadcasts.

"I enjoyed the experience, but I quickly realized I wasn't cut out for broadcasting," Smith said. "The thing that hurt me as a broadcaster was that I was too much a fan. At times during the game, I got caught up being a fan when I actually should have been announcing the game. But I was thankful for the opportunity."

Smith remains a loyal supporter of Texas A&M where he was inducted into the A&M Lettermen's Hall of Fame in 1997. Not bad for the frail kid who looked like somebody's younger brother when he first showed up on the A&M campus.

Homer Norton

Shortly after he'd been hired by Texas A&M officials to replace Madison Bell as head football coach, Homer Hill Norton spoke to the Houston A&M Club in the summer of 1934 about the bleakness of the athletic department's financial situation and the weakness of the football roster.

"This coming season doesn't look too good," Norton said, according to the book, *The Twelfth Man.* "We'll win a few games, and for the next year I can't raise your hopes by promising any better than we can expect this year. We need scholarships. Perhaps by 1936 we can offer scholarships. So maybe by 1937…"

Before he completed his sentence, a man in the audience interrupted, "Never mind telling us about 1937, Homer. If you haven't started winning by then, you won't be around."

Fortunately, it didn't take Norton long to show signs of progress. His first two years were predictably tough. A&M went 2–7–2 in 1934 and 3–7 the following year. But the Aggies won recruiting battles, landing Joe Routt, a guard who would become the first All-American in school history. Then in '35, Norton convinced Dick Todd, a sensational running back from a tiny West Texas town, to come to A&M.

The Aggies won eight games in '36, and in the spring of '37, Norton struck recruiting gold, signing Marion Pugh, Jim Thomason, Tommie Vaughn, Marshall Robnett, and many others who became the nucleus of the 1939 national championship team.

Once he had the talent in place, Norton was at his best, pushing all the right motivational buttons. In his first five seasons, Norton was just 22–23 as he built up the talent pool. But in 1939, the Aggies won the national championship behind an 11–0 record, a strong running game led by John Kimbrough, a dominating defense, and Norton's inspirational tactics.

"Homer, a great psychologist and master motivator, had Aggies from Houston, Austin, Dallas, and other locations send telegrams to our team before [the 1939 game against Texas]," Roy Bucek, the last living member of the 1939 team, wrote in his 2012 book, *Roy Story*. "We had a big blackboard in the locker room where we sat down and studied film. Prior to the Texas game, the blackboard was full of telegrams that were allegedly sent from [then Texas coach] Dana Bible, other coaches, and fans from the University of Texas.

"One of them, supposedly from Bible, said, 'We'll beat the hell out of you Aggies. You think you're smart; you're really not. You think you're good, but you are going down.' I realize now those weren't from Bible. They were sent by Aggies pretending to be Longhorns. But those telegrams fired us up, and in front of another record-setting crowd at Kyle Field, we kicked the crap out of the Longhorns, 20–0."

The Aggies went on to beat Tulane in the Sugar Bowl to win the national title, and Norton guided A&M to consecutive nine-win seasons in 1940 and '41. He did another masterful coaching job in 1943 by leading an extremely young team to the Orange Bowl, and he produced winning records in 1944 and '45.

But largely because of World War II and the toll it took on the A&M student body, Norton couldn't keep the talent pool stocked in Aggieland. In 1946–47, Norton produced a combined record of 7–12–1. Following the '47 season—his 14th at A&M—he reluctantly accepted the request from alumni to quit.

The Aggies quickly realized how good Norton had been once he was gone. In the first season after Norton's departure, A&M endured the only winless season in school history. And A&M attended just one bowl game in the nine seasons after Norton left.

After coaching, Norton entered the motel business in Galveston and later returned to College Station to operate a popular restaurant across from the main entrance to campus. In 1965, he died from a heart attack in his College Station home.

The 1940 Loss to Texas

Until the day he died on February 24, 2012—one week after celebrating his 92nd birthday—Roy Bucek, who lived longer than any other letterman from the 1939 national championship team, had one regret that superseded all others—the Aggies' loss to Texas in 1940, which ended A&M's back-to-back national championship hopes. In fact, he regretted it so much that Bucek wrote this to the 2011 A&M team prior to the Aggies' last-ever Big 12 game, which was also the last scheduled game against Texas for the foreseeable future:

"In my time on the varsity at Texas A&M [1939–41], we won a national championship, won two bowl games, attended three bowl games, and compiled an overall record of 29–3. But what sticks in my craw to this day is that two of those losses came to the University of Texas. We would have won back-to-back national championships if we had not lost to Texas in 1940. I am 91 years old, and that still makes me sick to my damned stomach. My one piece of advice to Coach [Mike] Sherman and the current team is to do everything possible to make sure they beat Texas this year. If you lose to Texas in the final game in the history of this series, you will carry that sick feeling with you to your grave. I guarantee it."

Despite Bucek's warning, the 2011 Aggies lost to Texas…just as the 1940 team had done. But Bucek was certainly not alone in

Don't Boo

One of the many things that makes the atmosphere at Kyle Field so unique is the Aggies—unlike most fan bases at other schools—do not boo their own players and coaches. Ever. Not even when the home team may deserve it.

Things will inevitably go bad on the field. But A&M fans do not boo. And they stay even after a loss at home to encourage the home team with a postgame yell practice.

Dating back to the earliest days of football at Texas A&M, students and fans came to the stadium to support the Aggies and to impact the game favorably with their yells and undying support... through thick and thin.

At the urging of the yell leaders, A&M fans occasionally give the officials the "horse laugh"—hissing—when there is a perceived unfair call that goes against the Aggies, but the lack of booing sets the A&M fan base apart from the rest of the sports-loving planet.

his strong feelings regarding the haunting memory of that loss to the Longhorns in 1940. Prior to their deaths, many members of the '39 national title squad swore that they were remembered more for one agonizing loss in 1940 than for all they had accomplished the previous season.

The '40 Aggies had picked up where the '39 team left off in terms of dominating the opposition. With the exception of a 7–0 nail-biting win over Jackie Robinson and UCLA in Los Angeles, A&M steamrolled most of its opponents en route to an 8–0 start in 1940. Dating back to the last game of the 1938 season, the Aggies had won 20 straight games and one national title under head coach Homer Norton. John Kimbrough had become one of the most famous names in college football, and times were indeed good as the Aggies went to Austin for the regular season finale.

The championship train was derailed, however, by a familiar name—Dana X. Bible, the former A&M head coach who had left

Nebraska for the University of Texas in 1937 to accept a 20-year contract valued at $15,000 a year.

Bible's first two teams at Texas were forgettable. The Longhorns went 2–6–1 in 1937 and 1–8 in 1938. The only UT win in '38 was a 7–6 victory over A&M. That one hurt the Aggies. But the loss to Texas in 1940 stung far worse.

Texas entered the game with a 6–2 record, but Bible believed he needed to hit the Aggies early to have a chance to upset them. The master psychologist read Edgar Guest's poem, "It Couldn't Be Done," to his players prior to the game, and he devised a quick-strike plan for the opening series. On the first play from scrimmage, Texas' Pete Layden faked a run and passed to Jack Crain to the A&M 35. One play later, Layden faked a sweep and passed to Noble Doss, who made an acrobatic catch at the A&M 1. Layden scored on the next play to give Texas a 7–0 lead 58 seconds into the game.

That's the way it ended. A&M tossed five interceptions and dropped from No. 2 to No. 6, settling for an SWC co-championship. The Aggies didn't immediately drop off the face of the planet, as A&M bounced back to beat Fordham in the Cotton Bowl. A&M also won the 1941 SWC title, going 9–2 and making a second consecutive Cotton Bowl appearance.

"Hell yeah, we did a lot of things right," Kimbrough said 55 years later. "But it's a damned shame we didn't go ahead and beat Texas [in 1940]. We just couldn't finish the job. I swear people remembered us losing that game more vividly than they recalled the national championship in 1939 and all the wins we had from 1939–41."

Kiddie Corps

Prior to the start of the 1943 season, many Texas sportswriters believed the Aggies were destined for doom, labeling the team in the preseason as "the beardless boys of Aggieland" and a "glorified high school team." One writer even asked A&M head coach Homer Norton if the Aggies would be better off by following the lead of Baylor and sitting out the '43 season altogether.

"Definitely not," Norton said at the time. "If I can find 11 boys on this campus who will suit up, we will have a football team." Norton found his boys, and those kids quickly became warriors, shocking sportswriters and fans across the region by reaching the Orange Bowl.

During a three-year stretch from 1939–41, A&M amassed an overall record of 29–3. But the school's football dominance began to change on December 7, 1941, when the attack on Pearl Harbor brought the United States into World War II and brought wholesale changes to the all-male military school in College Station.

Through the army's A–12 program and the navy's V–12 program, thousands of A&M upperclassmen were drafted into officer training schools. By the spring of 1943, A&M's football roster was decimated by the draft. Only one varsity player from the Aggies' 1942 roster returned for the '43 season.

"I came to school here in '43, and that was the year they had just cleaned out all of the upperclassmen because of the war," said former A&M star Red Burditt. "But what was really interesting was that if you were an upperclassman and a football player, you weren't going overseas directly. They sent you to college for a couple of semesters first. So all of these other schools—Rice, Texas, and so forth—that had A–12 and V–12 programs would recruit the best players. Ol' [Earl] Red Blaik really cleaned up at Army, picking up guys like [future Heisman Trophy winners] Doc Blanchard and Glenn Davis.

"These military bases also picked guys up, and they played against college teams, too. Randolph Field in San Antonio had 16 All-Americans on its team. And when we played Rice in 1943, there were seven guys on that team that had been playing at A&M in 1942. Practically all of our upperclassmen were gone."

But Norton didn't throw in the towel. In the true spirit of the 12th Man, he solicited what remained of the Corps of Cadets for football tryouts. When practices began in July 1943, 130 youngsters showed up in tennis shoes and shorts. The average age of the 1943 Aggies was 17.5 years old when A&M opened the year by trashing Bryan AFB 48–6 and blanking Texas Tech, 13–0.

By the time A&M pulled off back-to-back road upsets at LSU and TCU, the Aggies were 4–0 and developing some legitimate star power, as four players eventually earned All-SWC honors.

"We believed we were supposed to be good because we were Texas Aggies," Burditt recalled. "For me personally, it was a dream come true to be playing for the Aggies. I didn't even come to spring practice in 1943 because I weighed only 158 pounds. But that summer [Norton] put an article in the paper saying he needed football players. I was pretty cocky and said, 'Hey, give me a uniform and I think I can make your football team.' I had a burning desire to prove I could play."

Burditt and his teammates did just that, and heading into the regular season finale against Texas, the Aggies were 7–0–1 with the only blemish coming in a tie against North Texas Agricultural College (now UTA), which was loaded with V–12 players. With the SWC title on the line against Texas, the Aggies ran into a buzz saw, as the Longhorns were also stocked with "lend-lease" players.

Watch the Movie, *We've Never Been Licked*

In August 1943, United Artists released the movie *We've Never Been Licked*, produced by Walter Wanger and "inspired by the fighting sons of Texas A&M." In the movie, Brad Craig (played by actor Richard Quine) falls in love with a professor's beautiful daughter only to discover she is in love with his roommate. In the meantime, Craig unwittingly associates with Japanese spies intent on stealing a secret chemical compound developed in the A&M Chemistry Department. Craig is removed from the Corps for being a suspected accomplice to the spies, but he bravely infiltrates the spy network to sabotage the Japanese war effort.

Quite frankly, it's so corny that it is difficult to recommend to anyone with no A&M affiliations. On the other hand, it is a must-see film for any die-hard Aggie, as many A&M traditions are referenced in the film. The original Reveille, for example, makes a cameo appearance in the film. For many years, Reveille—Texas A&M's official canine mascot—has been a purebred American collie. But the original Reveille's blood lines were about as pure as the air around a petroleum plant. She was a lover with a golden heart, but she was also a dingy vagabond who was only slightly more attractive than the early bonfire heaps.

For many years, the bonfire on campus was nothing but a trash heap. But the bonfire was also referenced in *We've Never Been Licked*, and Universal Studios built a far more attractive-looking bonfire "stack" in 1942 as a prop. For the movie, logs were leaned on each other similar to a teepee, giving the bonfire a clean and conical shape. The logs were placed at an angle between 23 and 30 degrees, giving it vertical and horizontal resistance.

This design was adopted by the yell leaders of that era—the yell leaders were originally responsible for building bonfire—and by 1943, a stack of wood 25' high burned prior to the A&M-Texas game. Throughout the 1940s, the yell leaders continued to follow the teepee-style design, gradually adding to the height of the stack whenever possible. The first center pole (two telephone poles spliced together) was erected in 1946 to further anchor the growing structure. But bonfire first evolved from a trash heap to a structure thanks in large part to Hollywood.

Texas prevailed 27–13 and went on to tie Randolph Field in the Cotton Bowl.

Meanwhile, the second-place Aggies, who became known in media circles as the Whiz Kids and the Kiddie Corps, were extremely attractive to bowl representatives. A&M's 1943 defense recorded shutouts in six of its first eight games and set an SWC record for fewest pass completions allowed in a season (33).

With a 7–1–1 record, the Aggies accepted a bid to the Orange Bowl for a rematch with LSU and took 33 players to South Florida.

Burditt caught a 20-yard touchdown pass in the first quarter to give the Aggies an early 7–6 lead, but LSU's Steve Van Buren proved to be too much for the Aggies to handle. Van Buren rushed for 172 yards and two touchdowns and passed for another score as LSU beat A&M, 19–14.

The Aggies' magical 1943 run ended with a two-game losing streak. And by 1944, many of the key contributors of that team had been "drafted" into other lend-lease programs. As a result, A&M would not return to another bowl game until 1950. But because of the extenuating circumstances, the 1943 season remains one of the most poignant memories in Aggie football history.

Ray Childress

Following his 12-year career in the NFL, a 10-year run as the CEO of the Ray Childress Auto Group, and numerous other supervisory roles with non-profit organizations and businesses, former Texas A&M star Ray Childress started a new venture in the oilfield services industry called Childress Directional Drilling.

It seems like a perfectly appropriate business name. After all, opposing quarterbacks who'd been drilled by Childress through the years would probably argue that he's actually been a leader in that field for many decades.

Childress was one of the most dominant and imposing defenders in A&M history, earning All-American honors in 1983 and again in '84. While he was generally known to be a soft-spoken, mild-mannered presence in the locker room, Childress instigated one of the most significant turnarounds in Texas A&M history went he went on a verbal rampage prior to the 1984 TCU game.

Leading up to the game against the 8–2 and No. 17 Horned Frogs, the Aggies were 4–5 overall and 1–5 in the Southwest Conference. A&M was coming off a humiliating 28–0 loss at Arkansas, and Jackie Sherrill appeared to be heading for his third straight non-winning season in Aggieland. But a couple of days before the TCU game, Childress went on a tirade and inspired his teammates to be at their best on November 24 before a sparse crowd of just 38,209 fans at Kyle Field.

"I was livid about the direction we were headed," Childress recalled. "Basically, I just told everyone that we were not going down without a fight, and I was prepared to lead that fight."

He did just that as the Aggies dominated Jim Wacker's Frogs, 35–21. A&M followed up that win with a 37–12 victory over No. 13 Texas. In the previous two years against the Longhorns, the Aggies had been outscored by a combined total of 98–29.

Childress finished his collegiate career with two big wins, and in the years to come the Aggies continued to play with the passion that Childress helped to instill. A&M won the next three Southwest Conference titles.

"I am proud to have played some small role in getting things going," Childress said. "I was always proud to wear that A&M uniform."

Childress came to A&M after an all-state prep career at Richardson Pearce High School. He played on Tom Wilson's final team at A&M in 1981, and in his sophomore season in '82, A&M finished dead last in the SWC in total defense. But prior to the 1983 season, Sherrill and defensive coordinator R.C. Slocum switched from a 4–3 defensive look to the 3–4 and moved Childress from tackle to end.

The experiment obviously worked. Childress went from one sack as a sophomore to 15 sacks as a junior—four more than the Aggies had recorded as a team in 1982.

"I don't think there is any doubt that Ray was a part of the beginning of something very special," Slocum said. "He was an outstanding player for us. He could take control of a football game, and he literally changed games for us."

Childress finished his collegiate career in second place among A&M's all-time sack leaders. And in addition to breaking the Longhorns' hearts at the end of 1984, Childress also won the heart of a Longhorn. Childress began dating Kara Shipley, a University of Texas coed and a member of Texas coach Fred Akers' hospitality auxiliary known as "Akers Angels." Shipley later transferred to A&M and became Mrs. Ray Childress.

Together, the couple has four children, including a son, Wells, who walked on at Texas A&M in 2009 before transferring to play at Columbia University in New York. At Columbia, the younger Childress wore the No. 79 jersey that his father wore during a stellar NFL career.

Childress was the third overall pick of the Houston Oilers in the 1985 NFL Draft, and he was a five-time Pro Bowl selection. He finished in 1996 with the Dallas Cowboys, playing his entire high school, college, and professional career in the Lone Star State.

He has since been inducted into the Texas High School Hall of Fame, the Texas A&M Hall of Fame, the Texas Sports Hall of Fame, and the College Football Hall of Fame.

Kevin Sumlin

Eventually, Kevin Sumlin's name may be much higher on any list that celebrates or pays homage to the most powerful, productive, and prominent personalities in the history of Texas A&M football. In fact, if his first season as head coach at A&M is a foreshadowing of things to come, Sumlin's name may ultimately top this list.

In 2012, Sumlin became the most successful first-year head coach at A&M since Dana Bible went 8–0 95 years earlier. R.C. Slocum had previously been the only person to take the Aggies to a bowl game in his first year as head coach in Aggieland, but in 2012 Sumlin matched that and accomplished so much more than virtually anyone could have possibly imagined.

He guided the 2012 Aggies to the fourth 11-win season in program history and a No. 5 ranking in the Associated Press Top 25, the Aggies' highest final ranking since 1956. Under Sumlin, the 2012 Aggies also produced the school's first Heisman Trophy winner since 1957, won a January bowl game for the first time since 1987, and captivated the nation's attention by beating a No. 1-ranked team in the AP poll on the road for the first time in 118 years of Aggie football.

"This is a high I haven't felt in years, and it is all because [of] Kevin Sumlin's success at my school," former A&M offensive lineman Hunter Goodwin said after the Aggies beat Alabama in Tuscaloosa on November 10, 2012. "I never imagined that in his first year he could build a winning culture overnight and turn these kids into true believers."

Sumlin's first-year accomplishments are even more impressive considering that he achieved those feats in the first year of the Aggies' membership in the SEC and that he was inheriting what appeared to be a program with a fragile psyche.

From 2003–11, A&M had compiled an overall record of just 58–54. The Aggies had lost at least six games in seven of the previous 10 seasons prior to Sumlin's arrival, and they had not produced a double-digit victory total in a season since 1998—when Google was

Mike Sherman: Good Guy Did a Good Job

Ultimately, Mike Sherman's tenure at Texas A&M did not work out as he had hoped or planned. In four seasons as the head coach of the Aggies (excluding the 2011 Car Care Bowl of Texas, which he did not coach), Sherman compiled an overall record of 25–25. He had just one winning season (9–4 in 2010), and his final team was noted more for its collapses than its achievements.

In 2011, the Aggies started the year in the Top 10 nationally, but A&M blew double-digit leads in five games. The Aggies also suffered some rather humbling setbacks in the Sherman era, beginning with the first game he ever coached at A&M, an 18–14 loss to Arkansas State at home. The Aggies also lost nine games in Sherman's four years by 20 points or more.

Perhaps Sherman's greatest undoing as a head coach was that he gave his players too much responsibility. The longtime NFL coach treated his players like men, as he had in the NFL. Some of the players handled the responsibility well, but too many of them abused it and A&M underachieved as a result.

Sherman also made too many mistakes in hiring his first staff prior to the 2008 season. He made some extremely good hires two years later, bringing in Tim DeRuyter, Dat Nguyen, Nick Toth, and Terrell Williams, but his first staff was not particularly impressive across the board.

Sherman certainly deserves credit for a number of things he did right. He repaired relationships with high school coaches throughout the state of Texas that had been severed or damaged by Dennis Franchione. He also began developing a master plan for football facilities. He helped players like Von Miller and Damontre Moore immensely, and he recruited exceptionally well, as evidenced by the talent that Kevin Sumlin inherited in 2012.

Sherman was just a better offensive coordinator in the NFL than he was as a head coach in college.

founded, gas was $1.15 per gallon, and cell phones were only used for phone calls.

But Sumlin immediately brought back toughness, self-assurance, and swagger to the A&M program. The entire team appeared to adopt his confidence, which enabled his first A&M squad to win close games that the Aggies had dropped under Mike Sherman and Dennis Franchione before him. Sumlin coaches with an edge, and his team definitely played that way in 2012.

His golden touch continued into recruiting, as Sumlin signed a top-10 national class in February 2013, and he appears to have a transcending presence that makes him a charismatic attraction beyond the typical borders of Aggieland. Later in February 2013, for example, Sumlin served as the grand marshal for the Houston rodeo and was then presented with an honorary WWE World Heavyweight Championship Belt.

While most everyone associated with A&M has been surprised by how quickly Sumlin turned things around, one of his former players was not at all shocked. Terrence Murphy left A&M in 2004 with practically every receiving school record, and Sumlin had been his position coach at A&M in 2001–02.

"My perception of Coach Sumlin is that the dude is a winner," Murphy said. "That's the bottom line. I would take him into a bar fight, a basketball game, whatever, because I know he will find a way to succeed. Young men feed off of that."

Sumlin's former A&M boss, R.C. Slocum, also noticed something unique in Sumlin many years ago. In fact, Slocum first noticed Sumlin as somewhat of an annoyance to A&M's recruiting efforts in the Lone Star State.

"Newspapers would run recruiting lists [in the late 1990s] with the player's name and the universities they were considering," Slocum recalled. "I kept noticing that many Texas kids would have Purdue listed as one of the choices. At a staff meeting, I asked my coaches who recruits down here for Purdue, because he is doing a heck of a job, and they said it was a guy named Kevin Sumlin. I told them that the next time we are at a [coaches] convention, I want someone to introduce me to Kevin.

"At the national coaches convention, I first met him and put him in the back of my mind as a potential hire someday. Not long after that, we had an opening, and the first person I called was Kevin."

Sumlin took the job in 2001, and he became a head coach for the first time at the University of Houston in 2008—the same year A&M hired Sherman. When Sherman was fired following the 2011 season, A&M officials targeted Sumlin.

"I salute the A&M administration and leaders for hiring Kevin as the head coach, just as I applaud our leadership for making the decision about joining the SEC," Slocum said in December 2012. "You have to have courage enough to make the hard decisions, and the A&M leadership was right on the money with the decisions to move to the SEC and hire Kevin Sumlin. The future for this university and the football program [is] really, really bright."

Emory Bellard

Emory Bellard had already won three high school state championships as a head coach—two at Breckenridge in the late 1950s and one at San Angelo Central in '66—when he joined Darrell Royal's staff as an assistant at the University of Texas in 1967. The following summer, after he'd become Royal's offensive backfield coach, Bellard devised an offensive formation that contained three running backs lined up in a shape resembling the letter "Y."

Houston newspaper man Mickey Herskowitz eventually coined the "Wishbone" name, and after a slow start to the '68 season, the

Longhorns used the offense to win 30 consecutive games from 1968–70, including national championships in 1969 and 1970.

Bellard was hired by A&M prior to the 1972 season, and he used the Wishbone at A&M to lead the Aggies to a 48–27 record from 1972–78, including three straight bowl games. His '75 A&M team went 10–0 to reach No. 2 in the country before losing the season finale at Arkansas.

But the Wishbone that powered the Aggies to the brink of the national title in '75 was not Bellard's most important legacy at A&M. Nor was it a particular scheme that etched Bellard's place in college football history, particularly in the South. The Wishbone was an important chapter in Bellard's life story. But the theme of his book was much more important than football success in Burnt Orange or Maroon and White.

The big picture of Bellard's legacy was that he refused to see skin color as a barrier on the football field…or anywhere else.

Prior to Bellard's arrival at A&M, the perception among many football fans in Texas was that A&M had no facilities, no females, no nightlife, no minorities, and no chance to ever really contend with the Longhorns. But Bellard came to College Station intent on changing more than the record in Aggieland.

"Maybe I was foolish enough to believe I could recruit kids to A&M and change the culture," Bellard recalled. "The first thing I did was put together a really good staff. They arrived ready to out-work anybody. The second thing I did is tell those coaches, 'We are going to recruit the best football players. I don't care about skin color; I care about their hearts and their abilities.'"

The senior class of '75—the recruiting class of 1972—helped transform A&M's football reputation from mediocre to meaningful. That class moved the Aggies from obscurity in the Southwest Conference cellar to respectability in the national rankings.

"In the post–World War II, post–Korean War era, two men deserve the most credit for putting A&M on the national map—Gen. [James Earl] Rudder for having the wisdom to admit women, and Coach Bellard for having the courage to recruit black student-athletes," said R.C. Slocum, who was first hired at A&M by Bellard prior to the 1972 season. "Neither of those decisions was popular at the time, but those two visionary men weren't afraid to make the changes that desperately needed to be made."

Perhaps no single recruiting class in school history ever had a more meaningful impact on the university—not just the football program—than the 1972 group that Bellard and his new staff landed.

"There was some racial unrest at that time, and we were the first real wave of minority students, especially in football, to come through A&M," said Pat Thomas, the first African American player at A&M to earn All-American honors. "We had a group that stood out and stuck up for each other. There was no question that we were trendsetters. We had eight freshmen [who started in 1972], and five of them were black. So it was an opportunity for us to prove we could thrive at a place like A&M."

Thomas, Edgar Fields, Bubba Bean, Skip Walker, Carl Roaches, and other African American players from the 41-member signing class of 1972 did just that, and they also helped the Aggies land players like Lester Hayes, Tank Marshall, Robert Jackson, and George Woodard in ensuing years.

"It is still meaningful to me today because somebody had to make the first move to come to A&M," Bean said. "I'm proud of the fact that we were trendsetters, and I am proud to have played for a man like Emory Bellard."

Bellard later coached at Mississippi State (1979–85) before returning to the high school ranks at Spring Westfield (1988–93). He and his wife, Susan, retired and moved to a home near the No. 1 tee box at Meadowlakes in Marble Falls.

In the spring of 2010, Bellard and sportswriter Al Pickett authored a book called, *Wishbone Wisdom: Emory Bellard, Texas Football Visionary*. Later that year, Bellard returned to College

Station for the final time. The 12th Man Kickoff Team Foundation held a dinner to honor Bellard on November 19, 2010, and on the following night the largest crowd in A&M history saluted him prior to the Nebraska game, providing him with a roaring, demonstrative, standing ovation that moved him to tears.

"He was overwhelmed and amazed," Susan recalled. "It was a remarkable night."

It was the last time many Aggies ever saw Bellard. A condition called amyotrophic lateral sclerosis—or Lou Gehrig's disease—had taken a serious toll on his body. The disease attacks the nerve cells in the brain and spinal cord that control voluntary muscle movement.

On February 10, Bellard took his last breath inside a treatment home in Georgetown. He was 83, and he was ready to go. The Scott & White ALS clinic in Round Rock was later named in honor of Bellard.

Edd Hargett

According to former A&M quarterback Edd Hargett, the only reason he is on this list or others like it is because he played in an era when the Aggies had only one winning season (1967) in a span of 16 years (1958–73).

Hargett happened to be the signal caller for that '67 team, which he says is why he was inducted into the Lettermen's Athletic Hall of Fame in 1974 and why his name is still well known among many A&M fans more than 45 years after that '67 season when the Aggies overcame a truckload of early adversity in the season to win the SWC title.

"I was a pretty good quarterback on a pretty good over-achieving 1967 team," Hargett said. "Period. I'm convinced the reason I have continued to receive attention from Aggies all these years later is because we were so bad for so long before and after that one shining season."

Undoubtedly, that's part of the reason why Hargett etched his place permanently in the hearts of A&M fans, but that's not the only reason. Under any circumstances, Hargett was an exceptional collegiate quarterback, and he was easily the greatest quarterback in A&M history at the time of his graduation.

Hargett finished his three-year career at A&M (1966–68) with 5,379 passing yards, the most in school history at the time and still—as of this writing in 2013—the seventh most in A&M annals. His 418 yards of total offense against SMU in 1968 was a school record for 37 years until Reggie McNeal surpassed it in 2005. And his 40 career TD passes was a record that stood until Kevin Murray broke it in 1986.

In other words, Hargett is certainly worthy of his prestigious place in A&M history, especially considering how different the times and offenses were in the 1960s.

Hargett followed in the maroon footsteps of his older brother, George, who played football and baseball at A&M from 1961–63. The younger Hargett was part of Gene Stallings' first A&M recruiting class in '65, but because of a knee injury Hargett wasn't able to play freshman football in 1965.

In 1966, however, Hargett won the starting varsity quarterback job and passed for 1,532 yards as the Aggies showed some signs of improvement and went 4–5–1. After dropping the first four games of the 1967 season, Hargett engineered a late comeback against Texas Tech that kick-started a seven-game winning streak, including a 20–16 win over Alabama in the Cotton Bowl. Until Johnny Manziel led the Aggies past the Tide in 2012, Hargett had been the last Aggie quarterback to beat Bama.

Hargett was a first-team All-SWC selection at quarterback in 1967 and again in '68 when he passed for a career-best 2,321 yards. Unfortunately, A&M did not live up to the lofty preseason expectations in 1968, and the Aggies stumbled to a 3–7 overall record.

"I am certainly grateful for that one [winning] season in 1967, but more than that, I am thankful for my entire time at A&M," Hargett said. "I developed some lifelong friendships while at A&M, and I learned a lot about myself. Coach Stallings was so intense, and he expected so much of you. I remember working extremely hard in the off-seasons, going through workouts that would literally make us throw up on a daily basis. Coach Stallings made us tough and made us believe that we could be tougher than any circumstance that life threw at us. In that regard, my time at A&M had a tremendously positive impact on the rest of my life."

Hargett was selected in the 16th round of the 1969 NFL Draft and played five seasons in the NFL—first with the New Orleans Saints and then with the Houston Oilers. He also played in the WFL in Hawaii and Shreveport.

He and his wife, Shirley, were married during Hargett's collegiate days, and all three of their kids—daughter, Amy, and sons, Tedd and Thadd, attended Texas A&M.

Luke Joeckel

Luke Joeckel grew up dreaming about possibly winning an Outland Trophy for Texas Tech. His grandfather on his mother's side played for the Red Raiders and so did his father, David, an offensive lineman at Tech from 1979–82. Joeckel's mother, Reecanne, was also a Texas Tech graduate.

Fortunately for A&M, Luke and his twin brother, Matt, had a change of heart along the way. After graduating from Arlington High in December 2009, the Joeckel twins enrolled early at A&M and prepared for spring practices in 2010. Because of numerous deficiencies in the offensive line during the 2009 season, A&M head coach Mike Sherman indicated that Luke was the most likely candidate to become the first starter from the signing class of 2010.

Luke entered spring practices expecting to prove he could handle the challenges of starting at left tackle as a true freshman. But those hopes—as well as most of his long-term dreams—were initially dashed when Joeckel could rarely even touch the rush line-backer in front of him.

"It was a joke, but it wasn't funny to me," Joeckel recalled. "I was right out of high school, trying to make a big impression, and there were many times I couldn't even touch the guy. I'm dead serious. I remember thinking, *Man, is this the kind of talent I'm going to see every week in the Big 12?* I was pretty happy when we started playing games and realized that not everybody I faced was like Von Miller."

Not hardly. Miller led the nation in sacks in 2009, won the Butkus Award in 2010, was the Defensive Rookie of the Year in 2011, and was again among the NFL's sack leaders with the Broncos in 2012.

Joeckel started all 13 games as a true freshman in 2010, struggling at times early in the season but making major strides as the Aggies won six games in a row to end the '10 regular season. Joeckel continued to make progress throughout 2011, and he entered 2012 as a candidate for first-team All-SEC and All-American honors. He didn't disappoint anyone who projected great things for him.

Joeckel was absolutely dominant at left tackle in 2012, mauling opponents and helping the Aggies rank third nationally in total offense and scoring offense. Joeckel also played a major role in

Richmond Webb: The First Superstar OL from A&M in the NFL

In his 13-year NFL career (11 years in Miami, two in Cincinnati), Richmond Webb became one of the most respected and well-paid offensive linemen in the NFL, setting Dolphins records for most consecutive starts (118) and most consecutive Pro Bowl appearances (seven).

The monstrous Webb, who played tackle from 1990–2002 at 6'6" and 315 pounds, would be the first to admit that he never envisioned such a professional career when he came to A&M. When Webb began his collegiate career prior to the 1986 season, he had visions of terrorizing quarterbacks, not protecting them.

"I never dreamed things would work out the way they did, first of all because I was a defensive lineman coming out of Dallas Roosevelt high school," Webb said. "I was recruited for defense, and I played defense my first year before they moved me to offense where I was backing up Louis Cheek. I learned a lot from Louis and other guys on the offensive line, such as Jerry Fontenot. And then Joe Avezzano was the offensive line coach. He taught me a lot. But even with such great teaching, in no way, shape, or form did I expect to be a first-round draft pick in the NFL. It caught me by surprise. Basically, I was going to school to get an education and playing football for a university that I really loved."

Webb helped the Aggies to three bowl games, two conference titles, and an overall record of 34–14 from 1986–89. He earned first-team All-SWC and second-team All-American honors as a senior. But it was in the NFL, protecting Dan Marino at left tackle, where Webb truly blossomed into an elite player.

helping Johnny Manziel win the Davey O'Brien Award and the Heisman Trophy.

"Personally, I can't say enough about what Luke has meant to this team and our offense," Manziel said at the 2012 Home Depot College Football Awards Show in Orlando. "He is sensational."

Quite frankly, even though Joeckel chose to forgo his senior season to enter the NFL draft, he's probably the most outstanding

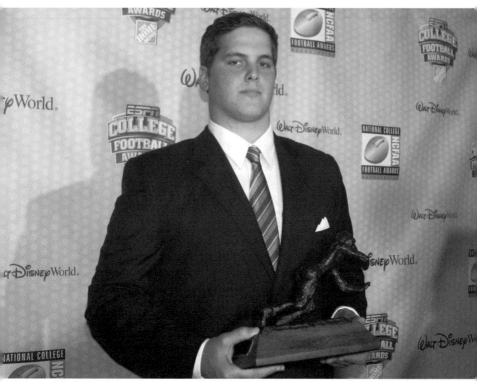

Luke Joeckel won the 2012 Outland Trophy. (Photo by Rusty Burson)

offensive lineman ever to play at Texas A&M. He has the hardware to prove it. At the 2012 College Football Awards Show, Joeckel was presented with the 67th Outland Trophy, beating out 2011 winner Barrett Jones from Alabama as well as North Carolina's Jonathan Cooper.

The 6'6", 310-lb. Joeckel became the first A&M player to ever win the Outland Trophy. In fact, he was the first Aggie to ever be a finalist for the award, which has been presented annually since 1946 to the nation's top interior lineman by the Football Writers Association of America.

"I did not expect to win at all," Joeckel said on the night of the awards ceremony. "This is all brand new to me. I've always thought of myself as my harshest critic, and just being invited [was great]. I didn't know if I deserved to be invited, and I sure don't know if I deserve to win this thing."

He definitely deserved it, and just to add validity to his sensational collegiate career, Joeckel joined Von Miller, Quentin Coryatt, John David Crow, and John Kimbrough as Aggies who have been chosen with the No. 2 pick in the NFL draft. Joeckel was selected by Jacksonville in April 2013.

36 The 1956 Texas Game

The University of Texas' football program moved from the wooden bleachers of old Clark Field into Memorial Stadium, originally a 27,000-seat concrete facility, in 1924. By the late 1920s, capacity had increased to 40,500, and by the late 1940s, the stadium had grown to seat more than 60,000.

While many things changed in the early decades of the stadium, at least one thing always seemed to remain the same—the Longhorns owned the Aggies on their home turf.

Beginning in 1924, A&M made 16 consecutive trips to Memorial Stadium and always returned home without a victory. Dana Bible took some great teams to Memorial Stadium but went 0–3. Madison Bell guided some lousy Aggie teams to Memorial and didn't score a point. Homer Norton took the defending national champions to Austin with a 20-game winning streak in 1940 but also lost to an inferior Texas team. Harry Stiteler managed one tie in 1948, but Ray George lost his only game in Austin. And Bear Bryant closed out his first season at A&M in 1954 with a 22–13 loss to the Horns at Memorial Stadium.

As the Aggies traveled to Austin to close the 1956 season on November 29, Texas A&M fans were certainly not overconfident about the chances of finally breaking through at Memorial Stadium. The Aggies, at 8–0–1 and ranked in the top five in the nation, were clearly the superior team, as the Longhorns had stumbled to a 1–8 record under Ed Price, including a 46–0 loss to TCU on November 17 in Fort Worth.

But there was still a perceived jinx in play in Austin. The A&M fans seemed to believe in it, and the players were made aware of it.

"We were certainly aware that A&M had never won a game there—and we wanted to do something about it," Jack Pardee, a senior in 1956, said in Brent Zwerneman's 2003 book, *Game of My Life: 25 Stories of Aggies Football.* "Coach Bryant wasn't one to bring it up and play the mental game with us. He was more interested in what we were going to do as opposed to any so-called jinxes."

One of the members of Bryant's staff, trainer Smokey Harper, was not opposed to bringing up the past and the Aggies' house of horrors in Austin. During a pregame prayer in the locker room, Harper interrupted, saying, "I hope you gentlemen pray you got some guts out there so we don't screw this thing up again, because we're better than they are."

A&M proved that early, building a 20–7 lead late in the second quarter. But the Longhorns scored just before halftime to cut the lead to 20–14 and keep A&M fans quite uneasy about the second half. Fortunately, the Aggies' worries began to subside soon after the opening kickoff of the third quarter.

Pardee fielded a bouncing kick near his goal line, received some clearing blocks and didn't stop running until Texas' Joe Clements tackled him 85 yards later. Two plays later, Pardee scored on an eight-yard run to give the Aggies a commanding 27–14 lead. A&M built the lead to 34–14 later in the third quarter as 61,000 fans at Memorial Stadium began to realize that history was indeed about to happen.

Texas scored midway through the fourth quarter, but it was too little, too late.

A&M wrapped up the Southwest Conference title with the victory and officially put an end to the jinx talk. The Aggies were on NCAA probation and were ineligible for a bowl game at the end of the '56 season, but the victory over Texas made for a memorable conclusion to a great year.

"This was our bowl game," John David Crow said in the victorious locker room. "We don't believe in jinxes, and we never thought much about it."

37 The 1975 Texas Game

In just his third season at Texas A&M, head coach Emory Bellard had completely revamped the roster, repaired the program's sagging image, and rejuvenated the masses of fans as the 1974 Aggies cruised to a 7–1 start and a No. 5 national ranking following a 20–10 win over Arkansas on November 2.

Unfortunately, the Aggies were upset 18–14 the following week by SMU in Dallas. After rebounding to beat Rice on November 16, Bellard took his eighth-ranked team to Austin to face No. 17 Texas on Thanksgiving night. A&M only needed to beat the Longhorns to go to the Cotton Bowl for the first time since 1968.

Instead of a bowl breakthrough, however, Bellard's boys were buried by Texas, 32–3. It was A&M's seventh straight loss to the Longhorns overall, and it marked the third straight year Darrell Royal had beaten Bellard, his former pupil. Despite an 8–3 overall record, the Aggies didn't even attend a bowl game. The Horns had again haunted the Aggies.

That memory—and so many other negative ones involving Texas—weighed heavily on the minds of most A&M fans as the undefeated and No. 2 Aggies prepared to play host to No. 5 Texas on the day after Thanksgiving in 1975.

The Longhorns (9–1 at the time) boasted the nation's top-ranked offense, while the Aggies featured the nation's most dominant defense, led by Ed Simonini, Robert Jackson, Tank Marshall, Lester Hayes, and Pat Thomas.

"We knew in the fifth game of the season we were going to beat Texas," tight end Richard Osborne said. "We were invincible."

Nevertheless, many of the fans among the fire code–breaking crowd of 56,679 inside Kyle Field (9,000 more than capacity) still worried about the Texas factor. Those concerns were eased, however, when Carl Roaches took a reverse 47 yards on the second play from scrimmage to set up a Tony Franklin field goal that gave the Aggies an early 3–0 lead. After the Aggie defense knocked out UT quarterback Marty Akins with a knee injury in the first quarter, A&M drove 80 yards to take a 10–0 lead when quarterback Mike Jay hit Osborne for a four-yard TD.

"We were a very confident group of guys," running back Bubba Bean said. "I know our fans were very worried because Texas had been so dominant in the series, but we felt very good about our chances, especially after we got off to the great start."

Texas closed the gap to 10–7 on a 64-yard punt return for a touchdown by Raymond Clayborn, and it stayed that way until the fourth quarter. But big George Woodard began to wear on the Longhorns, scoring on a one-yard run early in the fourth quarter, and Bean sealed the game with a 73-yard run that led to a field goal. Fans spilled onto the field afterward, celebrating the Aggies' historic victory. A few days later, Bean appeared on the cover of *Sports Illustrated* under a headline that read, "Texas A&M Stakes Its Claim."

At 10–0 overall and 6–0 in the Southwest Conference, the Aggies were in complete control of their own destiny and appeared to be in perfect shape to possibly play for the national championship in the Cotton Bowl. Only a December 6 trip to Arkansas stood between the Aggies and a perfect regular season.

"I would like to see something happen to [No. 1] Ohio State, so that if A&M takes care of its business, we will have another national champion down here," Texas coach Darrell Royal said after the Aggies' compelling win.

Ed Simonini

When Ed Simonini first arrived at Texas A&M from Las Vegas, Billy Pickard, the team's equipment manager and all-around care-taker of Kyle Field, thought it would be appropriate to give the kid from "the gambling capital of the world" the No. 77...or lucky double 7.

While it was an unusual number for a linebacker, it turned out to be quite fitting. The Aggies undoubtedly hit the jackpot with Simonini.

He was a key component of Emory Bellard's first recruiting class at A&M, a three-time All-Southwest Conference selection and the league's Defensive Player of the Year in '75, the same season he was selected as a consensus All-American. By the time he finished his collegiate career, Simonini was also the all-time leading tackler in school history.

He has since been passed in the A&M record books by stars like Dat Nguyen, Johnny Holland, and Mike Little. But it could be argued that the Aggies' tradition of great linebackers in the modern era started with Simonini, a third-round draft pick of the Baltimore Colts in 1976 who spent seven years in the NFL.

Bill Hobbs: From Hell-Raising LB to Soul-Winning Evangelist

Willie G. "Billy" Hobbs came to Texas A&M after a stellar prep career at Tascosa High School in Amarillo, and he immediately left a mark on Aggieland for his menacing, mischievous wild side. Hobbs was a terror on and off the field, earning All-American honors as a junior and senior in 1967–68. In A&M's memorable SWC championship season in 1967, Hobbs was the defensive leader, earning the league's Defensive Player of the Year honors.

Hobbs, who was drafted by Philadelphia in 1969, played three seasons with the Eagles and one with the Saints. But he found his calling in life and changed his wild reputation when he became a Christian in 1979.

His Christian ministry started in Amarillo and took him on mission trips to the villages and backstreets of Africa, India, and Brazil. After working several years as a minister at Amarillo's San Jacinto Baptist Church, Hobbs moved to San Antonio where he served as an evangelist for Alamo City Christian Fellowship.

Hobbs had founded a San Antonio–area missionary group called the Mercy Foundation, which he was building until his fatal traffic accident in 2004. In August 2004, Hobbs apparently ran a red light on his moped scooter and was struck by a vehicle, according to a police report.

He was a one-man wrecking ball before there was a Wrecking Crew. And he is the player who came to mind when A&M head coach R.C. Slocum was asked if he had ever seen anything like Dat Nguyen in the late 1990s.

"[Nguyen] reminds me of Ed, who was an undersized guy who had great intensity, great instincts, and was one of the best players that we've ever had," Slocum said during Nguyen's collegiate career. "They said [Simonini] was too small for pro football, but he played [seven] years in the pros. Ed was super."

Simonini, who lives and works in Tulsa, Oklahoma, still beams with maroon pride whenever he's asked about his playing days in

Aggieland, and he is incredibly proud of how far the university and the football program have come since he first arrived in College Station in the fall of 1972. Back then, A&M barely topped five figures in total enrollment, and the Aggies were typically football doormats in the SWC.

"By the time I got out of A&M, enrollment was close to 20,000," said Simonini, who has enjoyed a highly successful career with the Hilti Company, a Swiss-based manufacturer of construction-related products. "My freshman year was the first year of co-eds of any large amount. You just felt like you were a part of building something really special on and off the field and hopefully making it better. That's what I remember more than anything else. I still keep in touch with some of the friends I made at A&M, and I am ever so thankful I wound up at A&M.

"My dad was a pilot in the military, and we moved around quite a bit. He had been stationed in Abilene and El Paso when I was growing up. My oldest brother played at Abilene High when Emory was at San Angelo High. Emory remembered my brother, and the linebackers coach at A&M, John Paul Young, was a graduate of Abilene High. Some family friends in Abilene, who were Aggies, were very familiar with John Paul and me, so they recommended that A&M go to Las Vegas and take a look at me. Emory remembered my last name from my brother, and John Paul was probably looking for a nice trip to Las Vegas."

No matter the inspiration, Simonini and Texas A&M were just right for each other. He played like no other linebacker in A&M's past, and he obviously helped shape the Aggies' football future.

The 1967 Texas Game

Early in the fourth quarter of the 1967 Thanksgiving Day show-down between Texas A&M and Texas, the Longhorns finally pieced together a complete drive for the first time all afternoon, and with 11:11 left in the game, UT quarterback Bill Bradley scored on a two-yard run to give the Horns a 7–3 lead.

Plenty of time still remained for the Aggies to rally for a victory and earn a spot in the Cotton Bowl, but the record-setting Kyle Field crowd of 49,200 spectators grew eerily quiet after the Texas TD, squirming in their seats as a cloud of uncertainty filled the otherwise clear skies.

A&M had dominated most of this game. The Aggies, after an 0–4 start to the 1967 season, were also riding a five-game winning streak and a wave of momentum entering the Texas game. Even the breaks in the first half had seemed to go the Aggies' way.

For example, A&M took a 3–0 lead into the locker room at halftime on the strength of a 32-yard field goal by Charley Riggs in the second quarter. Riggs hit the ball too low, and the wind sent the ball soaring toward the left upright. But instead of missing wide to the left, the ball hit the upright and dropped over the crossbar to give the Aggies the lead at the intermission.

Then at the start of the second half, Texas lost Chris Gilbert, the leading rusher in the SWC, to a hip pointer. The Longhorns were also turning over the ball at an alarming rate. Texas was intercepted four times and lost two fumbles.

Everything seemed to be going the Aggies' way for much of the day. But with just one impressive drive, Texas took the lead and Texas A&M fans took a trip back in time, reliving one haunting memory after another involving the Longhorns.

Larry Stegent rambles for big yards in the Aggies' 1967 win over Texas.
(Photo courtesy of Texas A&M SID)

A&M had not beaten Texas at Kyle Field since 1951, and since that time there had been more maroon heartbreakers than any Aggie cared to remember. There were two-point losses at home in '57 and '63. There was the three-point loss in '59 and the four-point setback in 1965. Five of the last seven losses to Texas at Kyle Field had been decided by 10 points or less. And it had been 11 long years since A&M had beaten Texas anywhere.

A&M needed this win in the worst way. A win would send the Aggies to the Cotton Bowl. But a loss to the Longhorns would mean the Aggies would finish at 5–5 and spend the Christmas holidays at home looking toward the next year—again.

All those negative thoughts were running rampant through Kyle Field when the Horns took the lead. Fortunately for A&M, the Aggie players paid little attention to the trends and ghosts of Texas games past.

Eleven years of frustration would be put to rest—ironically—11 seconds after Texas took the lead. Following the kickoff, A&M took over at its own 20. A first-down incomplete pass set up second-and-10. The next play was designed for a short pass to tight end Tom Buckman—the same play the Aggies had run one series earlier.

But on the earlier play, A&M wide receiver Bob Long noticed that Texas safety Pat Harkins was cheating up, looking for the tight end and leaving the deeper route open. Harkins had intercepted A&M quarterback Edd Hargett earlier in the day, and the Aggies' signal caller listened with great interest as Long described to him how Texas was playing in the secondary.

"Bob said the [defensive back] was coming up," Hargett said. "The safety would come up to cheat toward that inside guy, and Bob was able to get in behind them. I just laid it up there for Bob."

Long caught the ball at around the Texas 45 and out-raced the Longhorns defenders into the end zone to give the Aggies a 10–7 lead.

"[Texas] scouted us well," Long said. "They knew our plays. On that particular play, it was a drag. I was supposed to clear out and our tight end, Tommy Buckman, was supposed to come over the middle. They knew that, and they weren't really biting [on the clear out]. I was supposed to clear out the safety, and he hesitated just enough for me to get open, and Edd threw the perfect pass."

Texas ran 32 more plays than A&M did in the second half, but that one 80-yard play was all the Aggies needed to pull out the victory. A&M went on to the Cotton Bowl where the Aggies beat Alabama to finish the season with a seven-game winning streak.

With a 6–1 conference record, A&M also became the first team in SWC history to lose its first four games and still win the league crown.

"It just all came together perfectly," Long said. "That play against Texas is still a memory that really sticks out in my mind. It's easier to forget about the tough losses and the losing seasons before and after that when you have a memory like that one. I'll never forget that one."

Bear Bryant

Shortly after the 1979 Sugar Bowl, where No. 2 Alabama defeated No. 1 Penn State to give Paul "Bear" Bryant his fifth national championship with the Tide, reporters asked the legendary head coach what he planned to do next.

Bryant told them that his next agenda item was to reunite with the "Junction Boys" of 1954 because that was his favorite team. The reporters could only have been more stunned if Bryant had told them he was leaving Bama to join the circus.

The '54 team at A&M went 1–9 overall and 0–6 in the Southwest Conference. It was Bryant's only losing season in his storied coaching career. It was the lone blemish and the ugliest black mark on his otherwise remarkable record of excellence.

But what the reporters couldn't fathom was that Bryant was more proud of what the men on that team accomplished later in life than he could accurately put into words. It wasn't just the fact that the survivors of Junction led the Aggies to a 7–2–1 record in '55 and a 9–0–1 Southwest Conference championship in '56.

Until the day he died, Bryant was proud of the members of that team for all they accomplished in business, how they served their communities, and the examples they set as husbands and fathers. He genuinely loved those guys.

Bryant proudly bought 1,000 shares in the Bank of A&M in 1967 to help Junction survivor and bank president Dennis Goehring with his business endeavors; Bryant continually acknowledged in his later years that he'd made so many mistakes in the way he treated the A&M players; he embraced Bill Schroeder—the man who came closest to dying from heat exhaustion in Junction—at the 25-year reunion of the '54 Aggies, which was held in May 1979; and the most cherished piece of jewelry that Bryant ever received—the one he was buried with—was the ring that the Junction survivors presented to him at that reunion.

Bryant left A&M following the 1957 season because, as he so famously stated, "Mama called." Alabama was undoubtedly home, but Texas A&M—and the Aggie players he grew to love—always occupied a special place in Bryant's heart.

It wasn't only the members of that Junction team that he loved, either. Nor was it merely the star players like John David Crow or Charlie Krueger. In 1977, Bryant wrote a letter to legendary high school running back Ken Hall—the "Sugar Land Express"—apologizing for the way he'd treated Hall, who quit the team in 1956. Hall rushed for 11,232 yards in four seasons (1950–53) at Sugar Land and set 17 national offensive records.

But at A&M, the defensive-minded Bryant didn't like the way Hall blocked or played defense. Bryant moved him to fullback and chastised him unmercifully. Years later, in a 1982 *Sports Illustrated* article, Bryant told the reporter who asked him what went wrong with Hall, "I don't think anything went wrong with him," Bryant said. "It was me. I was stupid. You're a fool to think, as I did as a young coach, that you can treat them all alike. He should have been an All-American for me. With him, we'd have won the national championship in 1957. Without him, we lost it."

Bryant always regretted the lost opportunity to win a national title in '57 as much as he cherished the titles he did win. In a 25-year career at Alabama, he won six national titles and 13 SEC championships while guiding the Tide to 24 consecutive bowl games.

In comparison, he spent four years at A&M, leading the Aggies to a 25–14–2 record, one conference title, and one bowl game. There's obviously no comparison between what he accomplished at the two schools, but there's also no denying that Bryant cherished his time at A&M—even though he grew to love his connections to Aggieland much more after he had departed than when he was actually at A&M.

After the 1982 season, the 69-year-old Bryant decided to retire. After his final game that season, Bryant was asked what he would do since he was no longer coaching. He replied, "I'll probably croak within a week." Four weeks later, Bryant suffered a heart attack and died on January 26, 1983.

41 The 1998 Nebraska Game

Defending co-national champion Nebraska entered Kyle Field on a sun-splashed picturesque October afternoon in 1998 with a No. 2 national ranking, a 40-game winning streak in regular season conference action, and a 65–3 overall record in the previous five years.

The dynamic Huskers were undoubtedly a modern-day dynasty, winning national titles in 1994, '95, and '97. En route to the '97 title, the Huskers steamrolled the Aggies in the second-ever Big 12 Championship Game, rolling up 536 yards of total offense and building a 37–3 lead at the half. Quite frankly, A&M was lucky it was that close, as the Huskers were forced to settle for three field goals in the first quarter.

Meanwhile, the Aggies entered the rematch with big, bad Big Red after struggling the previous two weeks against North Texas

Ja'Mar Toombs rushed for 110 yards in the Aggies' 28–21 win over Nebraska in 1998. (Photo courtesy of 12th Man Magazine)

and Kansas. A&M rallied to beat lowly KU 24–21 on October 3 to save face, but many college football observers expected Nebraska to administer another KO to A&M at Kyle Field.

As soon as A&M linebacker Dat Nguyen stepped onto the field and witnessed the first-ever Maroon Out (30,000 maroon T-shirts had been sold in the weeks leading up to the Nebraska game), however, the Aggies' defensive leader sensed there could be something special about this day.

"The crowd was incredible," Nguyen said of the 60,798 fans who packed into the stadium. (The north end zone was under construction and reduced the capacity of Kyle Field.) "We knew that if we could get off to a good start in our home stadium, it would be a lot different than the previous year in the Big 12 Championship Game."

That's exactly what happened. Midway through the first quarter, the Huskers ran an option play to the right on third-and-1 and to the left on fourth down from the A&M 31, needing one yard both times. The Aggies stuffed both attempts, and on third-and-25 from their own 19 on the ensuing drive, A&M quarterback Randy McCown dropped back under pressure, stepped up in the pocket, and delivered a perfect strike to Chris Taylor, who caught the ball in full stride and sprinted down the sideline for an 81-yard touchdown.

"Everybody in the stadium knew it would be different at that time," McCown said. "We knew we could not only play with them, but we believed we could beat them."

That belief increased after Nebraska tied the game. Ja'Mar Toombs raced 71 yards to set up A&M's second touchdown of the day, giving the Aggies a 14–7 lead at the half. Early in the third quarter, A&M sacked quarterback Bobby Newcombe on consecutive plays, setting up a third-and-19 from the NU 12. Ron Edwards sliced through a blocker and slung Newcombe toward the end zone where Warrick Holdman pounced on the loose ball for a 21–7 lead.

First OT Win in History in 1997 Against OSU

The first overtime game in Texas A&M history was significant, as it propelled Texas A&M to its first Big 12 South Division title in school history. It was also one of the more stunning wins for the Aggies in recent memory because, for most of the first three quarters, it didn't look like A&M had much of a pulse.

On November 1, 1997, No. 19 Oklahoma State came to Kyle Field and punched the Aggies square in the mouth. A&M, which entered the game on a two-game losing streak and with an overall record of 5–2, didn't respond well. The Cowboys, led by sensational freshman quarterback Tony Lindsey, stormed to a 22–7 lead early in the fourth quarter.

But that's when A&M quarterback Branndon Stewart caught fire. He completed 9-of-13 passes in the final quarter, rallying the Aggies for two long scoring drives. On the final drive of the fourth quarter, Stewart hit Chris Cole on a 25-yard TD pass to pull the Aggies to 22–20 with 43 seconds left in regulation. On the next play, Stewart connected with Sirr Parker for the two-point conversion.

The Aggies held OSU to a field goal on its overtime possession, and they celebrated wildly when D'Andre Hardeman scored on a 6-yard run to give A&M a thrilling 28–25 win.

Interestingly, it was a preview of things to come. One year later, Stewart rallied the Aggies from a 15-point fourth-quarter deficit to beat Kansas State for the Big 12 title. The game-tying two-point conversion pass went to Sirr Parker again. In fact, it was the exact same play.

The Aggies went up 28–7 when Toombs scored on a three-yard run early in the fourth quarter as Kyle Field went crazy.

The Huskers rallied with two quick, impressive drives within a four-minute span to cut the lead to 28–21 with 4:39 left in the game, and NU had one more opportunity on offense. But feeding off a frenzied crowd, the Wrecking Crew rose to the occasion. Reserve cornerback Sedrick Curry intercepted a Newcombe pass near midfield with 51 seconds left.

The win over the Huskers propelled A&M to its first Big 12 championship and sent some shockwaves across the country.

"We proved we were for real that day," Nguyen recalled. "It gave us the confidence that we could beat anyone in the country. And we needed that belief to knock off Kansas State later that season."

42 The 1967 Texas Tech Comeback

Entering the fall of 1967, Texas A&M was mired in a miserable streak of nine consecutive losing seasons. After starting the '67 season with four close losses, the Aggies looked well on their way to extending their dubious streak to double digits.

The Aggies had often played well in losses to SMU (20–17), Purdue (24–20), LSU (17–6), and Florida State (19–18), and aside from SMU, which eventually finished the year at 3–7, those teams ultimately proved to be quite solid. Purdue, for example, went 8–2 and finished the '67 season ranked ninth nationally, while LSU went to the Sugar Bowl and Florida State went to the Gator Bowl.

Nevertheless, the Aggies couldn't find any solace or satisfaction in close calls. A&M needed something big to happen to turn things around in order to salvage a season that was quickly slipping away.

"We really believed we had a solid football team," former A&M quarterback Edd Hargett recalled. "We easily could have been 3–1 as we headed to Lubbock [for an October 14 game against Texas Tech], but it seemed like we were snake bit or haunted by the ghosts of A&M's past."

A&M attempted to exorcise those demons early in the fourth quarter in Lubbock when Hargett capped a scoring drive with a

13-yard pass to Larry Stegent that gave the Aggies a 21–17 lead following Charlie Riggs' extra point.

But Tech responded late in the fourth quarter by driving 82 yards for a touchdown to regain the lead at 24–21 with less than a minute left on the clock. To add more agony to the Aggies, A&M had been penalized twice during the drive for unsportsmanlike conduct, accounting for 30 yards of the drive.

Once again, it appeared that the Aggies were being governed by Murphy's Law as Tech kicked off with 53 seconds left in the fourth quarter.

A&M moved the ball to the Tech 43 thanks to a 19-yard pass from Hargett to Stegent, but the Aggies later faced fourth-and-15 with 11 seconds left. At that point, the Aggies needed a minor miracle. That's just what Bob Long produced when he out-leapt three Tech defenders to make a sensational catch at the Red Raiders' 15 with three seconds left.

"At that point, we called a timeout and Coach [Gene] Stallings decided to go for the win as opposed to attempting a 32-yard field goal to tie it," Hargett said. "We called the play—Pass 62—where I would fake a handoff to the tailback and then look for my receiving options. The fullback would release into the flats, the tight end would run a crossing route, and our split end would run a curl. No matter what, though, we knew we had to get the ball into the end zone."

Just before the center snapped Hargett the ball on the final play, one of Tech's defenders jumped offside, so Hargett knew he had a free play. He rolled out and noticed that Tech had his receivers blanketed.

"I then looked back to my right and saw that Stegent had just one defender on him," Hargett recalled. "So I decided to tuck it and run. Stegent made a great block, and I ran into the end zone and kept on going into the locker room because the final gun had already sounded."

That dramatic victory turned around the season as A&M then rolled past TCU, Baylor, Arkansas, Rice, and Texas to win the SWC and earn a berth in the Cotton Bowl.

43 Quentin Coryatt and The Hit

Former Texas A&M linebacker Quentin Coryatt quickly credits all of the 12th Man Productions staff members through the years who have annually produced highlight packages that are shown on the video boards before and during Aggie football games at Kyle Field.

He also points out that his continuing popularity among the A&M masses probably has much to do with the Internet, specifically the YouTube website, where game footage from the early 1990s is readily available at the click of a computer mouse.

But no matter how rationally Coryatt discusses the reaction that A&M fans still have toward him, he admits that it defies logic.

"It's been a long time since I last suited up in my Aggie uniform, but I am often stunned to discover how many Aggies still remember specific games and plays I made while playing middle linebacker in 1991–92," Coryatt said. "What's more stunning to me now is that there are Aggie students and fans who were not even born when I first arrived at A&M who can vividly describe certain plays I made."

Actually, there's one play that still causes oohs and aahs among A&M fans of all ages at the mere mention of Coryatt's name. On November 7, 1991, in the midst of a 44–7 victory over TCU in Fort Worth, Coryatt delivered a smashing hit that was later dubbed by CNN as the detonation crunch of the season. Unsuspecting TCU receiver Kyle McPherson crossed the middle of the field and, Coryatt crushed him.

Moon Shots into Kyle Field

Mention "The Hit" to many Texas A&M fans, and there's a good chance vivid images of Quentin Coryatt's punishing blow against TCU in 1991 will instantly come to mind. But before ESPN or even color TV, "The Hit" probably had an entirely different meaning for many Aggies. It also involved TCU and a midfield collision, but it had nothing to with football.

Playing against the Horned Frogs in 1950, Texas A&M outfielder Wally Moon strolled to the plate in the rickety old baseball stadium that backed up to Kyle Field and launched perhaps the most monstrous hit in Aggie memoirs. The ball cleared the outfield fence and kept rising. It cleared the top of the first—and at that time the only—deck of Kyle Field, continued traveling over the seats inside the football stadium, and crossed the old cinder track. When it finally came to a rest, former A&M track coach Andy Anderson picked up the ball near midfield of the football playing surface.

Witnesses of the colossal crunch seem leery about estimating its distance, fearing a guess would fail to do it justice. But A&M historians claim it as the most unforgettable home run—at least in terms of pure length—in Aggie history. And it was done with a wooden bat.

"And a dead ball, for that matter," said Pat Hubert, a pitcher at A&M from 1949–51 and Moon's former roommate. "It was

Unfortunately, the hit ended up shattering McPherson's jaw in three spots. It wasn't a dirty hit, but it was a bone-crushing jolt.

"I knew at the time it would probably make the highlights on *ESPN SportsCenter*, especially since we were playing on a Thursday night on ESPN," Coryatt said. "But I could have never imagined that it would still be replayed, relived, and recited by A&M fans. I'll be at an airport or the grocery store or some place like that, and people will say, 'Hey, you're a pretty good-sized guy. Did you play football?' I'll tell them I used to play at A&M, and I tell them who I am. What usually comes up first is that unbelievable. I remember thinking, *My God, that thing is never going to come down.* It was easily 500', maybe 550', maybe more. It was a hit I will never forget."

Moon, a two-year letterman at A&M in 1949 and '50, won All-SWC honors in 1950, signed with the St. Louis Cardinals later that year, and enjoyed perhaps the most distinguished pro baseball career of any Aggie. After Moon spent 1953 in AAA, the Cardinals traded Enos Slaughter to make room for Moon in the lineup. As a rookie, he hit .304, scored 106 runs, and earned NL Rookie of the Year honors, beating out future Hall of Famers Hank Aaron and Ernie Banks.

After the 1958 season, Moon was traded to the Dodgers, who had moved from Brooklyn to Los Angeles the previous season. He hit .302 his first season with the Dodgers, clubbing 19 homers over the short porch in left field at the Los Angeles Coliseum. The homers became known as "Moon shots." It was a mere 250' down the line in left field, but a 42' net prevented many balls from going out.

Moon shots helped propel the ragtag Dodgers from a seventh-place finish in '58 to a World Championship in '59. Playing in a lineup that featured future legends such as Duke Snider, Maury Wills, and Gil Hodges, Moon helped the Dodgers land the first West Coast World Series in baseball history.

But the first Moon shot of all took place in Kyle Field—the baseball version and the football stadium.

TCU game. They'll say, 'I remember that.' They go on and on from there. It may have been years ago, but a lot of people haven't forgotten that one."

Coryatt, who was born in the Virgin Islands and raised in Baytown, is revered for "The Hit." But he did so much more than that for the Aggies in the early 1990s.

Coryatt's older brother, Jason, played football at Baylor, and after leaving for the military [he served in the first Persian Gulf War], he mentioned to his younger brother that he wished he had made the choice to go to A&M.

Quentin Coryatt was one of the most imposing linebackers in A&M history.
(Photo courtesy of Texas A&M SID)

"Just seeing the Aggie Spirit, the traditions, and support of the student body made him envious of A&M," Coryatt recalled of his brother. "He played against Kevin Murray and those really good mid-1980s A&M teams. A&M was also close to home, so it was easy for my parents to come to my games. It was only about 2½ hours from Baytown to College Station, so that was another big factor in me coming to A&M."

Coryatt had hoped to make an instant impact in Aggieland, but he was forced to sit out the 1988 and '89 seasons because of restrictions relating to Proposition 48. He broke onto the A&M

scene in a big way, earning Southwest Conference Newcomer of the Year honors in 1990. As a senior in 1991, he played on the nation's No. 1 defense and was selected as the SWC's Defensive Player of the Year.

The Indianapolis Colts then selected Coryatt with the second overall pick of the '92 draft.

Coryatt underwent wrist surgery in his rookie season and later had four shoulder surgeries. And in his most agonizing injury of all, he tore the pectoral muscle from the bone.

"They didn't think I'd ever be able to come back from that one, but I did," said Coryatt, who played eight years in the NFL. "I played the game 110 percent every play. It just caught up with me. The bottom line is that the human body is not built to play football. But in retrospect, I wouldn't do it any differently."

44 Chet Brooks and the Wrecking Crew

Growing up in South Oak Cliff on the southern edge of Dallas' city limits, Chet Brooks became a neighborhood star by the way he played football on some of the toughest streets. By the time he reached Carter High School, he was a street-savvy, hard-nosed cornerback who could have gone to a number of different schools.

When he was recruited by Texas A&M, Brooks knew the Aggies were struggling under new head coach Jackie Sherrill. A&M went 5–6 in Sherrill's first season in 1982 and followed with a 5–5–1 season in '83. Despite the records, Brooks said he could sense something special was brewing in College Station.

"Coach Sherrill was the big reason I went to A&M," Brooks said. "He came and visited with me, and he was very impressive. I was looking for a place where I could be myself, get a good education, and have the chance to play as a freshman. A&M offered me all those things, and I really bonded with Coach Sherrill. A&M fit my personality."

Nowadays, Brooks, who owns a construction company and is the father of four, acknowledges that his personality—especially back in his more youthful days—was loud. In fact, it was because of his trash-talking nature that Brooks was widely credited for creating and promoting the Wrecking Crew nickname in the mid-1980s. Brooks proudly says he played a part in popularizing the moniker, but he scoffs at the notion that it was a one-man production.

"It wasn't just me," Brooks said. "Our defense basically named itself. When we went to practice or played a game, we were thinking about wrecking the shop. It was a group effort, and the name fit us well. You would see 11 people flying to the ball, and everyone would be trying to get the hit.

"I may have gotten the credit for the simple reason I was kind of a loud mouth. To tell you the truth, I really don't remember how the name took off so big. Had I known, I might have taken advantage of it with a copyright or something. But I'm proud to have played a role in its early development."

Brooks played a prominent role in the development of the Aggies. He played as a true freshman in '84 and then helped to lead the Aggies to three consecutive Southwest Conference titles.

As of 2012, the former cornerback was still among the top 10 players in A&M history in career passes broken up with 26 from 1984–87. His career statistics would have been more glowing if not for injuring his knee in 1985 and breaking his ankle against Texas in 1987.

The broken ankle also cost Brooks considerably in the draft. He was originally projected as a third-round pick or higher, but he slid to the 11th round of the 1988 draft. The disappointing slide eventually worked out for the best. Brooks finished his college career with three straight SWC titles, and he began his pro career with back-to-back Super Bowl victories with the 49ers.

Five years, five rings. Unfortunately, he also ended up with much more than five scars, but Brooks says he wouldn't change a thing.

"My second year with the 49ers I started the entire year, and I was near the top of the team in tackles and we won another Super Bowl," Brooks said. "You can't complain about winning five championships in a row. But the game also took its toll on me. My rookie year I re-injured the knee I hurt at A&M in 1985 and wound up sitting out the last four of five games.

"When I decided to retire [in 1990], I was tired of the surgeries and all the rehab that went along with trying to get back into playing shape. My body was telling me, 'Chet, you're done.' But it was definitely worth it. I'll never forget how much fun I had playing the game, especially at A&M."

Nor will A&M fans ever forget Brooks, who left a legacy like few others before him.

The Rise and Fall of the '57 Aggies

More than 50 years later, former Texas A&M center Gale Oliver didn't remember if head coach Paul "Bear" Bryant showed up for the Wednesday practice prior to the Rice game wearing a tie or not. But Oliver—along with practically every other living member of the 1957 Aggies—clearly recalls Bryant being out of his typical coaching uniform.

Bryant, a chain-smoking, blue-collared and leather-necked mountain of a man, admired elbow grease and industrial grime as much as gridiron grit, and he talked often to his team about putting on his work clothes. Those speeches were much more than mere metaphors, as Bryant showed up for workouts in ready-to-sweat attire.

So when he arrived for a Wednesday afternoon practice in a business suit…

"We definitely knew something was up," Oliver recalled. "Those weren't his normal work clothes. On top of that, he showed up [to practice] late. Coach Bryant was never late. I can't remember if he was wearing a tie or not, but his clothes were the first indication something was up."

His attire was also the first indication that Bryant would soon be cutting ties with A&M. Bryant had dressed up to meet secretly with Alabama representatives in Houston about the possibility of becoming the Crimson Tide's head coach. A few days later—on the morning of the A&M-Rice game—a story in the *Houston Post* broke the news that Bryant had accepted the job at his alma mater and would be leaving Aggieland at the end of the season.

The Aggies, 8–0 at the time and ranked No. 1 in the nation, were devastated by the news.

"Coach Bryant had such a firm hold on that team," Oliver said. "When the article came out, we were shocked and, in my opinion, we didn't play with the same passion and intensity again. We found out we lost our coach, and then we went out and lost the game."

The Aggies actually dropped their final three games of the season and lost their No. 1 national ranking.

"To this day, I can't explain how it all fell apart so quickly, but it did," said Charlie Milstead, a sophomore quarterback in '57. "Those last three games, especially the Rice loss, are very vivid in my mind. We should have beaten Rice. We definitely should have beaten Texas. It could have been very different. We had a good enough team to [win] a national championship."

There's no telling how differently A&M's football fortunes would have turned out if Bryant had met with Alabama officials, for example, in Navasota as opposed to a high-profile hotel in Houston. Perhaps the story would not have leaked out until after the season—following the Aggies' second national championship in 18 years.

And perhaps if Bryant had not shown up at practice in his dress clothes, the A&M players would have never lost their focus.

"You can play the 'What if?' game until you make yourself sick," Oliver said. "There was no way we were going to keep Coach Bryant at A&M when Alabama came calling. That's where his heart was. But it is human nature to think about what could have been if things had been kept more secretive or turned out differently. I'd like to think we would have won it all."

A&M was in position to win it all when the 6–0 Aggies climbed to No. 1 in the AP poll released October 28, 1957. A&M then edged Arkansas 7–6 in Fayetteville and cruised past Don Meredith and SMU 19–6 at Kyle Field to move to 8–0 as the team prepared for a November 16 trip to Houston where a standing-room-only crowd was expected inside Rice Stadium.

Unfortunately for the Aggies, the biggest challenge of all would come away from the field as officials from Alabama arranged to meet Bryant on Wednesday morning at the Shamrock Hotel in Houston. During that meeting, Bryant agreed to become the head coach at Alabama. But he also specified that no announcement should be made until after the season.

It didn't happen that way, as the *Houston Post* dropped a bomb on Aggies everywhere. When the team awoke on Saturday morning, the upcoming game against Rice had become secondary in importance.

"We were stunned," Oliver said. "Absolutely deflated."

A few hours later, the Aggies would also be defeated. Before a crowd of more than 72,000—still the largest crowd ever to witness a game at Rice Stadium—and a regional television audience on

KPRC-TV, the Owls defeated the Aggies 7–6, which dropped A&M to No. 4 in the national rankings.

A&M also lost its final game of the regular season, falling to Texas 9–7 in College Station. The uninspired Aggies then traveled to Jacksonville, Florida, for the Gator Bowl and played like a team that had lost its direction. A&M's longest drive of the second half was only 18 yards, and Tennessee handed the Aggies a 3–0 setback in the final game of the Bryant era at A&M.

"It was difficult to stomach," John David Crow said. "Honestly, I can't even tell you what happened in the bowl game. By that time, Coach Bryant was basically gone and the season had lost so much of its meaning. We tried to win once the game got started, but our hearts probably weren't in it."

On January 1, 1958, Bryant officially reported to work at Alabama to begin one of the most storied careers in the history of college football.

The 2012 Ole Miss Game

After winning the Heisman Trophy on December 8, 2012, Johnny Manziel was asked by the media to describe his "turning point" moment of the season. Without hesitation, Manziel pinpointed the Ole Miss game on October 6 at Vaught-Hemingway Stadium in Oxford.

It was the Aggies' first SEC road game, and it easily could have been a loss. The Rebels were on the verge of taking control of the contest at several points, but A&M never buckled and produced just enough plays for a monumental win in terms of the confidence it gave the Aggies.

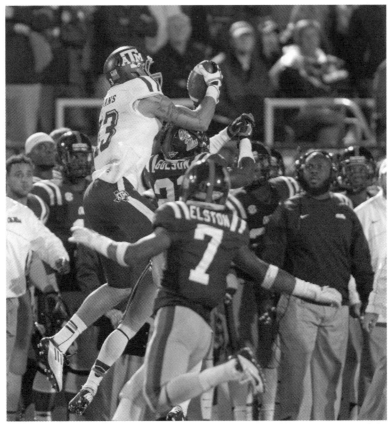

Mike Evans' 32-yard reception in the comeback against Ole Miss was one of the plays of the year in 2012. (Photo courtesy of Texas A&M SID)

"It was probably one of the best wins of my career," linebacker Sean Porter said after a spirited postgame locker room celebration. "I love these guys. It was a great win, a great comeback."

Porter played a big role in making sure the Aggies were within striking distance of a comeback. Following A&M's third turnover of the first half, the Rebels already up 17–10 were driving at their own 42 with 52 seconds left in the second quarter when quarterback Bo Wallace dropped back to pass and began looking down the sideline for a big play. But Porter, coming on a delayed blitz, hit

"Da-Monster" Blazing an Impressive Trail in Von's Footsteps

Coming out of Rowlett High School, Damontre Moore had several college suitors, including Baylor and Oklahoma State, but he committed to Texas A&M prior to his senior year in 2009 primarily because former Aggies defensive line coach Buddy Wyatt sold him on the idea of becoming the next Von Miller.

Moore didn't initially meet the All-American on a spring visit to Aggieland, but Miller, who led the nation with 17 sacks in 2009, served as Moore's host on his official visit. Miller instantly took a liking to Moore. In fact, Von liked Moore enough to introduce his new friend to his own parents, Gloria and Von Miller Sr.

"Von liked him right from the start, and I've always thought Von was a very good judge of character," Gloria Miller said from her home in DeSoto. "I was impressed with Damontre, too, and I told him I'd be watching out for him. I also talked to his momma, and I told Detra, 'I'm in College Station quite a bit, and I'm going to treat Damontre like one of my own. That means if he needs his butt kicked, I'll do it.'"

Eventually, he would need his butt kicked, which was part of the major maturation process he made. Moore was only 17 when he arrived in College Station in the summer of 2010. He played well as a true freshman, recording 5.5 sacks and 40 tackles while backing up

Wallace just as he was beginning to throw. The ball popped straight up, and fellow linebacker Steven Jenkins grabbed it and raced 37 yards for a momentum-altering touchdown.

Instead of going into the locker room facing a 7-, 10- or 14-point deficit, the Aggies were tied at the half. The momentum swing at the end of the first half allowed A&M to be in position for its most dramatic fourth-quarter rally of the season. With 8:35 left in the fourth quarter, Ole Miss held a 27–17 lead as A&M began a key drive at its own 12.

On the first play of the drive, Ole Miss nose tackle Issac Gross wrapped up Manziel near the A&M goal line. Manziel's knee clearly

Miller at the "joker" position during Miller's Butkus Award–winning season.

In the summer of 2011, however, Moore was arrested for possession of less than two ounces of marijuana. In the aftermath of that early-morning arrest on June 3, 2011, Moore says he was terrified that he may have thrown away a promising career. But head coach Mike Sherman gave him another chance, issuing a one-game suspension and arranging weekly meetings with Moore to talk about becoming more accountable.

Moore made the absolute most of his second chance. He finished 2011 with the fourth-most tackles (72) on the team and led the Aggies with 17.5 tackles for loss. He followed that up with a truly sensational season in 2012, leading the team in total tackles (85), tackles for loss (21), and sacks (12.5). Moore earned first-team All-America honors from the Walter Camp Football Foundation, the American Football Coaches Association, ESPN.com, and various other organizations. He was also a first-team All-Southeastern Conference selection and Ted Hendricks Award finalist.

Prior to the Cotton Bowl in 2013, he declared early for the NFL draft, and although he did not have a great performance at the NFL Combine, he was selected in the third round by the New York Giants.

And he may be well on his way to his ultimate goal—being the next Von Miller.

hit on the goal line, but he stretched the ball back across the stripe and into the green turf. Gross was livid that he missed recording a safety by inches, and Ole Miss challenged the call. But after further review, the call stood, and after a two-yard run by Ben Malena on second down, the Aggies faced third-and-19 from their own 3.

From the shotgun, Manziel dropped halfway back in the end zone and lofted a pass in the direction of 6'5" freshman receiver Mike Evans, who was covered extremely well by the Rebels' Senquez Golson. But Evans, utilizing all 77" of his long frame, leaped up and grabbed the ball over the 5'9" Golson's head for a 32-yard gain.

The "jump ball" was probably the pivotal play of the year, and Malena followed it with a 36-yard run to the Ole Miss 29. On the next play, Manziel raced 29 yards to cut the lead to 27–23.

But even after the Aggies cut into the Ole Miss lead with 6:24 left in the game, the Rebels had a golden opportunity to break their 15-game SEC losing streak by simply playing keep away from A&M.

Beginning a drive at its own 16, Ole Miss handed the ball to Jeff Scott on the first two plays of the drive, and he picked up 14 yards to the UM 30. Scott also handled the ball the next three plays, picking up almost 10 yards to set up a fourth-and-an-inch just shy of the Ole Miss 40.

That's when Mississippi coach Hugh Freeze gambled by going for it on fourth down for a third time that night. The Rebels converted the first two tries, but the third time was not a charm.

Running out of the shotgun, Ole Miss handed the ball to Scott for the sixth straight play. Jonathan Stewart beat Scott to the line of scrimmage and stopped him cold in his tracks for a loss.

The Aggies took advantage of the short field, and on the fourth play of the ensuing drive, Manziel tossed a 20-yard over-the-shoulder pass to Ryan Swope for the game-winning TD.

47 The 1990 Holiday Bowl

When recalling the 1990 Holiday Bowl, Defensive MVP William Thomas quickly points out that Texas A&M didn't completely shut out BYU on the night of December 29, 1990. Meanwhile, Bucky Richardson, the Offensive MVP of that game in San Diego, says he can still recall a few things that didn't go the Aggies' way.

In other words, it wasn't a perfect game for A&M. But both players used the same two words to describe A&M's 65–14 win over the ninth-ranked Cougars—near perfection.

"It was as close to the perfect game as I've ever been a part of," Richardson said.

"There's no such thing as a perfect game," Thomas said. "But from our standpoint, that was pretty close. It was one of those nights where everything seemed to work out in our favor. It was total domination in just about every aspect of the game."

It was an old-fashioned, behind-the-woodshed whipping in every sense, which ended with BYU coach LaVell Edwards first confronting A&M offensive coordinator Bob Toledo and then refusing to shake anyone's hand.

The 1990 Cougars had climbed to as high as No. 2 in the national polls early in the season. Then, following a late-September loss at Oregon, BYU went on the offensive, trying to run up the scores on opponents to move back into the national title picture and trying to run up the numbers for Heisman Trophy candidate Ty Detmer. In a nine-game stretch from mid-September to late November, the Cougars scored at least 45 points eight times, topping 50 five times.

But on December 1, BYU blew any national title aspirations when Hawaii crushed the Cougars, 59–28. The loss sent BYU to the Holiday Bowl, and the Cougars were extremely disappointed about the matchup against an unranked 8–3–1 A&M team.

"As soon as the bowl matchup was announced, we started hearing the talk about how disappointed they were," former A&M strength and conditioning coach Mike Clark said. "They talked to the media; they said things at banquets. They were extremely arrogant. It was very obvious that they did not deem us a worthy opponent. And beyond that, they didn't respect us. Those things really did have an effect on the way we prepared for that game."

Richardson said that once the Aggies traveled to the West Coast, the players certainly enjoyed themselves. The Aggies visited SeaWorld, they spent time on the beaches, and they explored the various sights and sounds of San Diego. But once practices began, A&M was all business.

"Looking back, we had some of the best practices I have ever been a part of at any level," said Richardson, who played three NFL seasons with the Houston Oilers. "We practiced at a junior college in San Diego, and we just got after it. We knew BYU was a very good opponent, and everybody knew Ty Detmer was a great quarterback who had just won the Heisman Trophy. We felt like we had our work cut out for us."

Once the game started, it initially appeared to have all the makings of a classic Holiday Bowl shootout. The Aggies took the opening kickoff and marched 80 yards for a touchdown, but BYU quickly answered with a seven-play, 65-yard drive to knot the score at 7–7 roughly eight minutes into the game.

"After that initial exchange of touchdowns, I remember going up to Coach [R.C.] Slocum," Richardson recalled, "and telling him this was going to be a shootout."

Instead, it turned into a blowout. Thomas intercepted Detmer on BYU's next possession, and the rout was on. A&M outscored BYU 58–7 the rest of the way, with Richardson stealing the quarterback spotlight from Detmer.

Richardson rushed for his first touchdown early in the second quarter, caught a touchdown pass from Darren Lewis later in the second quarter, and then threw his first touchdown pass of the night just before halftime.

When Richardson left the game early in the fourth quarter, he'd accounted for 322 yards of total offense. Meanwhile, Detmer also left the game, but not by choice.

Thomas drilled Detmer in the second quarter, causing the Heisman Trophy winner to separate his left shoulder. Detmer went into the locker room and then returned to action. But in the third quarter, Thomas again blasted Detmer, leaving him sprawling on the ground with a separated right shoulder.

When all was said and done, the Aggies had rolled up 680 yards of total offense and limited the prolific BYU passing attack to 197 net yards. And the Wrecking Crew, led by Thomas and Quentin Coryatt, held BYU to minus–12 yards rushing.

"It was one of those games that left an impression on everyone who watched it," said Thomas, who enjoyed an 11-year NFL career with the Philadelphia Eagles and Oakland Raiders. "I remember that during my rookie year with the Eagles Eric Allen, who was a Pro Bowl cornerback from San Diego, came up to me in the locker room when he found out I was from A&M. He had watched the game, and he said, 'Who was that No. 11 running all over the field?' I told him that was me. He was like, 'Man, that was a beat-down you put on those guys. That was unmerciful.'"

The 1975 Loss to Arkansas

Decades later, former A&M tight end Richard Osborne vividly recalled boarding the plane on that cold, dark, drizzly day in Little Rock. A fog of depression seeped from aisle to aisle, and the "Cotton Bowl Express" sign at the front of the plane had been ripped down and shredded.

It was over. The national title dream had died. So had visions of an outright Southwest Conference championship.

Arkansas 31, Texas A&M 6.

"I was thinking, *I can't believe we aren't getting ready to go drink beer because we're playing for the national championship*," Osborne recalled. "It was just total disbelief and shock."

Unbeaten A&M had beaten Texas 20–10 eight days earlier for the first time in eight years. The Aggies had soared to No. 2 in the Associated Press poll and sported a spotless 10–0 record. All the Aggies needed was a victory over the Razorbacks in the season finale and A&M would have faced Georgia in the Cotton Bowl for the chance to win the school's first national championship since 1939.

Instead, it was a Razorbacks rout. But it's not just the final outcome of the game that still haunts the A&M players, coaches, and fans who remember December 6, 1975, with such remorse. It's also the date.

The game wasn't supposed to be played in December. And if it had been played as originally scheduled—November 1, 1975—the Aggies would have likely rolled the Razorbacks, who entered the final game with an 8–2 record. Even the Arkansas players tended to agree with that.

"If we play them in November, it's a whole different ballgame, because we don't have the psychological advantage anymore," former Arkansas wide receiver Jesse Branch said. "Then it's just a matter of lining up against them and seeing who is a better team. And I don't ever remember seeing a better defense than that A&M team."

The '75 Aggies led the nation in total defense and rushing defense, allowing an average of 175 yards and one touchdown per game in the first 10 contests. But even the great A&M defense showed up flat after the emotional win over the Longhorns eight days earlier.

Prior to the start of the season, ABC-TV requested to move the A&M-Arkansas game from its original date to early December to accommodate its desire to broadcast the game nationally. That certainly worked to Arkansas' advantage.

"We were hoping A&M didn't have much emotion left in them after beating Texas the week before," former Arkansas coach Frank Broyles said. "We were planning on catching them at just the right time. We did. It was just right for us."

The emotionally flat Aggies battled throughout the first half, and it looked as if the game might go to the intermission in a scoreless tie. But with 34 seconds left in the second quarter, Arkansas quarterback Scott Bull lofted a prayer in the direction of 5'6" receiver Teddy Barnes, who was double covered by A&M's Lester Hayes and Jackie Williams.

Somehow, the ball descended through the outreached arms of both A&M defenders and lodged in the facemask of Barnes.

"The catch we made in the end zone right before the half was the luckiest thing I ever saw," Branch recalled. "Barnes didn't really even catch it. It just stuck in his facemask."

The Razorbacks rode the wave of momentum into the locker room and completely dominated the second half.

"Well, everybody's been telling us there was no way we could get up two weeks in a row," former A&M linebacker Garth Ten Naple said after the game. "That's all we heard all week—mental, mental. I thought we were up. But I guess everybody knows more than we do."

"What a great, great team Texas A&M had that year," Broyles recalled many years later. "We just got them at the right time. That's all."

Joe Routt

In 1936, Joe Routt became the first All-American in Texas A&M history. He was such a dominating blocker and strong tackler that he repeated the feat in '37, earning consensus All-American honors.

Not bad for a young man who failed to even make the freshman team in 1933.

Routt played high school football at Brenham, but he was primarily focused on farming and working horses, as he grew up on a ranch and cotton plantation. He decided to attend A&M College in hopes of learning the latest farming and ranching techniques, and he figured he would give football a shot while he was in Aggieland. It didn't initially work out.

Routt was cut from the freshman squad and decided to devote his time to boxing. The farm-tough country boy won the lightweight intramural titles at A&M in 1933 and '34.

After all of his accomplishments in the ring, Routt again tried out for the football team in 1935, and A&M head coach Homer Norton recognized his potential. Routt played well in 1935, and he was sensational in '36 when the Aggies went 8–3–1.

Routt was tough as nails on the field, and he was also an honor student in the classroom. He was such a good teammate that he was elected as a team captain in 1937, and he was universally liked in the locker room.

"Joe Routt was my favorite player on the team," said Routt's backup, Alvin "Block" Olbrich, in a 2013 interview with *12th Man Magazine*. "We would be practicing, and we would take a 10-minute break, and Routt would come over to me and say, 'Come on, Block, let's work on this together.' He wanted to help everyone to improve. He was a super player and a helluva good man."

Norton agreed wholeheartedly. When Routt was inducted into the National Football Foundation Hall of Fame in 1962, Norton said, "Joe Routt had the biggest heart and was one of the best fighters I ever saw."

Routt played on the 1938 College All-Star team in Chicago and in the East-West Shrine Game in San Francisco before he was selected in the third round (16th overall pick) of the 1938 NFL Draft by the Cleveland Rams.

Routt never actually played for the Browns, but he was commissioned as a second lieutenant upon graduation from A&M and went on active duty in the army in 1942. Also in 1942, he played for the Army West All-Star team against professional football teams.

In an effort to help fund the United States' World War II expenses, the NFL volunteered to play exhibition games against some of the top collegiate players who were enlisted in the armed services. The U.S. government organized two All-Star teams, and Routt played on the West squad along with former A&M star John Kimbrough. Overall, the 15 exhibition games produced a total purse of $680,384.07, which the NFL donated to the armed services.

After serving on the football field, Routt also distinguished himself on the battlefield. As an infantry officer in World War II, Routt and his troops advanced on German tanks in the Battle of the Bulge. He was killed in a flurry of gunfire on December 10, 1944, and was posthumously awarded the Bronze Star for his service.

He was inducted into the Texas Sports Hall of Fame in 1952, and the street just to the north of Kyle Field on the Texas A&M campus is named Joe Routt Boulevard in his honor.

Ryan Swope

Texas A&M fans already knew. They'd seen Ryan Swope race past defensive backs for years, shifting into another gear and accelerating like a NASCAR driver on the final lap. Swope isn't just fast like an ordinary sports car. He's Ferrari fast.

That's one of the primary reasons he broke A&M's career receiving records in 2012, finishing with 252 catches for 3,117 yards. And it's certainly one of the reasons he shattered the school record for most 100-yard receiving games with 14.

That doesn't happen without breakaway speed and sensational savvy in the open field. Swope possesses those qualities to go along with his great hands, fearlessness, and overall toughness. Swope is the complete package at wide receiver.

Aggies knew it. Appreciated it. Loved it.

And the so-called football experts received a taste of it in late February 2013 when Swope was among the most prominent stars at the NFL Combine, running a 4.34 40-yard dash. Scouts marveled as Swope's draft stock skyrocketed, and Swope later went on the *Dan Patrick Show* and said what most folks were thinking.

"I think a lot of people were pretty shocked," said Swope, who was drafted by the Arizona Cardinals in the sixth round in April 2013. "You don't see that every day, a white guy running a 4.3."

Swope certainly was a one-of-a-kind performer at A&M, and he—along with Von Miller—have become the "poster people" in terms of how valuable it can be for players to return for their senior season.

After the Aggies' disappointing 2011 season and the dismissal of Mike Sherman and his staff, Swope seriously considered forgoing his senior season to enter the draft.

"I prayed about the decision constantly and talked to my family members often," Swope wrote in a letter of thanks to the donors of the 12th Man Foundation following the conclusion of his senior season. "Finally, Coach Kevin Sumlin and former offensive coordinator Kliff Kingsbury reached out to me and essentially recruited me. They showed me how they ran their offense at the University of Houston and convinced me it would be beneficial to return for my senior year. I was leaning that way, and ultimately I followed my heart back to A&M. I am so pleased I did. Being a part of the historic first season in the SEC was more rewarding and satisfying than I could have ever imagined."

It started slowly for Swope, but he began rolling in a 58–10 win over Arkansas and then made one big play after another as the season progressed. He caught the game-winning TD pass against Ole Miss, went for 140 receiving yards against Auburn, produced 121 against Mississippi State, caught 11 passes in the upset of Alabama, and finished his career by shredding OU's secondary for 104 yards in the Cotton Bowl. Among all those great games, Swope says the Alabama victory is probably the most memorable.

"That game is unforgettable for so many reasons—the way we came out and built a 20–0 lead; the energy and volume of more than 101,000 fans inside Bryant-Denny Stadium; the big momentum swings; the Heisman moments produced by Johnny Manziel; the big interception by Deshazor Everett to seal the win; and so much more," he said. "Personally, I had one of the best games of my career, which included a couple of the most memorable catches of my career. I paid the price for them with big hits. But perhaps the most lasting memory of that win was the postgame celebration. I was standing on a brick column in front of thousands of Aggie fans inside Bryant-Denny Stadium and was amazed at how many fans and donors made the trip to be a part of that historic game. It was inspiring to me and my teammates, and it was equally stirring when we returned to College Station and thousands upon thousands of Aggies were waiting to congratulate us outside the Bright Complex.

"The support A&M fans provided—in donations, in attendance, in volume, and in so many other ways—made a lifetime impression on me and my teammates. A&M is an incredibly special place primarily because of remarkably generous people."

No wonder Swope is so adored in Aggieland. A&M fans have admired the person and the player for quite some time.

51 Lester Hayes

Standing on the Kyle Field sidelines during the final moments of Texas A&M's 1994 victory over Texas Tech, Lester Hayes soaked up the roar of the crowd and instantly displayed a smile that was as flashy as the purple leather suit he wore.

"I'll tell you this," Hayes shouted as the crowd noise reached a deafening pitch, "I've been all over the country and played in stadiums everywhere. But the best fans on the planet are at Kyle Field. This place just has a way of putting the fear of God into opponents."

So did Hayes…at Kyle Field and NFL stadiums across the country. As a safety at A&M and later as a cornerback with the Oakland/Los Angeles Raiders, Hayes didn't just cover receivers. He challenged them verbally—despite his stuttering issues—whipped them physically, and always stayed in their face and on their minds.

"I didn't play football to be a nice guy," said Hayes, who turned 58 on January 22, 2013. "I played as mean and as tough as I could. I came to A&M as a linebacker and then moved into the secondary. But I never lost that linebacker's mentality. Then Jack Tatum took me under his wing with the Raiders. Jack was the ultimate T-Rex. He'd rip you apart and eat your flesh. When I was on the field, I envisioned being in Vietnam, and the opponents were the Viet Cong. I'd jab [receivers], try to knock their heads into a different time zone, and stick with them."

Few defensive backs in the history of the game did a better job of sticking with receivers than Hayes. And not just because he spent the early portion of his glorious 10-year NFL career covered in Stick'um, a gooey substance that literally dripped off his hands before the NFL outlawed it in 1981 in a rule that included his name.

In the NFL, Hayes became known as "The Judge" and "Lester the Molester" because of his physical, no-mercy style of play.

But Hayes was sensational long before he earned his NFL reputation. He lettered at A&M from 1973–76 and was an integral part of probably the first great Aggie defense of the modern era. In 1975, the Aggies led the nation in total defense—thanks in large part to what might have been the best secondary in A&M history.

Before becoming a legend with the Raiders, Lester Hayes earned All-American honors at A&M. (Photo courtesy of Texas A&M SID)

With Hayes at strong safety and future All-Pro Pat Thomas at cornerback, the Aggies completely took away the passing game from many opponents.

"We were great, and that's not just a matter of opinion. Look at the stats," said Hayes, who was born in Houston and now lives in Modesto, California. "We had great linebackers [Robert Jackson, Ed Simonini, and Garth Ten Naple], who all turned out to be All-Americans. Teams couldn't run against us, and they sure as hell weren't going to pass against us.

"But we also had great coaches, and I owe a lot to them. The assistants like R.C. Slocum, Melvin Robertson, and all those guys helped me tremendously. And I think former A&M head coach Emory Bellard is, along with John Madden, one of the two best coaches I ever played for. A&M gave me a start, and I love that school with all my heart."

Hayes was a two-time All-SWC selection at A&M and an All-American in 1976 when he intercepted eight passes and broke up six more as the Aggies finished No. 7 in the Associated Press final poll.

In the NFL, Hayes switched positions and developed into the best man-to-man coverage cornerback in the league. He picked off 13 passes in 1980 (second most in NFL single-season history at the time), became the Raiders' all-time interception leader (39 in his career), made five Pro Bowls, and collected two Super Bowl rings.

Darren Lewis

Throughout his childhood and adolescence, Darren Lewis was hailed along South Oak Cliff's tough streets as the quintessential football superstar who was destined for fortune and fame. He was the can't-miss kid whose extraordinary combination of speed, elusiveness, and power earned him an immeasurable amount of adulation in his old neighborhood, which is just north of Interstate 20 and increasingly south of the poverty line.

"When he was 6, 7, or 8, hundreds of people—maybe thousands—would crowd the sidelines [at nearby Danieldale Park] to see him run in pee wee games," recalled his sister, Kimberly Lewis. "It was like some kind of cult following. He quickly went from being 'Darren' to becoming 'Tank' because he was unstoppable. When you're told all your life that you are Superman, you tend to believe it."

Lewis should know differently now. His Kryptonite is cocaine, which has corrupted and crippled his life, stopping Tank in his tracks with its addictive powers. Drug abuse ultimately wrecked his career, ruined his finances, shattered his marriage, uprooted his kids, destroyed his dreams, and ruined his reputation.

Many of his remarkable rushing records at A&M remain intact. But his once-revered status is as tainted as his criminal records, which include at least 15 theft charges, numerous probation violations, and a slew of drug-related incidents.

The most recent issue—at least at the time of this writing—occurred on January 29, 2013, when Lewis was charged with the aggravated robbery of a Duncanville 7-Eleven store that left an employee with a gunshot wound in the leg. Unfortunately, no one who has closely followed Lewis' life and his endless array of bad decisions was likely stunned that he was placed back behind bars.

"Darren is one of the most gracious, most caring, and most likeable guys I've ever coached," former A&M head coach R.C. Slocum said. "But Darren's biggest fault is probably that he wants everyone to be his friend. As a result, he's allowed many people—bad people—to influence him negatively, and he's been a magnet for trouble."

Cyrus Gray: An all-time great guy

After reading the Old Testament in the Bible during the latter stages of her pregnancy in 1989, Sharonia Gray decided that she would name her second son "Cyrus" after the king of Persia in 559 B.C., who is referenced in the book of Isaiah as the Lord's "anointed" one.

During his collegiate career at Texas A&M (2008–11), Gray certainly lived up to his namesake, who was known as "Cyrus the Great." On the field and off of it, Gray had a great influence on games, the locker room, teammates, and fans.

"He's always doing things the right way," A&M receiver Ryan Swope said of Gray in 2011.

"The one word that comes to mind when describing Cyrus as a player, a person, and a leader is 'selfless,'" former A&M running backs coach Randy Jordan said. "He defines the word, 'unselfishness.' He's generally a soft-spoken guy, but he leads by great example. He's a pretty remarkable role model."

Added former A&M head coach Mike Sherman: "Cyrus is not perfect, but his attitude is pretty close."

The humble, team-oriented, and unassuming Gray was one of the primary reasons the 2010 Aggies won nine games and reached the Cotton Bowl. After taking over as the starting tailback for an injured Christine Michael, Gray ended '10 with seven consecutive 100-yard rushing performances, including a 223-yard effort against Texas (the most ever by an Aggie against the Longhorns).

He also finished his A&M career as the third-leading rusher in school history (3,298 yards), which ranked him behind only Darren Lewis and Curtis Dickey. Gray, easily one of the most popular players on the roster throughout his A&M career, was selected in the sixth round of the 2012 NFL Draft by the Kansas City Chiefs.

Indeed, Lewis has left the crime-ridden neighborhood where he grew up many times. But he's never completely left the negative influences behind him.

He once dominated foes at Dallas Carter High School, where he became a Parade All-American and the Gatorade Player of the Year as a senior. He then rushed for 714 yards as a freshman at

A&M in '87 and burst onto the scene nationally as a sophomore by rushing for a school-record 1,692 yards despite only carrying the ball 10 times in the first two games because of a severe toe injury.

He earned first-team All-American honors in '88, and he repeated that feat as a senior in 1990. While rushing for 1,691 yards as a senior, Lewis shattered Eric Dickerson's all-time SWC career rushing record and established A&M career records for rushing yards (5,012), rushes (909), touchdowns (44), most 100-yard rushing games (27), most 200-yard rushing games (five), and all-purpose yards (5,138).

In the opinion of most NFL scouts, Lewis possessed first-round talent. But while training in Houston for the NFL draft, Lewis claims he befriended a couple of "runners" for his agent, and they introduced him to cocaine. Lewis says he'd tried marijuana in high school, but his first brush with cocaine came in the months leading up to the draft on April 21–22, 1991.

When Lewis attended the NFL Scouting Combine in February in Indianapolis, he submitted a urine sample for drug testing, which he failed. Lewis' draft stock plummeted.

When he was finally selected by Chicago in the sixth round, 19 running backs had been chosen before him. Lewis played in 15 games as a rookie, and he primarily became a special teams performer the following year. But following a publicized domestic dispute with his ex-wife during the 1993 season, Lewis was released by the Bears. The can't-miss kid played 33 games in his NFL career, starting six and totaling 431 rushing yards.

Lewis says he remained drug-free throughout his tenure with the Bears, but after he was released, he decided to experiment with crack cocaine. He also blew off an opportunity to try out with the Arizona Cardinals after Slocum had arranged for Lewis to work out with the team.

"That was a huge mistake," Lewis said of failing to show up in Arizona.

It was only one in a long line of huge mistakes Lewis would make in the ensuing years. By the time he was released from the Palestine Unit of the Texas Department of Corrections on October 27, 2010, Lewis' list of criminal records was as lengthy as his football records at A&M.

But he vowed to make the most of his freedom this time. He was the subject of a lengthy article in *12th Man Magazine* in January 2011, and he appeared on a panel of former players at a TexAgs. com function in College Station in the summer of 2012. He said all the right things in interviews, but by January 2013, he had obviously turned back to his destructive habits.

Greg Hill (left) and Darren Lewis (right) grew up in the same neighborhood in Dallas, but followed different paths later in life. (Photo by Rusty Burson)

Greg Hill

When Dallas Carter High's Darren Lewis departed A&M following the 1990 season as the all-time leading rusher in SWC history, it appeared to leave a gaping hole in the Aggies' ground game. And A&M had even more cause for concern when senior running backs Keith McAfee and Randy Simmons went down with injuries just a few days prior to the 1991 season-opener against LSU.

After the first game in the 1991 season, however, A&M fans were no longer worried about how to replace Lewis. The Aggies simply plugged in another Carter High product, and A&M was literally off and running once again.

On September 14, 1991, at Kyle Field, redshirt freshman running back Greg Hill enjoyed the finest debut game for a freshman running back in the history of college football at the time, slicing and dicing the LSU defense for 212 rushing yards and two touchdowns on 30 carries. Behind Hill's heroics, the Aggies coasted past the Tigers, 45–7.

"I knew I needed to step up in a big way," Hill recalled, "and I'm proud to say that is exactly what I did."

Hill scored on a 22-yard run on the Aggies' opening series, and by halftime he had surpassed 100 yards on the ground. He actually left the game early, missing most of the fourth quarter. Hill's performance broke the Kyle Field rushing record of Baylor's Walter Abercrombie, who torched A&M for 207 rushing yards in 1978.

"I went on to rush for at least 100 yards five times during my freshman season," said Hill, who was inducted into the A&M Athletic Hall of Fame in 2009. "I was able to carry the ball so many times during my freshman season as we ran out the clock in victories that fans, teammates, and even media members began referring to the fourth quarter as 'GHT,' signifying that it was 'Greg Hill Time.'"

Although Hill chose to forgo his senior season to enter the NFL draft, he finished his collegiate career as the third-leading rusher in A&M history with 3,262 yards. Hill obviously did a great job replacing Lewis, which was especially meaningful to him because from the moment he first saw Lewis run in his old neighborhood in South Oak Cliff, Hill mimicked Lewis' every move. Hill says his childhood heroes were NFL star running backs Tony Dorsett, Eric Dickerson, Bo Jackson, and Lewis. But not necessarily in that order.

"[Lewis] didn't even know who I was back then, but I watched him when he was on the A-team of the Cubs [of the youth Police Athletic League], and I was on the C-team," Hill recalled. "I followed his footsteps from Umphrey Lee Elementary School to D.A. Hulcy Middle School and on to Carter High and then to A&M. More than just about anything in the world, I wanted to be just like Tank. He was my inspiration."

Ironically, even when Lewis was at the depths of his self-destructive, drug-induced hell in the early 1990s, he continued to be Hill's inspiration. Hill says he cried in his dorm at A&M when he first heard Lewis had failed an NFL-mandated drug test in 1991. And with each devastating misstep Lewis would make in the ensuing years, Hill vowed to learn from his hometown hero's mistakes...and not repeat them.

Hill made a promise to himself that he would never try cocaine, marijuana, or even cigarettes. He also made the decision to never even have an alcoholic beverage. To this day, Hill says he has never celebrated a monumental moment or unwound from a long day with a beer or a glass of wine.

"[Addiction] caught my idol, so I don't drink, do drugs, or smoke," Hill said. "I have an addictive personality, and I came from the same streets as Tank did. In the back of my mind, I always knew that if it could happen to him, it could happen to me. I had to find a straighter route."

Hill's pathway has not been problem-free. But it has led him from his impoverished beginnings to financial independence. Hill, who now resides in the affluent north Dallas suburb of Frisco, played six seasons in the NFL. He seemed destined for stardom with the Rams in 1998, as he led the entire league in rushing early in the season.

A broken leg that same year seriously jeopardized his career, but even before he left the NFL for good in 2000, he became the co-owner of an audio-video business in Dallas that did well, and he then began a financing company in '04. He's maintained a golden touch in entrepreneurship, opening a high-end childcare location in '07. He's also held various media roles in recent years.

All of his successes have enabled Hill to be the kind of doting father to his kids, daughter Jordan and son Jayden, that he never experienced, as Hill was raised by his single mother.

Terrence Murphy

When Terrence Murphy departed Aggieland in 2004, he owned most of the school's career receiving records. Not bad for a guy who was barely even recruited by any major colleges in his own state.

"I thank God daily for sending me down the path that led me to A&M because that school helped to shape and mold me," said Murphy, who caught 172 passes for 2,600 yards from 2001–04. "Becoming an Aggie was such a blessing for me in so many different ways."

It was certainly an unexpected blessing for A&M. After overcoming severe bronchitis and seizures early in his life, Murphy became a star quarterback at Tyler's Chapel Hill High School and committed to following in the footsteps of his oldest brother, Kendrick Bell, who had been a standout running back at Baylor from 1991–94. But Murphy's stepfather, former Texas A&M defensive lineman Keith Guthrie (1980–83), also placed a call to R.C. Slocum, who examined a highlight tape and offered Murphy a scholarship.

Murphy promptly set a school freshman record with 36 catches, erasing the 29-year-old record set by Richard Osborne. His early success motivated him to work even harder.

Murphy was relentless in his workout routine, pumping iron, pounding the pavement, and working on his quickness into the wee hours of the morning while others partied. The hard work paid off, as Murphy left with the most total all-purpose yards by a receiver (3,583) in A&M history. And he was the only player in his class to be honored as a three-time Academic All-Big 12 selection.

Murphy was selected in the second round of the 2005 NFL Draft by the Green Bay Packers, where he was immediately among the NFC statistical leaders in kickoff returns during the first month of his rookie season.

"More significantly to me, I was just beginning to truly earn Brett Favre's trust in my role as a wide receiver," Murphy recalled. "I was beginning to fulfill all my dreams."

On the night of October 3, 2005, however, Murphy's life changed in the suddenness of a lightning bolt across the night sky. During the second quarter of a *Monday Night Football* game against Carolina, Murphy picked up a muffed kick and returned it seven yards before being hit by Panthers safety Thomas Davis. It wasn't a cheap shot, but Murphy's head was down when helmets collided.

He heard the pop. He heard the roar of the crowd. Then nothing.

Terrence Murphy departed A&M with most of the school's career receptions records. (Photo courtesy of Texas A&M SID)

"I couldn't feel my legs," Murphy said. "I couldn't feel my arms. I couldn't move."

For five minutes, Murphy was paralyzed from the neck down. He was later diagnosed with a spinal stenosis injury, and his football career was over after three NFL games.

"At that point, I relied on three things to refocus me, rejuvenate me, and put me back on the right track," Murphy said. "Those three things were my faith in Jesus Christ, my own resolve, and the relationships of so many people who cared for me."

In the aftermath of his injury, Murphy fell in love with his future wife, Erica. They were married in February 2008, and the couple settled in College Station, where Murphy also opened his own investment-acquiring company in '08.

The couple's first child, daughter Teryn, was born in September 2010, and she is growing almost as quickly as Murphy's business, TM5 Properties. Since first opening his business in '08, Murphy has displayed a phenomenal entrepreneurial touch. He earned his real estate license in 2010, and in 2012 Murphy was ranked in the top one percent of all realtors in the Bryan-College Station area. He was also one of 50 finalists for the National Association of Realtors prestigious 30 Under 30 Award, which honors the top younger than 30 realtors in the country.

"I've been blessed in so many ways, and being as passionate about my profession today as I once was about football is one of those blessings," said Murphy, who turned 30 on December 15, 2012. "To be able to come back to Aggieland to raise a family and build a career is especially rewarding. I've always worked hard, and I've always counted my blessings."

55 The Texas Special

Prior to the 1965 Texas A&M–Texas game, first-year Aggie coach Gene Stallings could barely contain his excitement. The 30-year-old head coach had a trick play up his sleeve, and he was so energized about the play's potential that he told a sportswriter just prior to the game:

"I've got a play that's guaranteed to score a touchdown against Texas if I have the guts to call it," Stallings said, asking the sportswriter to keep that nugget to himself.

Fortunately for Stallings, there was no Twitter in 1965. And fortunately for A&M, the Aggies' coach did have the guts to call it.

The Aggies entered the November 25, 1965, Thanksgiving Day game against the Longhorns at Kyle Field with a bit of momentum after beating Rice 14–13 the previous game. But the win over the Owls only improved the Aggies' overall record to 3–6. It was also the first SWC win of Stallings' A&M tenure.

Meanwhile, Texas entered the annual showdown with a mediocre 5–4 record. Although it was a down year for the Longhorns, Texas had still won eight in a row against the Aggies. Stallings knew his team needed something good to happen to it early in the game so the players might truly believe they had a chance to put an end to the losing streak.

His concoction was called, "The Texas Special."

After a scoreless first quarter, the Aggies took possession in the second quarter deep in their own end of the field. After a one-yard running play on first down, A&M faced second-and-9 from the Aggies' own 9. That's when Stallings decided it was time to pull out his secret play.

Just as it had been rehearsed earlier in the week, Texas A&M quarterback Harry Ledbetter bounced a lateral toward halfback Jim Kauffmann, who picked up the ball, stomped his feet in anger as the fans at Kyle Field thought it was a busted play, and momentarily took a step backward toward his own end zone. All of the Aggie players acted in disgust, as if Ledbetter had grossly underthrown an incomplete pass rather than a lateral.

But Kauffmann then looked up and connected with a wide-open Ken "Dude" McLean, who had jetted 15 yards past the Texas secondary. The field judge had been tipped off before the game by Stallings so that an inadvertent whistle would not be blown when the lateral hit the ground.

McLean caught the pass some 40 yards from the line of scrimmage and raced 91 yards for a TD and a 7–0 lead for the Aggies. The play, which was the longest in Texas A&M and Southwest

Conference history at the time, helped stake the Aggies to a 17–0 halftime lead.

"It was one of the most original, clever plays I have ever seen," Texas coach Darrell Royal said afterward.

The play helped McLean produce 250 receiving yards on 13 catches, an SWC record that stood until 1989. But it wasn't enough for the Aggies to win as Texas rallied for a 21–17 victory.

Nevertheless, it remains one of the most memorable and successful plays in A&M history, and it was one that McLean proudly talked about until the February day in 2009 when he finally lost his battle with cancer.

Jack Pardee

Jack Pardee, the first academic All-American in Texas A&M history and one of the greatest players and most humble personalities to ever wear the Maroon and White, insisted that he never envisioned winning championships or achieving individual acclaim when he arrived in Aggieland from Christoval, a tiny town approximately 20 miles south of San Angelo.

What he visualized the most upon arriving at A&M in the mid-1950s was air conditioning.

"My dad had severe arthritis, and I had five brothers and sisters, so money was tight," Pardee said. "During the summers—starting when I was about 14 and continuing through high school—I'd work nasty, dirty, hot oilfield jobs, and every once in a while I'd see guys drive up in a nice car or pickup to give instructions to my boss. What left the biggest impression on me was the fact that when they would roll down their windows, the air conditioning inside

Attend Aggie Muster on Campus

One of the greatest of all A&M traditions is Aggie Muster, a time-honored ceremony that celebrates the camaraderie of the school while remembering the lives of Aggies who have died, specifically those in the past year.

Muster officially began on April 21, 1922, as a day for remembrance of fellow Aggies. Muster ceremonies are now held at approximately 320 locations around the world. But the largest and most impressive Muster each year is held in Reed Arena on April 21 on the A&M campus. It's a must-attend event for every Aggie or Aggie fan.

The Roll Call for the Absent commemorates former students who died within the previous year or students who were enrolled at A&M when they died. Aggies light candles, and friends and families of Aggies who died that year answer "here" when the name of their loved one is called. Campus Muster also serves as a 50-year class reunion for the corresponding graduating class, and it usually features a well-known speaker. Off-campus Muster ceremonies are not typically as impressive as the one that is held on campus, so plan to at least make one trip to College Station to experience the event at Reed Arena.

the vehicle would pour out. It felt like a little bit of heaven. After asking a lot of questions, I discovered those guys inside the car were petroleum engineers.

"I didn't know the difference between a petroleum engineer and a train engineer at that time, but it stuck in my mind that being an engineer might be a good thing. Several years later when I began being recruited by Texas A&M, I was pretty intrigued by the fact that A&M had a program to help you become an engineer."

Pardee, an All-American fullback in 1956, ultimately helped Bear Bryant engineer one of the great turnarounds in college football, leading the Aggies from a 1–9 record in 1954 to an SWC championship in '56, Pardee's senior year.

Pardee played six-man football at Christoval, where the 6'2", 200-pounder scored more than 300 points during his senior year.

Partly because of his desire to be an engineer, he signed with A&M head coach Ray George and played on the freshman team under Willie Zapalac in 1953.

"I loved A&M right away, but coming from West Texas, I was in for a shock in terms of practicing," Pardee said. "At first, I didn't know if I could make it with the heat and humidity of College Station."

As Pardee would soon find out, those practices were a piece of cake compared to what Bryant put the Aggies through in Junction in '54. Pardee went to Junction as a fifth-team fullback and linebacker. After playing eight different positions and losing more than 10 pounds during the camp, he returned as one of the Aggies' key players.

After the 1–9 season in '54, Pardee helped lead the Aggies to a 7–2–1 record in '55 and a sparkling 9–0–1 mark in '56. The Los Angeles Rams chose Pardee in the second round of the 1957 NFL Draft, and he played for the Rams from 1957–70. When he was 28, Pardee was diagnosed with skin cancer. Fortunately, the doctors caught the cancer in time, but dealing with cancer changed his perspective on life.

"Football had been so much of my focus up until that point, but I really began focusing more on my family afterward," Pardee said. "I met my wife, Phyllis, on a blind date during my senior year at A&M, and we were blessed with five wonderful children— Steven, Judy, Ann, Susan, and Ted."

After being diagnosed with cancer, Pardee continued to play, and when head coach George Allen made the move to Washington, Pardee moved with him, joining Allen as a player-coach for the 1971 and '72 seasons. The final game he ever played in his 15-year career was in Super Bowl VII against the Miami Dolphins.

With his playing days behind him, Pardee accepted the head coaching position with the Florida Blazers in the World Football

Jack Pardee was an All-American fullback in 1956.
(Photo courtesy Texas A&M SID)

League in 1974 and led the team to the title game. He then coached the Chicago Bears from 1975–78 and the Redskins from 1978–80.

After sitting out of football for a brief time, he became the head coach of the USFL's Houston Gamblers in '84, introducing an exciting new offense known as the Run-and-Shoot. In 1987, the University of Houston hired him, and Pardee guided the '89 Cougars to a 9–2 record with quarterback Andre Ware winning the Heisman Trophy in the Run-and-Shoot.

Pardee was then chosen to replace Jerry Glanville as the Oilers' head coach in 1990. He guided the Oilers to four straight playoff appearances (1990–93) but was fired after a disappointing start to the 1994 season.

"But I had a great run in football and I have no regrets," said Pardee, who died in April 2013. "I've always felt very blessed that I was able to do what I loved to do as long as I did. Going all the way back to Texas A&M, I was very, very fortunate. Playing football and being a part of that university, with all the friendly people, kind of brought me out of my shell."

The opportunities he received after A&M also allowed him to buy many vehicles with air conditioning…just as he had hoped many years earlier.

57 Johnny Holland

Coming out of Hempstead High School—where he had been an All-State performer in football and basketball, a top-10 student in his class, and an all-around local celebrity—Johnny Holland had plenty of reasons to become a Texas Longhorn.

Holland's cousin, Roosevelt Leaks, was the first African American All-American at Texas, starring as a running back for the

Horns. Holland's sister also attended Texas, and it probably would have been easier for Holland to play quarterback right away at UT than at A&M, where new head coach Jackie Sherrill was stacking up QB prospects.

But for Holland, a small-town guy at heart, living in Austin was not nearly as appealing as establishing roots in College Station, only a 45-mile drive straight up Highway 6 from Hempstead.

"Texas A&M and College Station just made more sense to me," said Holland, whose No. 1 Hempstead High School jersey was retired shortly after his graduation. "I really liked the feel of the campus."

That proved to be a feel-good moment for A&M and a difficult decision for Longhorns fans to stomach for many years to come. Holland eventually became one of the greatest defenders in A&M history and a two-time All-American linebacker in 1985–86. He was a leader of SWC championship teams in 1985 and '86, a foundational building block of the Aggies' Wrecking Crew reputation, and perhaps the father of A&M's "Linebacker U" legacy.

Not bad for a guy who didn't appear to have a bright future at the original position he envisioned in college.

Upon his arrival in Aggieland in the summer of 1983, Holland was presented with his No. 11 jersey—a quarterback's number— and he began running drills with the numerous other quarterbacks on campus. Early in the '83 season, however, Sherrill approached Holland with an alternative option.

"When I was a freshman, we had seven or eight quarterbacks, including Kevin Murray," Holland said, as reported by Mary Schmitt of the *Milwaukee Journal* in a 1987 story. "Coach Sherrill wanted to redshirt all the freshmen quarterbacks. He asked me if I played defensive back, which I never had. But I said, 'Yeah.' I figured I was an athlete so I could play it. I played a little free safety my freshman year, and then they moved me to linebacker as a sophomore."

That was the Wrecking Crew recipe for success under defensive coordinator R.C. Slocum, who built his defenses around speed. Slocum always liked moving guys "up" in the defense—transitioning a defensive back to linebacker or a linebacker to defensive end—because it added speed.

Holland was one of the first speed linebackers to truly flourish in Slocum's aggressive defensive style. Throughout the 1980s and into the '90s, A&M became known as the Linebacker U of the South (Penn State had that reputation in the North), and that status probably began with Holland, who made plays from sideline to sideline from his inside linebacker position.

Holland was sensational throughout his final three years at A&M. He led the Aggies in tackles in 1984 (155) and 1986 (147) and left A&M as the school's all-time leading tackler with 455 stops (Dat Nguyen broke the record in the 1990s). He twice recorded 20 or more tackles in a game during his career, compiling 22 stops against Alabama in 1985 and 20 against Southern Miss in 1986.

Holland was drafted in the second round by Green Bay in 1987, and he played seven impressive years with the Packers. Former Green Bay linebackers coach Bob Valesente said of Holland, "He's one of the most consistent performers you'll find on the field on game day."

Holland was named the Packers' Rookie of the Year in 1987 and registered at least 100 tackles for six consecutive years (1988–93) during his career. In 1992 he suffered the first herniated disc injury that eventually cut short his career. After undergoing a corrective vertebrae fusion, Holland returned to lead the team with a career-high 145 tackles in 1993.

Following that season, a second herniated disk forced his retirement on May 20, 1994. He began his coaching career in Green Bay in 1995, moved to Seattle in 2000, and has also coached with Detroit, Houston, and Oakland.

Holland was inducted into Texas A&M's Athletic Hall of Fame in 1993, the Cotton Bowl Hall of Fame in 2000, and the Packers' Hall of Fame in 2001.

58 Stay in the Stands for the Fightin' Texas Aggie Band

At most football stadiums across America, halftime represents an opportunity to stretch the legs, grab something to eat, or visit the bathroom.

Not at Kyle Field. And not when the Fightin' Texas Aggie Band travels with the football team to out-of-town destinations.

Unlike many other collegiate bands with frilly and exaggerated uniforms, superfluous flag corps performers, and sequin-covered, ballet-mimicking baton twirlers, the nationally famous Fightin' Texas Aggie Band is not a sideshow, show tune–playing distraction; it's long been a main game-day attraction, which is why Aggie fans have been trained to stay in the stands until after the band's performance has concluded.

In fact, while the Aggie football team has frequently been outscored by opponents through the years, most A&M former students, fans, and current students believe—with all their hearts— that Texas A&M has never, ever lost a halftime. And most opposing fan bases would not disagree. The A&M Band, with its patriotic music and jaw-dropping precision, has regularly received standing ovations following performances on the road as spectators marvel at the pinpoint maneuvers performed by the nation's largest military marching band.

The band has performed at inauguration parades for several Presidents of the United States, as well as parades celebrating many

The nationally famous Fightin' Texas Aggie Band is one of the main attractions of a football game day at Texas A&M. (AP Photo/Pat Sullivan)

other occasions. But the band owes its national reputation to the grand stage that Aggie football has presented it throughout the years.

The band traces its origins to Joseph Holick, who initially worked in a Bryan boot shop in the late 1880s. Lawrence Sullivan Ross, the president of A&M at the time, was impressed with Holick's work at the boot shop and requested that he relocate to College Station to service the footwear needs of the cadets at A&M College.

Holick accepted the proposal and moved to College Station to work at Texas A&M. In addition to his cobbler work, Holick was also a talented musician, who was asked to play the bugle for Corps of Cadets functions. Holick eventually asked the commandant for permission to start a band comprised of cadets. Holick, who also manufactured senior boots, started the first band in 1894 with approximately 14 members.

The band grew in the ensuing years, and for a rousing marching squad that desired a place to perform for more than just the standard campus functions, the football stadium became the grand stage, especially as Kyle Field expanded from one generation to another.

As the university grew, so did the band, which typically consists of about 300 to 400 members today. All of the members are part of the Corps of Cadets, so they eat together, sleep in the same dormitories, and practice up to 40 hours per week in addition to their academic demands.

Through the years, the extensive practice has allowed the Aggie Band to expand its marching maneuvers and increase the difficulty of the performances. The maneuvers, designed by the directors and drum majors, are often mesmerizing to fans. According to an article in the student newspaper, *The Battalion*, some of the Aggie Band's maneuvers—like the four-way crisscross—are so complex that some drill-charting software describes them as impossible because they require multiple members to be in the same place at the same time.

As the popular Adidas slogan states, "Impossible is nothing" for the Fightin' Texas Aggie Band.

59

12th Man Kickoff Team

Jackie Sherrill climbed to the second stack of Aggie Bonfire on a cool November night in 1982 and gazed at the activity below him. He was fascinated by the fanaticism, tantalized by the toughness of the students, and captivated by the camaraderie.

As Sherrill continued to survey the surroundings, the students handed him pliers and provided him with instructions on how to wire the mammoth logs together on the 55' stack. Sherrill clearly saw the passion in their eyes. He instantly understood their commitment to the cause.

Suddenly, a thought crossed his mind.

What if he could find 10 of these maniacs—10 of these Bonfire-building, reckless renegades who were obviously willing to risk life and limb for Texas A&M—to run down on kickoff coverage? What kind of positive marketing could that generate? What kind of raucous reaction would that create inside Kyle Field? How could he possibly honor the original 12th Man, E. King Gill, any better than actually pulling students out of the stands and suiting them up in uniform?

"If these kids are this tough and crazy and give so much back to their school," Sherrill recalled thinking that night, "then I can find 10 [plus a scholarship kicker] to go down the field on my kickoff team."

That's how the 12th Man Kickoff Team at Texas A&M was born. A couple of months later, Sherrill stopped by Duncan Dining Hall and announced his idea to the 2,327-member Corps of Cadets. He invited anyone interested in being part of this walk-on group to a tryout. He then placed three advertisements in the student newspaper, *The Battalion*, about the tryout.

More than 250 Aggies, including two women, showed up for the tryout. Sherrill cut that group to 17, and by the summer of 1983 *Sports Illustrated* was on campus to write a positive, six-page article on the unique squad.

The first 12th Man Kickoff Team debuted on September 3, 1983, against California—the team that in 1982 returned the famous, multilateral kickoff against Stanford and the Cardinal band for a game-winning touchdown.

Against the Golden Bears, the 12th Man Kickoff Team performed well, and it played exceptionally well at home all season (the walk-on unit did not travel to regular season road games), allowing just 13.1 yards per kickoff return. In fact, no opposing team managed to score a touchdown against the 12th Man Kickoff Team in its first seven years of existence.

The end of the 12th Man Kickoff Team as Sherrill originally designed it came in 1990 when Texas Tech's Rodney Blackshear returned a kickoff for a touchdown. Head coach R.C. Slocum then modified the tradition to feature one walk-on player on each kickoff.

That tradition continued throughout the Slocum years, survived the Dennis Franchione and Mike Sherman eras, and continues today with Kevin Sumlin.

Many members of all the previous 12th Man Kickoff Teams under Sherrill and subsequent coaches are still having an impact on Aggieland today through the 12th Man Kickoff Team Foundation (12th MKOTF), which was chartered in 2007 by Sherrill.

"Back in 2007, Coach Sherrill called four or five of the original members of the 12th Man Kickoff Team and pitched the idea of putting something together that was similar to what Bear Bryant helped to create at Alabama, where a foundation could provide scholarships to heirs [of the 12th Man Kickoff Team members]," said Warren Barhorst, a member of the 1987 12th Man Kickoff Team. "The group came back to Sherrill and said, 'Coach we would love to put a foundation together, but not for our heirs.

We want to raise scholarship dollars for Aggies who really need the help.' Coach was surprised, but we made sure it was in the bylaws that if you are an heir of a 12th Man Kickoff Team member, you can't accept a scholarship."

The organization has also been influential in raising funds for various causes. In 2010, for example, the 12th MKOTF raised $125,000 to name the ALS clinic in Round Rock in honor of former A&M coach Emory Bellard. The following year the 12th MKOTF raised $25,000 in honor of Billy Pickard, who started as a student trainer at A&M in 1952 and has spent the next six decades working at A&M in so many roles that he simply became known as the "caretaker of Kyle Field." Pickard donated the money to the 12th Man Foundation's Campaign for Aggie Football, targeting the money specifically to the R.C. Slocum Nutrition Hall.

60 The 2010 Nebraska Game

Perhaps no other fan base in college football appreciates great defense more than Texas A&M's famed 12th Man. So it was fitting that the largest crowd in the history of Kyle Field and the largest student crowd in the history of college football was treated to a game without a single touchdown.

Texas A&M 9, Nebraska 6.

Don't be misled by the final score. It was such an electrifying night that many of the 90,079 fans stormed the field afterward to join the Aggie football team in singing the "War Hymn" in the postgame celebration. As an added bonus, the mayhem on the field after the masterful defensive effort further infuriated the hot-headed, red-faced, foul-mouthed Nebraska coach Bo Pelini, who spent much of the evening storming the sideline and berating officials and his own quarterback, Taylor Martinez.

Pelini was livid about the loss and incensed that officials called 16 penalties against Nebraska (including one against him for unsportsmanlike conduct) for 145 yards, both school records. Meanwhile, the Aggies were penalized twice. After the game, Bo Pelini tried to chase down one of the officials, while his equally hotheaded and confrontational brother, defensive coordinator Carl Pelini, assaulted TexAgs.com cameraman/CEO Brandon Jones for having the audacity to film the postgame celebration.

Bo Pelini apologized the following week for being such a meathead, saying: "I always believe it's okay to disagree with a call. It's not okay to make it personal. At times during that game, probably in my quest to fight for the kids on our football team, I let it get personal. For that, once again, I'm sorry."

While Pelini was apologizing, the Aggies were basking in the glow of a defensive battle for the ages, and the 12th Man played a major role in securing the victory. The 31,005 student tickets sold broke the Guinness World Record for number of students in attendance at a university football game. A&M officials sold 1,217 standing-room-only spots and an additional 1,800 folding chairs were placed on the track surrounding the playing field to achieve the record.

"I can't say enough about our students and former students who were at the game to get us over 90,000 fans," A&M head coach Mike Sherman said. "The noise that they made and the energy they generated was phenomenal, and I can't thank them enough."

The scene was phenomenal, as well. The students twirled their 12th Man towels throughout the game in a dizzying wave of emotion, and when A&M secured the victory in the final moments, the students tossed the towels into the air.

Running back Cyrus Gray and the A&M defense gave the fans plenty of reasons to celebrate. Gray produced 202 yards of total offense in a game where the Huskers limited the Aggies to only 310 total yards. Gray rushed for 137 yards—his fifth-straight 100-yard rushing performance of the season—and caught nine Ryan Tannehill passes.

"We knew we needed to run the ball, and Cyrus carried that load," Tannehill said. "He got so many tough yards. It seemed like he was going to get a three-yard gain, and he took it 15. He fought for every yard."

Likewise, the Aggies fought for every point. The game was tied at 6–6 when the Aggies took the lead on Randy Bullock's 19-yard field goal in the fourth quarter, his third of the game. To Pelini's dismay, the drive was kept alive by a roughing-the-passer penalty on Nebraska on third-and-11 at the Cornhuskers' 49.

Martinez, who missed the last five minutes of the first quarter and the entire second quarter after injuring his right ankle, had one more chance to rally the Huskers in the fourth quarter. But he was flagged for intentional grounding on first down on Nebraska's last drive and then sacked on third down. His desperation heave on fourth down was incomplete, sending the standing-room-only crowd into a jubilant celebration.

61 Attend Yell Practice

Perhaps the single most impressive tradition associated with a Texas A&M game day in College Station—aside from the actual game—occurs at the stroke of midnight when Friday evening officially turns into Saturday. Midnight yell practice at Kyle Field may lose some of its luster and majestic appeal to A&M students, former students, and fans who've attended their fair share of them.

But the event, which is also held at various locations for road games, is so unique among all college football traditions that it never ceases to amaze visiting fans or first-time media members who are covering the next day's game at Kyle Field.

There are plenty of excuses for not going—it's late, it's inconvenient for numerous reasons, it's a hassle entering and exiting the stadium, etc. But if you've never been, forget the excuses. It's an absolute must-experience event. And that's not just a maroon-colored-glasses opinion, either.

Prior to their first *College GameDay* visit to College Station in November 2000, ESPN's Chris Fowler and Kirk Herbstreit were most excited about experiencing midnight yell practice for the first time.

Each week during the season, Fowler (since joining the *GameDay* set in 1990) and Herbstreit (since joining the crew in 1996) travel to the premier venues in college football to preview the weekend's most anticipated and high-profile matchup. It would be accurate to say that—at least in college football circles— Fowler and Herbstreit have practically seen it all. Except they both acknowledged afterward that they'd never seen anything quite like midnight yell practice.

"On Friday night, the school holds yell practice at midnight, where 25,000 people practice their yells in a pep rally," Herbstreit wrote on ESPN.com after his 2000 trip to Aggieland. "It is amazing to see that many people that fired up. They have five yell leaders, who use hand signals to communicate each cheer. It's an incredible scene that carried over into Saturday's game."

Added Fowler, "Aggie fans are accustomed to it, but packing 25,000 to 30,000 fans inside the stadium the night before the game is one of the great spectacles in college football. Not many schools could pull something like midnight yell practice off on a continuing basis. Once, maybe. But week after week and year after year, no way. A&M is unique."

The Yell leaders: A tradition as unique as A&M

When it comes to its one-of-a-kind game-day atmosphere, Texas A&M can stand toe-to-toe with any program in the country, as Kyle Field continually achieves national recognition for the unmatched, ear-splitting, goosebump-inducing environment generated at its home football games.

Although they are rarely cited by the media and often ridiculed by opposing fans, much of the credit for the awesome atmosphere at Kyle Field is due to yell leaders, the five guys in white uniforms who generate maroon mayhem, calculated clamor, and a symphony of spirit with the mere gesture of hand signals.

From the earliest documented yell leader—Tom Armstrong Adams in 1907–08—the yell leaders have played an instrumental role in defining, refining, building, maintaining, and showcasing the Aggie spirit.

The yell leaders are woven into the fabric and culture of the university like no other spirit group or athletic support organization at any other university. Cheerleaders may turn a few heads in the lower rows of a stadium and encourage handfuls of spectators to participate in chants or cheers. But the five yell leaders at A&M impact the crowd noise and even the opponent's game plan unlike cheerleaders could ever fathom, directing a trained crowd with the precision of an orchestra conductor and rallying the 12th Man troops like an infantry leader directing his men to roar in unison at the drop of his hand.

Today, being a yell leader at A&M involves so much more than leading yells at football games or numerous other sporting events. The scope and responsibility of the position have grown dramatically over the years, and it is not uncommon for more than twice as many students to vote in annual yell leader elections than those who vote in the student body president elections.

As Wayne Drehs of ESPN.com wrote in a 2003 article, "Their white jumpsuits give them the look of hospital orderlies, but A&M's yell leaders are the only students who receive a varsity letter without competing in an intercollegiate sport…. Before games, after games, and during countless public appearances, they're treated like the Backstreet Boys, with 12-year-old girls wearing braces jumping up and down and hoping for a picture…all while their girlfriends, some of the most sought-after women on campus, look on."

It has been practically since the start of the university. According to the university's official Aggie Traditions website, the first sanctioned, on-campus yell practice was held in 1913. But according to numerous articles from *The Bryan Weekly Eagle*, it's quite possible that yell practices were held on campus as early as 1905 or '06.

Regardless of when they started, it's clear they quickly became must-attend, must-participate events. By the 1920s, yell practices were held multiple times per week, and by the late 1930s and early '40s, they were held at least three times a week during football season.

For roughly the first two decades of yell practices, the events were held regularly right after supper had been served. In the fall of 1930, however, it appears that cadets gathered in T.D. "Peanut" Owens' dorm room at Puryear Hall days prior to the annual A&M-Texas game, where someone suggested that the freshmen should "fall out" and meet on the steps of the YMCA building at midnight. The midnight tradition was officially born then.

During the 1940s, yell practices were held at both the YMCA and on the steps of Guion Hall. In the late 1940s, it appears that yell practices moved to the Grove, where they remained until 1960. According to 1960–61 head yell leader Sonny Todd, yell practices moved to Kyle Field in '60. It's been a spectacle to behold ever since…and one that every Aggie fan should experience.

Shane Lechler

In arguably the most meaningful victory in Texas A&M history— at least from an emotional healing/uplifting standpoint—Matt

Shane Lechler is the only punter in A&M history with a career net average of more than 40 yards. (Photo courtesy of 12th Man Magazine)

Bumgardner caught the winning touchdown, Ja'Mar Toombs ground out the tough yards, Jay Brooks forced the key fumble, and Brian Gamble recovered it. But from the opposing standpoint, the player who may have been most critical to the Aggies' 20–16 win over Texas eight days after the collapse of bonfire was punter Shane Lechler.

"Lechler was the difference in the ballgame," Longhorns coach Mack Brown said after watching Lechler hit 53- and 54-yard punts toward the end of the game, both of which were killed inside the Texas 12. "He pinned us, and we couldn't get off the goal line."

That type of game was not an isolated incident for Lechler. He not only won the field position battle for the Aggies in numerous contests—he was often the difference-maker. As far back as his freshman year, Lechler was determining games with his terrific right leg. In a 24–21 win at Iowa State in 1996, for example, the Cyclones rallied from 17 points down to cut the A&M lead to three with five minutes left. The ISU fans were worked into a frenzied state on the ensuing drive when the Cyclones forced the Aggies to punt from the A&M 21.

Lechler then entered the game and hit a 76-yard punt that was killed by Jason Webster at the ISU 3. It was Lechler's second 70-yard punt of the game, and it may have been the most pivotal play as the Aggies held on for the win.

There are many other examples of individual games where Lechler, who was originally recruited out of East Bernard as a quarterback/punter, was invaluable to the Aggies' efforts. But what truly makes him the most valuable punter in A&M history—and there have been some really good ones through the years like Steve O'Neal, Justin Brantly, Todd Tschantz, David Davis, etc.—is the consistency with which Lechler performed.

Lechler is the only punter in A&M history (with at least 100 punts) who has a career net average of more than 40 yards at 40.6 from 1996–99. Lechler also holds school records for season average (47.0 in 1997), career average (44.7), season net average (42.7), most career punting yards (11,977), most consecutive punts without a block (268), and single-game average with a minimum of five punts (57.2 against Texas Tech in 1999).

"As I've said before, Shane Lechler has been the most valuable player on this football team, by far, for a couple of years now," former A&M head coach R.C. Slocum said in 1999. "He's the best punter I've ever coached."

The versatile Lechler also held for field goal and extra-point attempts, and he threw a key touchdown pass to Dan Campbell on a fake field goal in a 17–10 win over Texas Tech in 1998. During that '98 Big 12 championship season, Lechler had at least one punt of 57 yards or more in close wins over Nebraska (64), Missouri (69), and Kansas State (57), and he had 21 "coffin corner" punts for the season.

Lechler, a two-time All-American in 1998–99, is probably one of the greatest punters in college football history. And he's been even better in the NFL. Oakland used its fifth-round draft pick on Lechler in 2000, and in the ensuing 13 years with the Raiders, Lechler earned seven trips to the Pro Bowl and six first-team All-Pro selections. He was so valuable in Oakland that in 2009 the team made him the NFL's highest-paid punter with a contract worth $16 million over four years.

He proved his worth time and time again. For example, he hit an 80-yarder against Chicago in 2011, breaking the previous Oakland record of 77 yards by…Shane Lechler.

Ray Guy, the other legendary punter in Raiders history, is still awaiting a call from the Pro Football Hall of Fame. So it's uncertain if Lechler is destined for enshrinement in the Pro Fotball Hall of Fame in Canton, Ohio, but he at least deserves serious consideration.

63 The Rice Comeback in 1955

On November 12, 1955, Bear Bryant's heavily favored Aggies trailed Rice 12–0 before a stunned crowd of 68,000 at Rice Stadium in Houston.

The Aggies had been placed on NCAA probation earlier in the year for recruiting violations regarding two prospects, which seemed to further alienate the Aggies from the rest of their foes in the Southwest Conference. And Bryant was livid about the sanctions.

"We had out-recruited everybody in the state," Bryant said. "There was no way for that to go down easy. People were out to get us. No big daily [newspaper] like the *Dallas News* or *Houston Post* was there to protect us. We were stuck [in College Station] and fair game."

With no bowl prospects on the horizon at the end of the 1955 or '56 seasons, every regular season game became even more meaningful for the Aggies. A&M traveled to Rice on November 12, 1955, with a seven-game unbeaten streak and a top-10 national ranking. After losing the opener at UCLA, the Aggies had beaten LSU, Houston, Nebraska, TCU, Baylor, and SMU while tying Arkansas.

A&M, which had gone 1–9 and 0–6 in the Southwest Conference in 1954 after the famed trip to Junction, appeared to have hit its stride after losing the opener 21–0 at UCLA. But against Rice, the Aggies seemed to be in serious danger of being shutout for the second time in the 1955 season as the fourth quarter neared the midway point.

But instead of enduring a blanking, the No. 9-ranked Aggies battled back in one of the most stunning turnarounds in Texas A&M history.

Leeland McElroy: Many Happy Returns

Unfortunately for Texas A&M, Leeland McElroy's 1995 Heisman Trophy hopes died prematurely—along with the Aggies' national title aspirations—on September 23, 1995, in a bitterly disappointing 29–21 loss at Colorado.

McElroy finished the '95 season with an impressive 1,122 rushing yards. He then chose to forgo his senior season to enter the NFL draft, which was probably a mistake in judgment. McElroy, who had 2,442 career rushing yards, possessed first-round talent, but he slipped to the second round of the '96 draft.

Despite some disappointment at the end of his time at A&M, though, McElroy began his collegiate career in an incredibly explosive manner that earned him the nickname 'Lectric Leeland. He was certainly as explosive as a bolt of lightning.

In addition to being an exceptional backup tailback in 1993 and '94, McElroy may have been the most electrifying kickoff returner in school history. He set the single-season school record in '93 by averaging 39.3 yards per kick return. And in one of the most memorable days in A&M's history at Rice Stadium—October 23, 1993—McElroy returned the Owls' first two kickoffs 93 and 88 yards for touchdowns, tying an NCAA record and sparking the Aggies to a 38–10 victory.

He ended the year with three kickoff returns for touchdowns, including a 100-yard return against Texas that played a huge role in the Aggies' 18–9 win on Thanksgiving night.

"It looked pretty bleak for the ol' Maroon and White heading into the fourth quarter," said personable former quarterback Jimmy Wright, who would come off the bench to direct perhaps the most spectacular comeback in Texas A&M history. "I was just hoping Coach Bryant might give me the opportunity to throw the football if times were desperate enough."

Reluctantly, the run-oriented Bryant finally put the game in Wright's capable hands, and he and Loyd Taylor made the Owls pay.

With only four minutes left in the game, Taylor, a versatile running back, raced 58 yards to set up his own three-yard scoring run. That cut the Rice lead to 12–7 with 3:18 left.

Jack Pardee then booted a perfect onside kick that Gene Stallings recovered at the Rice 43. On first down, Wright hit Taylor on a 43-yard scoring pass. Taylor then added the conversion kick to give A&M a 14–12 lead with 2:32 left. That gave A&M 14 points in a span of 46 seconds, but the Aggies were not done.

Pardee later intercepted a pass from Rice quarterback King Hill and returned it 37 yards to the Owls' 8. From there, Don Watson scored an insurance touchdown with 1:09 left in the game to give the Aggies 20 points in a span of 2:09.

The 20–12 victory over the Owls ended Rice's 10-game winning streak in the series against the Aggies.

"Rice outplayed us and deserved to win," Bryant said afterward. "We were very, very lucky. But let's not forget Loyd Taylor. He's a back that no one seems to notice, but he does a fine job each week."

Aaron Wallace

Former Texas A&M outside linebacker Aaron Wallace knows it's coming. After all, it has come up in practically every conversation he's had with Aggies since that memorable moment in Kyle Field.

No matter where a conversation starts or where it seems headed, A&M fans usually bring Wallace back to October 14, 1989. That's the day the Houston Cougars, led by eventual Heisman Trophy winner Andre Ware, came to College Station with a No. 8 national ranking and the country's top offense.

Texas A&M's "Blitz Brothers," Aaron Wallace (left) and John Roper (right).
(Photo by Cathy Capps)

The Cougars entered that game averaging almost 60 points per contest. They left Aggieland bruised, bloodied, and beaten.

The unranked Aggies intercepted three Ware passes and sacked him six times in a 17–13 win. The image that summed up the entire day appeared in newspapers the next day and in *Sports Illustrated* later that week. It was of Wallace, following a sack, holding up Ware's helmet like a trophy, and it sent the crowd of 66,423 inside Kyle Field into a frenzied celebration.

In the big picture, it represented just one of Wallace's record-setting 42 sacks in his sensational A&M career, but it was also the image Aggies have held on to ever since.

"Aggies don't forget," Wallace said of the triumphant moment. "That was obviously a moment that made a lasting impression."

Wallace made many positive impressions at A&M from 1986–89 as he shattered Jacob Green's previous record of 37 career sacks. Additionally, Wallace and fellow "Blitz Brother" John Roper combined for a phenomenal 78 sacks in the mid-1980s.

"Roper and I weren't that tight or anything like that, but we really competed against each other," said Wallace, a Lombardi semifinalist in 1989. "After a game, we would always check to see who had more sacks. We pushed each other hard. I guess it was *The Sporting News* that came out with the 'Blitz Brother' tag. It may seem a little cheesy now, but at the time it was fun. We had a nice little following."

Wallace continued to win fans and turn heads at the next level. A second-round draft pick of the Raiders in 1990, Wallace wasted no time in making an immediate impact in the NFL. He recorded nine sacks his first season, making the NFL's All-Rookie team.

He started for four seasons and helped lead the Raiders to three playoff appearances. Later in his career, he played primarily in pass situations and on special teams before retiring in '98. It was at that time that Wallace began seriously thinking about returning to school, and he earned his degree from A&M in 2002.

"In some ways, I felt like coming back to A&M was part of my opportunity to get things right," Wallace said. "It took some sacrifices, but I know it was the right thing to do for a lot of reasons. When Coach [R.C.] Slocum recruited me way back when, all he could talk about was getting that Aggie ring. I ended up with three Cotton Bowl rings instead of an Aggie ring the first time around. But I came back to finish what I started."

Wallace said one of the primary reasons he wanted to earn his degree was to serve as an example to his own two kids, and after walking the stage, he began coaching at Dallas Sunset High School before moving on to Spruce and Conrad High Schools. In 2011, Wallace's son, Aaron Jon Wallace Jr., signed to play football with UCLA. He redshirted in '11, and he played 10 games in 2012 as a reserve linebacker for the Bruins.

Tony Franklin

During his freshman season in 1975, barefoot placekicker Tony Franklin proved to possess an exceptionally strong leg, hitting five field goals of more than 40 yards, including his longest from 59.

A&M head coach Emory Bellard developed so much confidence in Franklin that he began taking more and more risks the following year, sending Franklin into the game in situations where he might have otherwise chosen to punt.

That was certainly the case on October 16, 1976, an overcast, windy day at Kyle Field when the 5'10", 170-lb. Franklin stood particularly tall in a must-win game against defending SWC champion Baylor.

The Aggies were 3–2 overall but 0–2 in the SWC after losses to Houston and Texas Tech to open league play. A&M desperately needed a win against the Bears, and Franklin did more than his fair share.

Franklin opened the scoring for the Aggies by hitting a 24-yard field goal in the first quarter with a strong wind in his face. And when a later A&M drive bogged down near midfield early in the second quarter, Bellard elected to send his kicker onto the field. The tee—which is no longer used in college football—was placed at the A&M 46, making it a 64-yard attempt. With the wind at his back, Franklin nailed the kick, splitting the uprights to set an NCAA record and give the Aggies a 6–0 lead.

Later in the quarter, A&M extended its lead to 14–0. Then in the third quarter—with the wind again at his back—Franklin was called to show off his remarkable leg once more. Placing the tee this time at the A&M 45, Franklin nailed a 65-yarder to break his own NCAA record.

The sellout crowd of 52,241 roared its approval, and the A&M players carried Franklin off the field following the second kick of more than 60 yards. All three of his field goals helped A&M to a 24–0 win over the Bears. That victory kick-started a six-game winning streak to end the '76 season for the Aggies, and Franklin was selected as a consensus All-American.

A&M's 9–2 regular season earned the Aggies a trip to the Sun Bowl on January 2, 1977, and Franklin once again stole the spotlight in the 37–14 win over Florida. Franklin hit three field goals, including an NCAA bowl-record 62-yarder. He was chosen as the MVP of the game, and in 2006 the Sun Bowl honored him as one of the legends of the bowl game. He was also chosen as a member of the Sun Bowl's 75th Anniversary All-Star team.

When he left Texas A&M following his senior year in 1978, Franklin was the Aggies' all-time scoring leader with 291 career points. He also finished his collegiate career with 18 NCAA records, including most career field goals (56), most field goals of 50 yards or longer in a career (16), and the longest average for field goals made in a career (39.5 yards).

A third-round draft pick of the Philadelphia Eagles, Franklin spent 10 seasons in the NFL with Philadelphia, New England, and Miami. He played in Super Bowl XV with Philadelphia and Super Bowl XX with New England. In 1986, he led the NFL in scoring (140 points) and field goals made (32).

In 1989, he was also inducted into the Texas A&M Athletic Hall of Fame.

Jacob Green

As a student-athlete at Texas A&M, Jacob Green would frequently stop by the old offices of The Aggie Club on his way to football practice. At the time, he didn't know much about the purpose of The Aggie Club, which became the 12th Man Foundation in 1988, but he did enjoy the people in the office.

He especially enjoyed his visits with former Aggie Club executive director Harry Green, who was a fundraiser ahead of his time.

"I couldn't have told you all of the specifics of what Harry did, but I knew he loved A&M athletics, and I knew he was a real people person," Jacob Green said. "Little did I know that I would one day come full circle."

Nowadays, Green is no longer a visitor in the offices of A&M's fundraising organization. He accepted the position of Assistant Director of Major Gifts for the 12th Man Foundation in February

Rodney Thomas: Great RB, Better Person

The statistics clearly show that Rodney Thomas was one of the best running backs in the history of Texas A&M. The stories about him reveal he was an even better role model than a running back.

From 1991–94, Thomas rushed for 3,014 yards—the fourth-most in A&M history when he completed his eligibility. Thomas possessed a rare combination of speed and power. He could run away from opponents, but it appeared he loved running them over even more.

Off the field, Thomas was one of the most universally liked and admired personalities in A&M history. In one of the legendary stories of old Cain Hall—the athletic dorm at one time—a vending machine went haywire, spewing out free candy bars. While many of his teammates grabbed as many freebies as they could carry, Thomas attempted to keep count as chaos ensued. After the machine was empty and virtually everyone had emptied the hallways, Thomas went to his room, grabbed his change jar, and began inserting all the coins he had into the machine to pay for what his teammates consumed.

The humble Thomas refused to ever talk about that incident that a teammate witnessed—or many others like it—but he was a man of impeccable character and integrity.

Thomas, who was chosen in the third round of the 1996 NFL Draft by the Oilers, was also a legendary high school player in the Lone Star State. He led Groveton to back-to-back Class 2A state championships in 1989 and 1990. As a senior in '90, Thomas became the first back in state history to rush for 100 yards or more in all 16 games, finishing the year with 3,701 yards. His prep career rushing total of 8,441 yards was fifth on the all-time list when he graduated.

2006, and he has been instrumental in working with former A&M students and former athletes ever since.

Green has also played a major role in the fundraising efforts for such projects as The Campaign for Aggie Football, which raised money for the construction of the Monty and Becky Davis Aggie Football Player Development Center, the R.C. Slocum Great Hall/Nutrition Center, and the expansion of the Lohman Center at the front of the Bright Complex.

At the time of this writing, Green is also turning his attention toward tackling the fundraising challenges associated with a completely renovated and redesigned Kyle Field. It should be a perfect role for Green, who has certainly proven in the past that he has the abilities to tackle challenges—or anything else—at Kyle Field.

Green came to A&M from Kashmere High School in Houston, and he was part of some very good teams in 1976 and '77, going a combined 18–6 in his first two years in College Station. The Aggies started off the 1978 season in outstanding fashion, too, whipping Kansas, Boston College, Memphis State, and Texas Tech by a combined score of 170–21 to move to 4–0. Unfortunately, things quickly went awry from that point. A&M lost its next two games to Houston and Baylor, and head coach Emory Bellard was essentially forced out of his job in mid-season.

"That was terribly disappointing, and so was much of my senior year in '79," Green said. "We lost a bunch of close games in my final season, and we went into the Texas game with a 5–5 record. We weren't going to make a bowl game for the first time in my A&M career, but we had one more chance to do something special against a Texas team that was coming into Kyle Field with a 9–1 record. The night before that game our team gathered with 40,000 or more A&M students and former students for the burning of Aggie bonfire.

"I'm normally a pretty laid-back guy, but something overcame me that night. When I was handed the microphone and given a chance to address the crowd, I said, 'We're gonna kick their ass.'"

It may not have been an actual butt-kicking, but A&M did beat Texas that next day 13–7 to keep the Longhorns from winning a share of the SWC title.

Green, a two-year captain and two-time All-SWC selection, was chosen as an All-American defensive end in 1979, the year he posted a school-record 20 sacks. He went on to become a first-round draft pick of the Seattle Seahawks in 1980, becoming an All-Pro and finishing his 12½-year NFL career with 116 quarterback sacks, which ranked fourth in AFC history at the time of his retirement.

All three of Green's daughters—Janelle, Jessica, and Jillian—have attended A&M, and Janelle is married to former A&M defensive lineman Red Bryant, who is playing with the Seahawks and following in his father-in-law's big-time footsteps.

Ryan Tannehill

In the week after the Ravens defeated the 49ers in Super Bowl XLVII in New Orleans, NFL Network ran a segment asking its analysts to name the quarterbacks most likely to lead their teams to the Super Bowl within the next few years. Former Eagles, Redskins, and Vikings quarterback Donovan McNabb suggested this name:

Ryan Tannehill of the Miami Dolphins.

Most A&M fans would probably agree with McNabb. After all, Tannehill is a trendsetter who seems to ultimately succeed wherever he's placed.

Tannehill grew up dreaming of following in his mother's and father's footsteps to Texas Tech. In fact, if former Tech coach Mike Leach would have offered him a scholarship in the summer of '06, the Big Spring High product would have been Lubbock bound. Instead, he signed with A&M, redshirted in Dennis Franchione's last season as head coach (2007), and developed a close friendship with the Aggies' quarterback at the time, Stephen McGee.

The following spring when Mike Sherman replaced Franchione, the new head coach announced that every position was open for competition. At quarterback, the top three candidates were McGee, Jerrod Johnson, and Tannehill. The battle was intense, but a couple of weeks before the '08 opener Sherman named McGee the starter, Johnson the backup, and Tannehill as third string.

"It was then that [Sherman] asked me if I would run a few routes at practice the next day," Tannehill said. "I said, 'Sure, I'll do anything to get on the field.'"

Tannehill actually led the Aggies in receiving in 2008 with 55 catches for 844 yards, and he again led the team in '09—when Johnson was the full-time starting QB—with 46 catches for 609 yards. And he was on his way to another strong season as a receiver in 2010, until Sherman decided to insert Tannehill at quarterback in the second quarter against Kansas. It was the seventh game of the season, and the Aggies (3–3, 0–2 in the Big 12) were mired in a three-game losing skid.

Tannehill gave the Aggies a spark, and he earned the start the next week against Texas Tech. In that first game as a starter, he set the school record for single-game passing numbers with 449 yards. Most significantly, he led the Aggies to six straight wins to end the season.

In 2011, Tannehill started every game at quarterback for the first time in his career and passed for a school-record 3,744 yards. While the '11 Aggies didn't live up to expectations as a team, Tannehill played well enough to become the first A&M quarterback to be selected in the first round of the NFL draft, going to the Dolphins with the eighth overall pick.

In Miami, Tannehill was reunited with Sherman, who became the Dolphins' offensive coordinator after he was fired by Texas A&M. Tannehill then earned the starting job over Matt Moore and David Garrard and started all 16 games for Miami in 2012, throwing for 3,294 yards with 12 touchdowns and 13 interceptions.

And perhaps, as McNabb suggested on NFL Network, the best is yet to come for Tannehill.

"He's got [36] starts under his belt [as a quarterback in college and in the NFL], and that's huge," Dolphins general manager and former Baylor kicker Jeff Ireland said after the 2012 season. "I think we're better for it. I think Ryan is better for it. So now we're kind of going to hopefully see a big jump in his development."

Billy Liucci

Walking along the streets of New York City in early December 2012, Billy Liucci was first recognized by a group of Texas A&M college girls who yelled his name and introduced themselves near Rockefeller Center. Later, near the 9/11 Memorial, a vacationing former A&M student in his sixties stopped Liucci to tell him how much he enjoyed his work. And on the subway near the Stock Exchange, a recent A&M graduate who'd just landed a job on Wall Street thanked Liucci for keeping him updated on Aggie football during A&M's first season in the SEC.

Over the course of the day and later that night, it was evident that Liucci was probably the second most recognizable Aggie in New York City on December 8, 2012...behind only Johnny Manziel, who picked up a rather prestigious bronzed trophy that evening. But the gap between the two in terms of their popularity among A&M fans—at least at that point—was probably not as wide as some would think.

Both are Tweet-producing, headline-generating, media-savvy rock stars who essentially stepped into stardom out of nowhere. Manziel may have more star power, but Liucci has staying power. His popularity keeps on rising, his product keeps on improving—and unlike Manziel, Liucci won't be leaving College Station any time in the foreseeable future.

"If I am comparing us to a sports team, then Billy is our franchise player," TexAgs president and CEO Brandon Jones said. "He's our Johnny Manziel or LeBron James. Billy by himself doesn't make TexAgs because it's bigger than any of us. But as far as our content and the reporting attached to our brand, he's our marquee name and star attraction."

Not bad for a man who first enrolled at A&M to become a chemical engineer. Liucci was born in Yonkers, just outside the NYC borough of the Bronx. He moved to Houston with his family when he was five, attended Sugar Land Kempner High School, and applied to an array of colleges, including Columbia, Colgate, USC, Baylor, Texas, and Texas A&M.

He ultimately chose A&M over Texas because he had so much fun attending the 1991 Aggie bonfire. Liucci arrived at A&M in the fall of '92. He was initially doing well in his chemical engineering classes, although he didn't believe it was his long-term calling. While considering other majors, Liucci met some A&M football players during his sophomore year and began hanging out with guys like Ryan Kern, Robert Danklefs, Brad Crowley, and Hunter Goodwin.

Those friends and others that followed proved to be instrumental in Liucci finding his true calling. He first lived with players such as Steve McKinney, Dan Campbell, and Crowley as he switched majors from chemical engineering to business. He actually earned his degree in industrial distribution in 1998, which is when he received a phone call from the owners of a recruiting news–based newsletter called *Maroon & White Report*, which was typically faxed or mailed to subscribers. The previous editor, Doug Walker, was leaving to take a sports information job at TCU.

Liucci, who had been writing occasional recruiting stories for *Ags Illustrated* since 1996, leapt at the opportunity to stay in College Station and delay his pursuit of a "real job."

"I didn't even ask how much I would make," said the personable and unassuming Liucci. "I just said yes because I could stay in

College Station. That was prior to the '98 season, and I thought A&M was going to have a good football season. I was living in a two-bedroom place with Dan, Seth [McKinney], and Shane [Lechler]. I graduated in August, and a week before the Florida State game, the owners of *Maroon & White Report* dumped off a computer at my home. I had no idea what I was doing or how to work the software.

"I was trying to call the SIDs to set up interviews, but they didn't know who I was, so I just started interviewing the guys I lived with. My first interview was with Dan Campbell in our living room. It wasn't supposed to be a long-term deal, but I liked it and I thought subscribers liked it. I started putting together the numbers, and I figured if I could get 1,500 email subscriptions, I could make a good living."

The plug was nearly pulled on *Maroon & White Report*, but Liucci and Goodwin eventually bought it in '99 from the Austin owners. Liucci's insight, his strong relationships with A&M players and coaches, and his work ethic transformed the newsletter into a success and generated plenty of subscriptions. But he needed a first-class web presence to really make any money.

"I started to eyeball TexAgs because I needed to go real time with recruiting news," Liucci said. "At that time, when there was breaking news, I would write up an email and send it to people and then fax information to 100 people. It was very rudimentary. After exploring the possibility of building my own website, I figured I would go to TexAgs and see if we could partner up. I wanted to basically pay them rent space on their site for the premium content. We cut a deal, and by 2001 it really started to take off. Hunter and I eventually bought out 50 percent of TexAgs' investors—25 percent each—and it was a really good fit."

Liucci steadily built a following with his premium content, and TexAgs increased its advertising base thanks to more visitors to the site. But the big explosion came in the summer of 2011 as A&M

moved toward membership in the SEC. In the summer of 2010, as Texas tried to push A&M and other Big 12 schools toward membership in the Pac-16, Liucci had plenty of pertinent information, including that A&M was investigating the possibility of moving to the SEC. But he chose not to write anything about it at the request of his sources.

While he didn't write, Chip Brown of Orangebloods.com did. And the entire conference alignment story became Texas-driven and Longhorns-sided. Liucci vowed to take a more aggressive approach if something similar ever happened again.

"I was really disappointed in myself for not pushing my sources to allow me to shape the story in 2010," Liucci said. "But in 2011, I got out in front of it, and people really became obsessed by it. The exposure I received from that was amazing. I'd been doing this for 10 years, but it just exploded when I started being contacted by all these national media outlets. One morning I was lying in bed in my pajamas and ESPN called and asked if I wanted to be on *SportsCenter*. Then I was on one national show after another. I think the whole thing legitimized us nationally and also made all Aggies want to go to TexAgs, and then [it] made the people who were really wanting the inside scoop to get the premium subscription. That was a tipping point for me and TexAgs."

While the summer of 2011 made Liucci famous, what has always made him so unique and popular is his ability to relate to all types of people—ranging from 17-year-old college prospects to 70-year-old donors. Liucci never takes himself too seriously and never betrays someone's trust. He's a genuine people person, and he possesses a magnetic personality. All of those traits along with his entrepreneurial efforts have made him the most well-known and well-liked media/information source associated with A&M athletics.

He's so popular that he's even a big deal in the Big Apple.

Bob Smith

When Bob Smith departed Texas A&M following the 1951 season, he left as the Aggies' all-time leading rusher with 2,415 yards. In the ensuing 61 years, 13 Aggies surpassed Smith in the record books. Through the 2012 season, however, no A&M player had ever topped Smith's remarkable one-game performance on an unforgettable autumn afternoon in 1950.

In leading the Aggies to a 25–20 victory at SMU on November 11, 1950, Smith dismantled the Mustangs for 297 rushing yards. During regular season games, no Aggie has ever come within 60 yards of matching that monumental mark.

Ironically, Smith didn't know at the time his performance had been so spectacular. All he really cared about was the victory and that he had made a lasting impression on one SMU co-ed. The summer before the 1950 season, while Smith was taking summer school classes at the University of Houston, he met an outgoing girl named Betty Lu, a full-time student at SMU. The two began dating in the summer, and by the fall, they were an item.

Prior to the opening kickoff against SMU, Smith was shagging punts during warm-ups when a ball bounced toward the stands and landed close to where Betty Lu and her friends were sitting. When Smith went to retrieve the ball, he caught a glimpse of Betty Lu. They didn't say anything to each other, but she smiled at him, providing all the motivation Smith needed.

"It was the first time we'd seen each other right before a game," said Smith prior to his death in January 2005. "I just went out there and did my best to show off for her. But I honestly had no idea I rushed for 297 yards. During the game, it didn't seem so impressive."

A Scoring Record that is Still Standing

In today's fast-paced, high-flying, pass-happy offensive attacks, perhaps no scoring record should ever be considered impossible to beat. But one school record has stood so long at A&M that it is at least becoming rather improbable that someone will break it.

On October 16, 1926, V.W. "Jelly" Woodman scored 44 points in Texas A&M's 63–0 win over New Mexico in College Station. Woodman scored seven touchdowns and added two extra-point kicks, establishing an NCAA and SWC single-game scoring record at the time.

In 1990, Illinois' Howard Griffith broke the NCAA record by scoring 48 points in a game against Southern Illinois. San Diego State's Marshall Faulk also tied Woodman's record with 44 points against Pacific in 1991.

But no A&M player has come remotely close to breaking Woodman's record. Jorvorskie Lane is second on the A&M single-game scoring list with 26 points against Fresno State in 2007, followed by Preston Smith's 25 points against Ellington Field in 1945. Five A&M players—Ryan Swope, Cyrus Gray, Uzoma Nwachukwu, Leeland McElroy, and Lane (twice)—have scored 24 points in a game.

Apparently, the New Mexico defense was not particularly strong. The week before playing New Mexico, the Aggies scored six points in a 6–3 win against Sewanee, and the week after scoring 63 against the Lobos, A&M managed a single TD in a 9–7 loss to SMU.

Betty Lu, however, was obviously impressed. A year later, she married Smith during his senior year at A&M. And she was certainly not alone in her admiration of Smith.

The win over the Kyle Rote–led Mustangs enabled the Aggies, who were just 1–8–1 in 1949, to secure their first bowl berth since the 1943 season in the Presidential Cup in Washington, D.C. The SMU game also helped Smith become the first A&M All-American running back since John Kimbrough in 1939–40. And as impressive as he was during the 1950 regular season, Smith may have been even better in the Aggies' 40–20 victory over Georgia in the Presidential Cup.

He set the tone for that game by returning the opening kickoff 100 yards for a touchdown and added an 81-yard scoring run as the Aggies jumped to a 33–0 halftime lead against the nation's No. 1 defense. Overall, Smith accounted for 303 all-purpose yards, which still ranked as the No. 1 performance in A&M bowl history through 2012.

After graduating from Texas A&M in 1952, Smith first served his country as a lieutenant in the United States Air Force during the Korean Conflict. Upon returning home, he learned that his NFL draft rights had been purchased by the Detroit Lions. Smith then joined Doak Walker and former A&M teammate Yale Lary in Detroit, helping the Lions to the 1953 NFL title.

After just two seasons in the Motor City, Smith made a decision to leave the game because of financial reasons. He had a good job in the off-season with an oil field company in Houston, and the Lions were paying him only about $10,000 per year. After leaving football, Smith later opened several businesses.

He died in early January 2005 after suffering a heart attack and stroke earlier in the week. He was 75.

The 1968 Cotton Bowl

During his renowned 323-victory coaching career, Paul "Bear" Bryant developed a reputation as one of the fiercest competitors in the history of college football. His competitive drive was celebrated, and his absolute disdain for losing was legendary.

Bryant anguished over every one of his 85 career losses as a head coach…with the possible exception of one.

On January 1, 1968, Bryant suffered a 20–16 loss to Texas A&M in a mistake-filled Cotton Bowl in which No. 8 Alabama often seemed like its own worst enemy. Bryant didn't like losing, but afterward he was so proud of the coach on the other sideline that he could hardly keep the smile off his face.

The other coach was Gene Stallings, a former "Junction Boy" and one of the captains of Bryant's 1956 Southwest Conference championship team at A&M. Stallings had also been an assistant coach at Alabama under Bryant from 1958–64, helping the Tide to the '64 national title. Bryant practically loved Stallings like a son, and he was especially proud of his former player for leading the Aggies to the 1968 Cotton Bowl after beginning the year with an 0–4 start.

And when the pupil led the Aggies past his mentor in a monumental upset before a crowd of 73,800 in Dallas, Bryant walked to the middle of the field after the contest and grabbed Stallings in a gigantic Bear hug, carrying him around proudly for a few steps before placing him back on the ground.

"He sure is strong, isn't he?" Stallings mused when Bryant finally let him down.

Heavily favored Alabama, which began the year ranked No. 2 nationally, scored first as quarterback Kenny Stabler capped a 10-play, 80-yard drive with a three-yard scoring run midway through the first half. Stabler, who went 28–3–2 as a starter in his career at Bama, looked to be in control early in the game, but the momentum changed in A&M's favor when Tommy Maxwell intercepted the southpaw's pass later in the first quarter at the Alabama 43.

Four plays later, A&M quarterback Edd Hargett hit Larry Stegent for a 13-yard TD pass that knotted the game at 7–7 and sent a message to everyone inside the Cotton Bowl that the Aggies were not intimidated by the Tide.

Alabama regained the lead early in the second quarter on a field goal, but the Aggies again capitalized on an Alabama mistake that gave A&M the lead at the intermission. Texas A&M's Jim Piper recovered a Tide fumble late in the second quarter, and Hargett hit Maxwell for a seven-yard score with 16 seconds left in the half to put A&M up for good, 13–10.

The Aggies added to the lead in the third quarter when Wendell Housley scored on a 20-yard run to put A&M up, 20–10. Alabama answered with a score later in the third quarter, but the Aggies, playing in their first bowl game in 26 years, were able to hold off the Tide throughout the fourth quarter to preserve the 20–16 win.

Hargett was the less-heralded quarterback entering the game, but he did a much better job protecting the ball than Stabler. Hargett completed 11-of-22 passes for 143 yards and two scores, while Stabler was intercepted three times. Alabama also lost two fumbles, while A&M had just one turnover. Hargett was later awarded the MVP honors for his poise under pressure.

"I'm glad to see you won in spite of Stallings," Bryant joked with the A&M team captains afterward.

71 Jake Matthews and His Brothers

By his senior year in 2004 at Elkins High School, Kevin Matthews had blossomed into a solid offensive lineman who was receiving scholarship offers from numerous "directional" schools, as well as one Big 12 university.

Naturally, Matthews took a visit to Oklahoma State, the biggest program to actually offer him a scholarship. But at the time, the Cowboys were transitioning from Les Miles to Mike Gundy, and Matthews did not feel comfortable in Stillwater.

The Krueger Brothers Leave a Legacy in Aggieland

Many families have left a positive impression on Texas A&M's football history. But few have ever left a legacy quite like the Krueger boys from nearby Caldwell.

Charlie Krueger was an offensive tackle and warrior for Bear Bryant's mid-1950s teams. Charlie became just the fourth two-time All-American in Texas A&M history in 1956–57, helping to pave the way for John David Crow's run to the '57 Heisman Trophy.

A decade later, Charlie's younger brother, Rolf, earned All-American honors as a defensive tackle in 1968, making the Krueger boys the first All-American brothers in A&M history.

Rolf played three years (1969–71) with the St. Louis Cardinals and then joined the 49ers in 1972, where his brother was wrapping up a historic career. Charlie Krueger played 16 seasons for the 49ers, twice reaching the Pro Bowl before retiring in 1973.

But Charlie made some of his biggest headlines after his stellar NFL career. He won one of the most significant injury settlements in NFL history in August 1989, when a judge awarded him $2.36 million in damages stemming from knee surgery that was performed in 1963. Krueger eventually settled out of court for $1 million.

"These people," he said, referring to NFL owners, "are the meanest and cheapest employers I've ever worked for. They retired my jersey in San Francisco. That means if they can [mess] with me, they can [mess] with anybody. I gave them 16 years. I played every game I ever dressed for. But they fight everything right down to the last nickel."

After his NFL career ended, X-rays revealed that Krueger had been living without a ligament in his knee since 1963 when surgery was performed by team physician Lloyd Milburn. Milburn had removed the ligament but never told Krueger, who missed only one game during the next 10 seasons. Upon learning of his condition, Krueger filed for the NFL's $65,000 disability benefit but became enraged when he was told he could not receive the money because he had not filed his request within the allotted 36 months after retirement. Krueger was eventually granted the $65,000 by an arbitrator, but he sued the 49ers for damages. After nearly a decade of appeals, Krueger finally received the settlement from the 49ers.

"I went up to Oklahoma State, but I didn't like it at all," Kevin recalled years later. "It didn't feel right. Besides, I had started dating a girl from Houston, and I didn't want to get away from her. Her name is Amanda Hinkle [now his wife]. But anyway, I came back from Oklahoma State and the next day I called A&M, and I said I wanted to walk-on. There was something about A&M that just felt right."

That decision proved to be significant at the time, and it is still paying huge dividends for A&M. Kevin Matthews walked on for Dennis Franchione in 2005, earned a scholarship in '06, backed up All-American Cody Wallace in '07, and started the final 25 games of his A&M career under Mike Sherman.

Kevin, who went on to play for the Tennessee Titans, enjoyed A&M so much that his younger brother, Jake, decided to sign with the Aggies, as well. Jake, who began starting as a true freshman in 2010, became one of the most impressive and imposing offensive linemen ever to play at A&M. In 2012, right tackle Jake and left tackle Luke Joeckel combined to form the most outstanding bookends in the history of Aggie football. Those tackles played a huge role in Johnny Manziel winning the 2012 Heisman Trophy.

Both juniors were projected as first-round picks if they decided to forgo their senior seasons to enter the 2013 NFL Draft, which is what Joeckel did. But Jake further endeared himself to A&M fans by deciding to return for his senior year in 2013. He wanted a chance to play left tackle and play with his younger brother, Mike, who could be a dominant center for the Aggies for years to come.

In other words, the Matthews family has already etched a prominent and permanent place in the hearts of Aggie fans. And what a football family it is. The Matthews name is synonymous with big-time football. "NCAA" is part of their DNA.

The Baldwins act; the Kennedys run for political office; the Jacksons sing; and the Matthews play big-time football.

Kevin, Jake, and Mike Matthews' grandfather, William Clay Matthews Sr., was an All-American at Georgia Tech who made it to the NFL. Their dad, Bruce, was an All-American lineman at USC and is now in the Pro Football Hall of Fame. Their uncle, Clay Jr., was also an All-American for the Trojans and a first-round pick in the NFL draft who played 19 years with the Browns and Falcons. And three of their cousins played college football, including Clay Matthews III, who became a linebacker for the Packers and made his fourth straight Pro Bowl in 2012.

Fortunately for A&M, Bruce Matthews was drafted with the ninth overall pick in the 1983 draft by the Oilers and chose to make his home in Houston. Bruce, who played 19 years along the offensive line with the Oilers and Titans, entered the Pro Football Hall of Fame in 2007 after playing in more games (296) than any positional player in NFL history at the time of his retirement in '01.

Bruce Matthews played so long that his former USC teammate, Jeff Fisher, became his NFL head coach. Bruce's 14 consecutive Pro Bowls (nine at guard, five at center) tied Hall of Famer Merlin Olsen for the most ever, and Bruce was selected as a guard on the NFL's All-Decade Team of the 1990s.

Ironically, Bruce says he didn't initially like anything about Texas A&M when he first moved to the Lone Star State to play for the Oilers. But Kevin's experiences in Aggieland changed his mind.

"I heard so much about A&M and UT while playing in Houston—from the guys I played with and the media—that I just got sick of A&M and UT," Bruce said. "But in Kevin's time up there, I was totally won over. For Kevin to go up there as a walk-on and to earn a scholarship first and then to be starting…well, Carrie [his wife] and I were so proud of him. Our experiences with A&M have continued to be very positive."

Likewise, A&M's experiences with the Matthews continue to be exceptional.

72 Dave Elmendorf

During his sophomore year at Houston's Westbury High School, Dave Elmendorf almost quit playing sports altogether. He was inflicted with an extremely painful condition called Osgood-Schlatter Disease, which was so debilitating that he could barely run.

Osgood-Schlatter Disease can cause a painful lump below the kneecap in children and adolescents experiencing growth spurts during puberty. The condition occurs most often in children who participate in sports that involve running and jumping, but the good news is that it often goes away in a year or two when the child outgrows it. Elmendorf was in such immense pain as a sophomore in the mid-1960s, however, that he nearly quit everything athletics-oriented.

Imagine how bad those A&M teams he played on would have been without him. They were rather wretched with him, as A&M won only eight football games in Elmendorf's three varsity seasons (1968–70). But at least he gave Aggies fans something worthwhile to watch.

A&M went 3–7, 3–7, and 2–9 in Elmendorf's final three years in Aggieland, but head coach Gene Stallings was so pleased with "Elmo's" effort and attitude that he wrote a letter to the defensive back's parents.

"I just wanted to drop you a note to let you know what a pleasure it has been working with Dave the past four years,"

Stallings wrote in a December 16, 1970, letter, as reported by Brent Zwerneman, to Ed and Patricia Elmendorf. "Earning All-American honors as a defensive back is even more of a compliment considering the win-loss record we had this year."

No doubt about that. Elmendorf earned consensus All-American honors in 1970 after intercepting six passes, averaging 10.0 yards per punt return, and setting a school record for total kick return yards. On top of all that, Elmendorf was such a talented all-around athlete that he became the first athlete in A&M history to earn All-American honors in two sports.

Elmendorf played on much better baseball teams at A&M, including the 31–9 squad that finished second in the Southwest Conference in 1971 under Tom Chandler. Elmendorf was a three-time All-SWC centerfielder from 1969–71 and an All-American in '71. He was drafted first out of high school by the Braves and later by the Red Sox in '70. Finally, he was drafted by the Yankees in the first round in '71, but he instead chose to pursue a career in the NFL after he was selected in the third round of the '71 NFL Draft by the Los Angeles Rams.

It was a wise decision. Elmendorf, also an Academic All-American at A&M, played nine seasons with the Rams, intercepting 27 career passes and earning All-Pro honors. He played on some great defensive teams with the Rams, including the '75 squad that also featured Fred Dryer, Jack Youngblood, Merlin Olsen, and Isiah Robertson. The '75 Rams went 12–2, holding opponents to just 9.6 points a game, the second-lowest average in NFL history.

Elmendorf was just as successful in business as in football. Among other things, he spent 10 years as a general manager for American Golf Corporation, the world's largest golf course management firm; he served as the Dolce International Director of Golf; he was the general manager of Bear Creek Golf World in Houston; he was the GM of the Quail Valley Golf Course in

Missouri City; and he was the managing director of Miramont Development Corp. in Bryan.

He has also endeared himself to many Aggies over the years with his outstanding work as the color commentator of Texas A&M football games, joining play-by-play commentator Dave South in the broadcast booth.

Curtis Dickey

As a sophomore at Bryan High School, Curtis Dickey was so shy, withdrawn, and docile that his football coaches figured he did not really care about playing. Dickey's passive personality was his most dominant trait in those early high school days, which is why he wound up playing on the junior varsity.

At least temporarily.

"When he was a sophomore—this is how brilliant we were—we didn't put Curtis on the varsity at first because we didn't think he wanted to play," former Bryan High coach Merrill Green told *Sports Illustrated* in 1979. "He was so introverted we thought he was indifferent. He didn't seem to care. He certainly didn't jump out at you. But then one night he gained more than 300 yards in a junior varsity game, which kind of woke us up. Soon we realized that not only could he run with a natural ability but also that he had a natural sense for football and was very smart about plays and things.

"And all the time he was here he did everything we asked him. Everything. If he only knew how great he really is, there's no telling what he could become."

Dickey always remained exceptionally humble. But he managed to become rather sensational, as well.

Playing first in Emory Bellard's wishbone and later in Tom Wilson's I formation, Dickey rushed for 3,703 yards in his A&M career from 1976–79, leaving school as the Aggies' all-time leading rusher. More than three decades later, he still ranked No. 2 on the all-time A&M rushing list behind Darren Lewis.

But with Dickey, it wasn't just the amount of yards gained that was so impressive. What really turned heads and kept defensive coordinators up late at night was how quickly he covered those yards.

Curtis Raymond Dickey could absolutely fly. He won three consecutive NCAA indoor track championships in the 60-yard dash, clocking identical 6.15 times in 1978–79 and running a 6.12 in 1980. Dickey won All-American honors in each of those years in the 60, and he was also cited as an All-American in the 100 meters in '78 and the 400-meter relay in '79.

In one of his most impressive outdoor meets, Dickey won the SWC championship in the 100 meters with a time of 10.05 and then anchored the 400 relay team that also won the league title with a time of 39.54. And unlike so many track stars, Dickey's speed translated to the football field.

"Curtis is the kind of player who makes your eyes light up every time he touches the football," said former A&M offensive coordinator George Haffner, who had once coached Tony Dorsett at Pitt. "He has the same type of speed or better than Dorsett has. Curtis isn't as evasive as Tony, but he's in a class by himself in his explosiveness. And when the pro scouts ask about Curtis, which is often, I tell them he's got stuff inside of him, too. I think he's a winner."

Dickey was particularly sensational in '78 when he earned first-team All-SWC honors after rushing for 1,146 yards and averaging 104.2 per game. Dickey finished that year by rushing for an NCAA bowl-game record of 276 yards against Iowa State in the Hall of Fame Bowl.

His senior season in '79 was hampered by injuries, and his Heisman hopes never really developed because of those injuries.

But he was still selected with the fifth overall pick of the 1980 NFL Draft by the Baltimore Colts. Dickey went on to play seven seasons in the NFL with the Colts and Browns.

74 Sam Adams

As the temperatures turned cold in December 1990 and January 1991, Texas A&M was hot on the recruiting trail of Cypress Creek High School defensive lineman Sam Adams. Of course, so were most of the other major powers in college football.

Adams was among the bluest of blue chips, a 6'4" monster of a young man who was considered by virtually every newspaper and recruiting service as a "can't-miss" prospect. Adams wasn't only projected to play right away; he was expected to dominate right away. The only question at the time was: Where he would do it.

As the 1991 signing day approached—back then many top prospects actually waited until after their senior seasons to commit to a school—Adams had narrowed his short list to Texas A&M, Texas, Oklahoma, and USC.

A&M's coaches, looking for something to give the Aggies an edge in the recruiting race, decided to utilize their "closer" for Adams' official visit to College Station.

"And I was the closer," said former A&M star running back Greg Hill, a member of the Texas A&M Lettermen's Association Hall of Fame. "I also closed the deal on Rodney Thomas and Leeland McElroy. Unlike some guys, I wasn't concerned about somebody coming in and stealing my spotlight. I wanted Texas A&M to have the best players, so I was selling A&M the best I could. The thing I remember about Sam coming in was that he was a man-child even back then. I knew I had to close that deal because I knew Sam was going to dominate in college and was going to be able to play for a long, long, long time in the NFL."

Fortunately for the Aggies, Hill closed the deal. And he was right in his observations about Adams, who proved to be one of the most dominant defensive ends in school history.

Adams immediately excelled at A&M, earning SWC Defensive Newcomer of the Year honors in 1991 as a 280-lb. defensive end. He followed up with an All-SWC year in '92, and in '93—his last season at A&M—Adams was a consensus All-American and was selected as the National Defensive Player of the Year by *Sports Illustrated.*

Adams then began fulfilling Hill's other prediction. After leaving school early, he was selected in the first round of the 1994 NFL Draft (eighth pick overall) by the Seahawks. He spent six outstanding years with Seattle and then helped Baltimore win Super Bowl XXXV in 2001. He played with the Raiders in 2002, spent the next three years in Buffalo, joined the Bengals in '06, and started 11 games with Denver in '07. He played in three Pro Bowls and 206 regular season games in 14 years.

Adams' father, Sam Sr., was an outstanding collegiate player at Prairie View A&M University who then played as an offensive lineman with the New England Patriots from 1972–80 and finished his NFL career with the New Orleans Saints in '81.

At a very early age, the younger Adams began training with his father each spring and summer. And there was never even the slightest doubt that Sam would eventually follow his father into the NFL.

"Because my father played, making it to the NFL wasn't something that was a dream of mine; it was just something I was supposed to do," Adams said. "I thought of it as a family business, something I was born to do. I would go and train with him in the off-season when I was a little boy, not really knowing what I was doing. I was just out there jumping and running with my dad.

"Once I got a little older, I had more of an appreciation for what my dad was doing and what he was teaching me to do. I thank God it worked out for me. I was very, very fortunate throughout my career. I continually count my blessings."

Dave South

Since he first became the permanent Texas A&M radio play-by-play announcer in 1985, Dave South has literally broadcast tens of thousands of Aggie events. South, who was raised in North Texas, began by broadcasting A&M football games. Men's basketball followed. Then baseball. And coach's shows, pregame shows, daily syndicated shows, and so much more.

Nowadays, he estimates that he does at least 140 to 150 live broadcasts each year. So when fans ask him—and they inevitably do—to describe one or two of his favorite calls, it's practically impossible for him to narrow it down so succinctly.

In a span of 28 seasons from 1985 to 2012, South broadcast 346 football games alone. During that stretch, he broadcast seven conference championship teams, 21 bowl games, two conference championship games, two A&M upsets of the No. 1-ranked team, and two Aggie wins over the No. 2-ranked team in the nation.

"Fortunately, I've been around here long enough and been fortunate enough to call some great games in a variety of sports," said South, who first began his college radio play-by-play career with the Exxon Radio Network back when Exxon service stations throughout the Lone Star State gave pennant-shaped window decals of each of the Southwest Conference schools to its customers. "The 2012 Alabama game had a number of memorable calls. When we went to the College World Series in 1999 with Casey Fossum getting the big strikeout to end the game, that was a lot of fun.

"There was the Acie Law shot at the buzzer against Texas [2006], the pass to Sirr Parker for a TD against Kansas State [in the 1998 Big 12 championship game], and so many other dramatic finishes. Beyond the great games, though, there have been so many special players, from the greatest ones with the most talent to the walk-ons like Jarod Jahns and Chris Walker. Dominique Kirk is another guy I loved, as well as Jeff Granger and John Scheschuk. Getting to know these guys is so rewarding. I always get a kick when those guys come back and say hello to me. That's the real reward to me. A lot of the games are memorable, but so many of the people—the players and the coaches—have been really unforgettable to me."

Likewise, South has left an unforgettable legacy in Aggieland. In addition to possessing a great voice, South is passionate about his love for Texas A&M athletics. He does not consider himself a journalist of any sort; he says he is a public relations extension of the athletic department and a promotions specialist for each of the teams.

Regardless of how he defines it, South's voice has become synonymous with Aggie athletics. The Yankees had Phil Rizzuto; the Cardinals had Jack Buck, the Rangers have Eric Nadel, the Cowboys have Brad Sham, and the Aggies have Dave South, who so thoroughly enjoys his job and working in Aggieland that he typically replies to the question, "How are you doing?" with the response, "The best I've ever been."

South was purely the voice of the Aggies from 1985–90, but he was then hired by athletic director John David Crow to sell advertising for the athletic department. Since then, South has had various roles within the athletic department in marketing, promotions, and sales.

South is extremely dedicated to broadcasting all Aggie sports, and even when seasons overlap, he does his absolute best to make sure he attends as many games as possible…even if that means juggling his travel schedule.

"In 2013, I wanted to make sure I could do the opening game for baseball, so I elected to not fly with the basketball team on the charter to Nashville for the Vanderbilt game the next day," South said. "I stayed the night in College Station and then had [my wife] Leanne drive me to Houston Saturday morning where I caught a plane out of Hobby. One time back in the Big 12, in order to do a baseball game on Friday night, Leanne agreed to drive me to Lubbock from College Station the next morning at 6:00 so I could do a 3:00 PM basketball game at Texas Tech. She dropped me off at the United Spirit Arena at about 2:00 and started driving back immediately. I did the game and flew back with the team. I was waiting for her on the front porch swing when she drove back into the driveway. That's quite the wife to do that for me."

South acknowledges that the A&M losses used to be especially hard on him, causing excessive heartache. But the deeply devoted Christian and family man says that God has given him a better sense of perspective through the years, and he regularly receives reminders about what is really important.

"In the [2013] Kentucky game [at Reed Arena], someone came down prior to the broadcast and asked me if I had a radio so somebody in the arena could listen to our broadcast," South recalled. "They told me about a wounded warrior named Matt Bradford, who had lost both his legs and his eyesight in combat. I had them bring him down to the arena floor and sit him between [color commentator] Al [Pulliam] and I during the broadcast. He was from Lexington and was a big Kentucky fan.

"Before he left us that night, he reached in his pocket and pulled out a Wounded Warrior's coin. He handed it to me and told me that this had been a great moment in his life because he had always wanted to be the color guy on a basketball broadcast of a Kentucky game. That was really special to me and put it all in perspective. He thanked me for allowing him to do it. I have Matt Bradford on my prayer list, and that coin is in my pocket. I want the Aggies to win every game, but when we don't, it's not the end of the world. There were times that we would lose a game and it would stay with me for weeks. But I am able to keep it in perspective much better these days thanks to people like Matt Bradford."

Gene Stallings

At the 2012 SEC media days in Hoover, Alabama, Gene Stallings strolled through the hallways and meeting rooms of the Wynfrey Hotel, shaking hands with adoring Alabama fans, signing autographs for youngsters, and conducting interviews with hordes of media representatives who had gathered for the annual event.

Stallings, the head coach of Alabama's 1992 national championship team, is obviously still revered among the Tide fans in the heart of Dixie. But many of those fans were surprised—perhaps even a little offended—when Stallings replied to a question he was asked about who he would be rooting for when Alabama played Texas A&M in early November.

"When Texas A&M plays Alabama, I'll be for Texas A&M," Stallings said. "Love Alabama, no question about that, but that's who I'll be for. I still bleed maroon."

Alabama fans should understand. After all, when push came to shove, the legendary Bear Bryant chose to leave A&M for Alabama in 1957 because Bama was home. It was where he had played, where he had graduated, and where he'd first made a name for himself in college football.

Texas A&M was all of those things for Stallings. And so much more.

Ironically, Stallings, who grew up in Paris, Texas, never envisioned going to A&M and had never heard of Alabama when he was in high school in the early 1950s. Stallings had wanted to go to Baylor, but his girlfriend, Ruth Ann Jack (who later became his wife), wanted Stallings to attend A&M because there were no girls at the school.

She eventually talked him into signing with Ray George and the Aggies in 1953. But he never played for George. After Stallings played on the freshman team in '53, A&M hired Bryant prior to the '54 season. Stallings said he had never heard of Bryant, but he was actually fairly excited when the new head coach took two busloads full of Aggie players to a little town called Junction in the summer of '54.

"[Bryant] told us to get a pillow and a blanket and a couple changes of clothes," Stallings told Brent Zwerneman in the 2003 book, *Game of My Life: 25 Stories of Aggie Football*. "He wouldn't tell us where we were going. He even bought us some candy at a little rest stop along the way—we were all just having a good ol' time. Finally, we pulled into Junction, and it was a pretty place. It had these little Quonset huts for us to stay in and even a river behind the back of the facilities. We thought it was going to be great."

Instead, it was torturous. But Stallings survived Junction, and he became one of Bryant's favorite players. Stallings earned first-team All-Southwest Conference honors as an end in 1955, and he was a captain of the '56 SWC champions. And when Bryant left for Alabama in '57, he hired Stallings as an assistant.

Stallings stayed at Alabama until he was 29. At that point, A&M hired him to return as head coach for the 1965 season. In seven seasons at his alma mater, Stallings compiled an overall record of just 27–45–1. His only winning season was in 1967 when the Aggies won the SWC title and beat the Bryant-coached Tide in the Cotton Bowl. Bryant was so proud of his pupil that he lifted Stallings off the ground in a hug after the game.

Stallings was fired by A&M following the 1971 season, and he spent the next 14 years as an assistant under Tom Landry with the Dallas Cowboys. He then served four seasons as the head coach of the St. Louis/Phoenix Cardinals before returning to Alabama as head coach in 1990. In seven seasons at Bama, Stallings won a national title and compiled an overall record of 70–16–1. He was beloved in Alabama, but he eventually returned to the Lone Star State and ultimately represented A&M one more time in a different role.

After his retirement from football, Stallings served on President George W. Bush's Commission on Intellectual Disability and wrote a book about his late son, John Mark, who was born with Down's Syndrome. And in 2005, he was appointed to the Texas A&M Board of Regents by Governor Rick Perry. In that role, Stallings was an outspoken proponent of A&M's move to the SEC. Once an Aggie, always an Aggie.

77 Joe Boyd

As Joe Boyd waited in the hospital for the doctor's diagnosis in November 1938, he knew something was terribly wrong. Boyd was as tough as a $2 steak and possessed a mean streak wider than the

Brazos River. He boxed for fun, wrestled as a hobby, and regularly went for blood like a shark on a feeding frenzy.

Following Texas A&M's season-ending victory over Rice in '38, however, even Boyd's battle-tested pain tolerance was pushed to the limit. The throbbing in his neck was so severe that Boyd wasn't the least bit surprised when doctors discovered cracked vertebrae. He also suffered broken ribs and endured temporary paralysis in his legs from the beating he took in the game. But it was his neck that was causing him the most torment.

"The man came out of the X-ray room and said my neck was broken," Boyd recalled in the late 1990s in an interview with *12th Man Magazine* from his home in West Union, West Virginia. "I said, 'I knew something was wrong.' I was a tough old bird, but it absolutely bothered me."

It did not, however, prevent Boyd from playing the following season. In one of the ultimate testaments to Boyd's toughness, he not only played the entire 1939 national championship season with a broken neck, but he was also named to six All-American teams.

A&M coaches hired a masseuse to give Boyd regular neck massages during the 1939 season. The massages were grueling, as bone chips crackled like fireworks. He endured plenty of pain on and off the field in 1939, but he was still the anchor of an unyielding defense that allowed just 31 points the entire season.

"Joe Boyd was one tough son of a gun," Kimbrough said prior to his death in 2006. "As a player, he'd fight and battle you until hell froze over."

On June 1, 2009, Dr. Joe Boyd finally lost a fight, succumbing to an array of health issues. The former A&M legend, who had devoted most of his adult life to Christian ministries, was 92.

For several years Boyd had been relegated to an assisted living facility in West Union. He had suffered several mini-strokes that limited his communication skills, and his overall health had continued to deteriorate. His cause of death was listed as complications resulting from hardening of the arteries.

"But he never lost his great spirit and happiness [until the day he died]," wrote Dr. Randy E. Taylor, president of Randy Taylor Revivals, Inc. at Mt. Salem Revival Grounds in West Union. "When one reflects upon the history of America's great preachers, evangelist Dr. Joe M. Boyd will be ranked among the greatest. He was a statesman of the sermon and a scholar of the scriptures. His biblical knowledge made him a theologian; his delivery made him a legend. Dr. Boyd was always on the soul winner's trail.

"He tangled with the devil and wrestled against sin while preaching as an evangelist for almost 70 years.... His life was fascinating."

Indeed it was. Long before Boyd became the leader of Christian revivals around the world, he was a self-proclaimed renegade. He was a hell-raiser whose background was as hard as his backbone. By the time he was a teenager, Boyd was a member of one of the numerous gangs in the Dallas area in the early 1930s.

The city's answer to the gang problem was to organize them into sports teams—the West Dallas gang, the Fair Park gang, and so forth. Each gang fielded a football team, and it was there that Boyd's gridiron career began to flourish.

"I played for one of the gang teams, and it was so rough that we drank wine at the half," Boyd said. "We'd guzzle it down. All the games wound up in free-for-all fights. By the time I got to Crozier Tech High School, I was already tough, and I thought I could whip anybody."

Boyd's fortunes first began to take a turn for the better when he found a home at Texas A&M. Playing strongside tackle, Boyd was a two-time All-Southwest Conference performer and was later named to *Sports Illustrated*'s 25-year All-American team.

Later in life, the Rev. Joe M. Boyd started numerous churches and a youth camp—Mt. Salem Revival Grounds in West Union—in

1976. He preached the gospel in every state in the union and around the world, and he authored 15 Christian books.

"Dr. Boyd also trained hundreds of young evangelists, held thousands of revivals, and saw millions saved," Taylor wrote. "Those who heard him speak savored the taste of his endless southern colloquialisms. Nothing ever slowed him down. After the [death] of his wife of 62 years, Edith Boyd, on July 6, 2000, and the passing of Dr. Jack Hyles, his pastor of over 50 years on February 6, 2001, his travels at the age of 84 increased. He began to travel worldwide with less time at home than ever before in his ministry. He was an amazing man and servant of God."

78 Pat Thomas

As a school senior at Plano High, Pat Thomas rushed for two touchdowns in the 1971 Class 4A state championship game against Gregory-Portland, leading the Wildcats to a 21–20 victory at Memorial Stadium in Austin.

Thomas then became part of Emory Bellard's first recruiting class at Texas A&M in 1972. He played a prominent role in helping the '74 Aggies post the school's first winning season in seven years, and he was instrumental in the Aggies' 10-win season in 1975. Thomas was selected as an All-American in 1974 and '75, becoming just the sixth two-time All-American in A&M history at the time.

But for all the magical moments and defining games that he played at A&M from 1972–75, it was the role that Thomas and several of his teammates played off the field that ranks most prominent in his memory banks.

Attend Silver Taps

On the first Tuesday of each month, Texas A&M takes a reverent moment to honor any graduate or undergraduate student who passes away while enrolled at A&M in a moving ceremony called Silver Taps. It is just one of the sincere and moving traditions that distinguishes A&M from so many other universities.

The first Silver Taps was held in 1898 honoring Lawrence Sullivan Ross, the former governor of Texas and president of A&M College.

Silver Taps is currently held in the Academic Plaza. On the day of Silver Taps, a small card with the deceased student's name, class, major, and date of birth is placed as a notice at the base of the academic flagpole, in addition to the memorial located behind the flagpole.

At about 10:15 that night, lights are extinguished and hymns chime from Albritton Tower. Students silently gather at the statue of Lawrence Sullivan Ross, and at 10:30 PM, the Ross Volunteer Firing Squad marches into the plaza and fires three rifle volleys. Buglers then play a special rendition of Silver Taps.

Taps is played three times from the dome of the Academic Building: once to the north, south, and west. It is not played to the east because the sun will never rise on that Aggie again. After the buglers play, the students silently return to their homes.

"I am definitely proud of becoming an All-American at A&M, but I am more proud of becoming a trendsetter for African Americans at A&M," Thomas said. "There was some racial unrest at that time, and we were the first real wave of minority students, especially in football, to come through A&M. We had a group that stood out and stuck up for each other. There was no question that we were trendsetters. We had eight freshmen who started in 1972, and five of them were black. So it was an opportunity for us to prove that we could thrive at a place like A&M.

"It was really not all that different from what I had experienced in Plano. Growing up in that community gave me some experience in breaking down racial barriers. Plano was predominately a white upper-income community in the 1960s. So I think coming from Plano did make the transition to A&M at that time easier for me. I was able to communicate and to get along with people of all ethnic backgrounds because that's the way I was brought up. It wasn't a strange environment for me, which was the case for some of the other black players who had not experienced what I had experienced. It maybe helped me to bridge the gap a little between some of my fellow black athletes and the predominately white student body at that time."

Thomas was a great leader at A&M on the field and across the campus. He was also a tremendous playmaker who intercepted 13 passes in his collegiate career. He was drafted in the second round of the 1976 NFL Draft. One of the amazing things about the '75 team was that 21-of-22 starters went on to play in the NFL.

Thomas made two Pro Bowl trips during his seven-year career with the Los Angeles Rams, and he landed his first assistant coaching job with another former A&M standout, Jack Pardee, who was the head coach of the USFL's Houston Gamblers in 1984. From there, Thomas also had coaching stints with the University of Houston, the Houston Oilers, the Indianapolis Colts, the Buffalo Bills, and an arena team in Dallas.

He later started his own business, a certified 8A company in commercial construction that is headquartered in Buffalo, New York, but also has operations in Texas, where he settled in Galveston.

79 Ray Mickens

Shortly after it was revealed that Ray Mickens had torn the anterior cruciate ligament in his left knee in early September 2004, Herm Edwards, the head coach of the New York Jets at the time, dejectedly addressed the media regarding what a big loss for the team it would be to lose the diminutive Mickens.

One of Mickens' Jets teammates also summed up the sentiment of the entire team when he was asked about Mickens' season-ending injury.

"It hurts," defensive end Shaun Ellis said. "It hurts."

Texas A&M fans and Mickens' former A&M teammates understood completely. While "Ray-Ray" was small in stature—media guides listed him at 5'8" and 180 pounds—he played with a huge heart and was consistently a big-time force in the locker room and on the field throughout his career in Aggieland (1992–95).

Mickens first made a big name for himself at A&M as a sophomore in 1993, earning consensus All-Southwest Conference honors in a secondary that featured All-American Aaron Glenn on the other side. With opponents hoping to avoid Glenn, Mickens was tested time and time again. In fact, among all his great memories of his playing days at A&M, Mickens says the '93 game against Texas—an 18–9 A&M victory at Kyle Field—was his favorite.

The Longhorns tried exposing Mickens by matching him against the 6'5" Lovell Pinkney. But Mickens limited Pinkney to only two catches and batted away a key jump ball in the end zone to preserve the win that sent the Aggies to their third straight Cotton Bowl.

"It was Aaron and me against Mike Adams and Lovell Pinkney of Texas," Mickens recalled. "I remember so much about that game.

There was a play in the end zone, where everyone in the whole stadium knew they were going to be throwing to Pinkney. I broke it up, and that kind of put me on the map. My confidence was so high after that game, and it had a carryover throughout the rest of my career."

The personable and highly quotable Mickens went on to become a three-time All-SWC performer and a first-team All-American as a senior in 1995.

Mickens slipped into the third round of the 1996 draft because of concerns about his height. But he did much more than merely make it into the NFL. He thrived on some of the biggest and brightest stages in the league. Mickens played for the Jets from 1996 to 2004 when the knee injury threatened his career. But he returned to play for the Browns in 2005 and finished his career with the Patriots in 2006.

Overall, Mickens played 146 games in his NFL career, posting 324 tackles, six sacks, and 11 interceptions. However, the most impressive thing about Mickens is his charity work.

Beyond all the accolades he received in the NFL, Mickens is most proud of the fact that he used his position and his name recognition to do charity work across the country. In 2004, for example, he started the Ray Mickens Champions Fund, a non-profit organization designed to serve underprivileged kids in the Dallas area and in his original hometown of El Paso.

In fact, one of El Paso's highest-profile fundraising events is The Ray Mickens Celebrity Weekend. In 2010, the free football camp and health fair attracted 568 kids. The Fund also offers a mentor program for high school students, which is aimed at motivating students to continue their education and attend college.

"I have my foundation, it's called the Ray Mickens Champions Fund. I help underprivileged kids in the Dallas area and El Paso. We have reading programs, and we reward the kids with trips to the Cowboys games. It's fun to do; I enjoy working with kids."

Mickens also keeps close tabs on the Aggies. Prior to A&M's 2013 Cotton Bowl victory over Oklahoma, for example, Mickens and former A&M defensive lineman Ty Warren sponsored the Lettermen's Association happy hour and reunion on the night before the game. Roughly 400 people attended the gathering, and Mickens had the opportunity to share some stories about the last time he played OU in 1994 at Kyle Field.

"That was a good year for us and a memorable game," Mickens said. "We whipped them pretty good [36–14] that day, and I always let my teammates in the NFL who went to OU know about that."

80 Aaron Glenn

During the course of his 15-year NFL career, which included more than 200 games with the Jets, Texans, Cowboys, Jaguars, and Saints, cornerback Aaron Glenn was often spotlighted against the best receivers in the game on the league's biggest stages.

The 5'9", 185-lb. Glenn welcomed the challenges each week with supreme confidence and a steady, calm demeanor. Glenn was occasionally beaten by opponents, but he was never rattled. His poise under pressure allowed him to intercept 41 passes in his career, return six of those passes for touchdowns, and earn three trips to the Pro Bowl.

The perpetually cool "A.G." may never have been overly anxious on the field—except for the time he was invited by the Texas A&M baseball team to throw out the ceremonial first pitch in 2002, the same year he returned to the Lone Star State to play with the Houston Texans.

Former A&M baseball coach Mark Johnson hands the ball to Aaron Glenn to throw out the first pitch at a 2002 game. (Photo by Rusty Burson)

"I was a nervous wreck," Glenn admitted in regard to his first pitch. "I was completely out of my element. If I do that again, I'm going to practice for at least a couple weeks. I like to be fully prepared."

That's the mentality that made Glenn so great for so long on the football field, and it's what will likely make him great in his quest to become a general manager in the NFL. In 2012, Glenn returned to the New York Jets as a pro personnel assistant 18 years after he first arrived as the team's first-round draft choice out of Texas A&M.

Robert Jackson: Another Great JUCO

Prior to the 1975 season, A&M head coach Emory Bellard took a chance on Henderson County Junior College (now Trinity Valley) prospect Robert Jackson. It was a wise decision.

Along with fellow linebackers Ed Simonini and Garth Ten Naple, Jackson helped A&M lead the nation in total defense in 1975 and earn a share of the SWC title. All three starting linebackers from that team were selected to All-American teams during their collegiate careers.

"There have been so many great linebackers come through A&M, and it's an honor to have been part of that great tradition," Jackson said. "You look out there today...and see guys flying around the field and making plays all over the place, and it brings back a lot of great memories of my time at A&M."

Jackson was a consensus All-American in '76 and a finalist for the Lombardi Award after leading the Aggies with 143 tackles. Jackson was then a first-round draft pick of Cleveland in 1977. He played four seasons with the Browns and one with the Falcons.

"I know if I want to get where I'm trying to go, just like as a player, I've got to put in the work," Glenn told NewYorkJets.com. "My ultimate goal is to be a general manager in the NFL. I'm here to pay my dues. I was always the first in the training facility and the last one out as a player. I know it takes time to be a GM, and I will put in the time."

Former A&M teammates and coaches who remember Glenn putting in the extra time in the early 1990s have little doubt that Glenn will once again rise to the top of his profession as he did in Aggieland when he arrived from Navarro Junior College in 1992 and left in 1993 as one of the best defensive backs ever to wear the Maroon and White.

Taking over the premier cover cornerback spot that was held by All-American Kevin Smith in 1991, Glenn started every game of his first season at A&M and was selected as a first-team All-SWC defensive back in '92 when he shattered the SWC record for passes broken up in a season with 20.

The following year opponents practically refused to throw in his direction, yet Glenn still broke up 13 passes and picked off three more. In 1993, Glenn was the SWC's Defensive Player of the Year and a consensus All-American. He was also the runner-up to Alabama's Antonio Langham for the Thorpe Award, which is given annually to the nation's best defensive back.

In addition to blanketing opposing wide receivers, Glenn also led the nation in 1993 in punt returns, averaging a school record 19.9 yards and scoring two touchdowns.

"My experiences at A&M were great," said Glenn, whose younger brother, Jason, was also a standout defender for the Aggies from 1997–2000. "I considered it an honor to be part of the Wrecking Crew, and I look back on my decision to go to Texas A&M as one of the best I've made."

81 Larry Jackson

When Larry Jackson accepted a job as an assistant strength and conditioning coach on Bob Stoops' Oklahoma staff in 2004, the former standout Texas A&M linebacker/defensive end viewed it as a wise career move. When he went to the University of Houston in 2006 as Art Briles' strength and conditioning coordinator, it was purely a business decision. And when he declined Briles' offer to go with him to Baylor in 2008—opting instead to stay at UH with new head coach Kevin Sumlin, whom he'd known well at OU—it was all about business.

When Jackson accepted Sumlin's offer in January 2012 to oversee the strength and conditioning program at Texas A&M, however, it was much more than a calculated career move based solely on bottom-line business pros and cons.

"This wasn't about business; this is personal," said the perpetually vibrant and energetic Jackson, a letterman at A&M from 1991–94. "This is home. I met my wife, Amy, here in the spring of 1994. We both graduated from here. I came back here after playing, and now I am thrilled to come back here and be in a role where I am in charge of the strength and conditioning program.

"Coach Sumlin is going to keep recruiting great athletes. I am going to keep bringing firepower in here. We are going to keep pushing the program and fine-tuning all the stallions the best we can. When I was here as a player, we used to say that you better never give your backup a chance to shine because we had so many players here. If your backup shined brightly enough, you might not see the field again. The competition was intense. That is what we are trying to create here now. The competition to be on that field representing Texas A&M is just getting started."

That should be a scary thought to the rest of the SEC. In his first season at A&M, Jackson didn't merely make a difference in Aggieland. He reshaped the players, reinvigorated the program, and reawakened the Aggies' swagger.

In 2011—Mike Sherman's last year as head coach at A&M— the Aggies lost five games in the second half in which A&M had held a double-digit lead. The often-exhausted Aggies simply couldn't finish games in '11.

But after just one spring and summer under the tutelage of Jackson, the Aggies showed a killer instinct and an ability to finish games in 2012, going 11–2. Even in the two losses, to Florida and LSU, it was obvious that the Aggies were in superior physical condition.

"Coach Jackson gave us a tremendous edge," said 2012 Aggie Heart Award winner Spencer Nealy. "He made a huge difference in our physical, mental, and emotional condition. He pushed us very hard, but he was invaluable in that we felt like we were in better shape than every team we played [in 2012]."

Jackson, who celebrated his 41st birthday in October 2012, knows all about what it takes to win at Texas A&M. The former Rockdale High School running back arrived in Aggieland in 1990 and began making the weight room a second home. He redshirted his first season, played sparingly at linebacker and on special teams in 1991, and started 22 games during the next three seasons at linebacker or defensive end.

In four seasons as an A&M letterman, the Aggies compiled a 42–2–1 regular season record (excluding bowl games) and never lost a game at Kyle Field. A&M also led the conference in all four defensive categories (rushing, passing, scoring, and total defense) three seasons in a row, which had previously never been done in SWC history.

The exceptionally quick and physically imposing Jackson was a destructive force on those outstanding Wrecking Crew defenses. In fact, he developed enough in the weight room and on the field to play with the Denver Broncos, Arizona Cardinals, and Miami Dolphins from 1995–97 and with the Barcelona Dragons of NFL Europe in 1998.

While Jackson was an exceptional player, he has proven to be an even better coach. He's personable, professional, passionate, and he still looks like he could step onto the field and dominate opponents like he did in the early 1990s.

"First off, Larry is a good friend. Second, he is a great person. Third, he is an outstanding coach," said fellow A&M strength and conditioning coach Allen Kinley who first set foot in Aggieland as a graduate assistant coach in 1984. "I've known Larry since he was

18 coming out of Rockdale High, and he was always a very hard worker, very conscientious, and always did everything we asked of him. The same approach he took as an athlete, he now takes as a coach. He works very hard and is very diligent. He is extremely resourceful and knowledgeable, as well. He's a big addition to our program, and we are all very pleased to see him return. He'll make a difference with these [football players]."

He already has, and perhaps the best is yet to come—another scary thought for A&M's opponents in the SEC.

82 Alan Cannon

Sitting on a plane bound to New York from Orlando in early December 2012, Texas A&M freshman quarterback Johnny Manziel leaned over and asked veteran Associate Athletic Director for Media Relations Alan Cannon what to expect when the A&M contingent arrived in the Big Apple for the Heisman Trophy ceremonies.

Manziel figured that Cannon had seen or experienced just about everything in a sports information career that dates back to the early 1980s when Cannon gave up his dreams as a walk-on baseball player at A&M and began volunteering in the media relations office under Spec Gammon.

But to the initial surprise of Manziel, Cannon informed the future Heisman winner that even traveling to New York for the ceremony was unchartered territory for him.

"We had a couple of guys finish in the top 10 in the Heisman voting with Darren Lewis [eighth overall in 1990] and Bucky Richardson [10th in 1991]," Cannon said. "So I was really excited

Johnny had an opportunity just to be invited to New York. When he asked me what to expect with the Heisman presentation and schedule, I told him I didn't know. My advice to him initially was the same thing I was telling myself—enjoy the moment because as much as you want to look ahead to even more opportunities, you never know if you will ever be back in this situation."

Good advice from one of the great professionals in the business. Cannon, a 1984 graduate of Texas A&M, is one of the most respected sports information specialists in the country. He's a statistics-generating, quote-facilitating, press release–producing, and interview-moderating machine.

And no one runs a press box more efficiently than Cannon, who was a student assistant in the SID office for four years in the early '80s where his main responsibility was baseball for head coaches Tom Chandler and Mark Johnson. Cannon was then hired as an assistant SID in 1985, and his prime responsibility became men's basketball under former head coach Shelby Metcalf.

Cannon served in that capacity until being named the sports information director at Texas A&M in March 1989 when he began overseeing the football program. Throughout his time at A&M, he has been winning professional accolades and friends in the media. Cannon is an even-tempered detail-oriented pro who is known by media across the country for his willingness to be accessible to the deadline needs of those who cover college athletics for a living.

But he is also a stickler for regulations, which has also won him fans and friends in the media. In some stadiums across the country, the press box is practically another cheering section for selected donors, former athletes, or staff members of the hometown school.

But when Cannon makes the announcement that his domain is a "working press box" and "no cheering is aloud," he means it. He is not afraid to toss violators who test him.

Cannon, a past president of the National Collegiate Baseball Writers Association and the 1999 winner of the prestigious Wilbur

John Thornton: From Student-Athlete to Student-Athlete Role Model

Including his time as a basketball player in the mid-1970s, John Thornton dedicated more than 35 years of his life to Texas A&M athletics, and he was undoubtedly one of the most loyal, dependable, and outstanding athletic department employees ever hired by A&M. His commitment to developing student-athletes at A&M was unparalleled.

Thornton, the son of former Yell Leader Bill Thornton (Class of 1950), was practically raised on the campus, and he fulfilled a childhood dream by leading the 1974–75 Aggies to the SWC championship as a senior captain.

Taking full advantage of the opportunities presented to him by A&M, Thornton graduated *cum laude* from A&M in 1975. He spent two years as a graduate assistant basketball coach on Shelby Metcalf's staff and earned his master's in educational administration. He then became the basketball head coach at Athens High School and spent a brief time at UT–San Antonio before taking the athletics director and head basketball coaching job at Hill Junior College in Hillsboro.

In 1981, Thornton returned to A&M to serve as an assistant basketball coach under Metcalf until the middle of the 1990 season when Thornton was promoted to interim head basketball coach.

After finishing the 1990 basketball season, Thornton turned his efforts to athletics administration with his focus on student-athlete development, including academics, strength and conditioning, athletic training, financial aid assistance, and community involvement. He headed up Aggie Athletes Involved (AAI), as well as the Student-Athlete Advisory Committee (SAAC), and he was the chairman of the Professional Sports Counseling panel.

Thornton, who was extremely involved in the lives of the student-athletes in so many other ways in his role as Sr. Associate A.D./ Student-Athlete Development, took over as interim athletic director in 2012, bridging the gap between Bill Byrne and Eric Hyman. Thorton resigned in the summer of 2012 after Hyman was hired.

Snypp Award presented by the organization, has also done a great job through the years of adapting to ever-changing media formats as newspapers have faded and electronic and social media outlets have increased dramatically.

Cannon, who is married to the former Kaye Miller of Bryan and has two daughters, is committed to evolving as technology and times constantly change.

"The Heisman race is one example of something that has changed over the years with the evolution of the Internet and social media," Cannon said. "I remember in 1990 when BYU sent out ties to the media to promote Ty Detmer. And we had Leeland McElroy's picture on some notepads that we gave media covering the team in 1995. It was more of a season-long promotion that started with the sports information department efforts in the summer. But now there is so much instant communication that a guy like Johnny can come out of nowhere, so to speak, to become a contender, especially when you have a stage like the SEC.

"The fact that Johnny won it really hit me on the plane ride back to College Station. I was so busy up until that point, but on the plane I had an opportunity to try to put it into context. I was so happy for Johnny and his family, but beyond that, I was happy for our entire football program and the athletic department. It was something that our entire team can celebrate—the web staff, 12th Man TV, Jason Cook and university marketing, the 12th Man Foundation, and everyone else who covers Texas A&M, from the newspaper reporters to TexAgs. So many people were there to cover it, and it was just wonderful for it to all come together."

Likewise, it was fitting that Cannon was there to experience it, moderate it, facilitate it—and add yet another feather to his professional hat.

83 Homer Jacobs

Maybe it was all the bowling results he typed in each week or the endless array of Little League games he covered across Galveston County. Perhaps it was editing the daily fishing report or gathering the nightly results from the greyhound racetrack in La Marque. Most likely, it was simply the perpetual grind of finding three local stories every day and writing them while also laying out the paper, organizing the agate, and often working 10 consecutive days without time off.

Whatever the case, Homer Jacobs had finally had enough. Covering Mardi Gras fun runs and documenting the best locations on Galveston Island to catch redfish were not the reasons he first pursued sportswriting. Jacobs earned his degree in journalism from Texas A&M in 1987 with hopes of one day covering college football—hopefully Aggie football—for a living.

In 1992, he mustered the courage to tell the management of *The Galveston Daily News* that his two-person sports department was going to cover college football whether they liked it or not.

Or maybe he just started doing it…and hoped nobody would tell him to stop.

"I was so desperate to cover college football that my one other sports reporter and I would take turns covering a Southwest Conference game each week and we would pay our own way, mileage and all," said Jacobs, now the editor of *12th Man Magazine* and one of the most well-known, talented, and respected journalists covering A&M athletics. "We covered good games like A&M-Houston in the heydays of the Cougars' Run-and-Shoot and really crappy ones like Rice-Baylor in front of 55,000 empty seats at Rice Stadium.

"Covering college football kept us sane while we were doing the other minutia we were required to do. It also allowed us to be in press boxes, so sports information directors and other sportswriters knew who we were and knew we were willing to do anything to cover college football."

Jacobs' willingness to pay his own way paid off one year later when a Dallas-based company that was already producing *Sooners Illustrated*, *Huskers Illustrated*, and *Hogs Illustrated* contacted Texas A&M's sports information department about who might be interested in helping them start *Aggies Illustrated*. A&M's assistant SID Brad Marquardt gave the company Jacobs' name. He leapt at the opportunity to leave beach volleyball tournaments behind and cover the Aggies.

It was a dream job for Jacobs who grew up in El Paso with visions of one day attending A&M. Jacobs' father, a longtime doctor in El Paso, attended A&M for two years in the 1950s, and Jacobs' older sister, Carol, began school in College Station in 1977. That was also the first year Jacobs saw the Aggies in person, as he and his father attended A&M's 37–14 victory over Florida in the Sun Bowl on January 2, 1977.

"As a kid in the '70s, I'd watch A&M with my dad whenever they were on," said Jacobs, the sports editor of the A&M campus newspaper, *The Battalion*, in 1986–87. "It wasn't on very often in El Paso, but if it was the ABC Game of the Week, we'd be glued to the TV. The first A&M game I saw in person was at the Sun Bowl. I remember going to get a hot dog, and I saw these guys in leather boots walking around the concourse. I thought that was pretty cool. I didn't know who they were, but it was impressive. Then my first game at Kyle Field was the 1978 Baylor game, which was not a good one. Baylor's Walter Abercrombie went nuts on the Aggies, but I was hooked on everything A&M."

After attending high school in Alexandria, Virginia, Jacobs enrolled at A&M in the fall of 1983 and was working for the school paper in 1986. His first job out of college was at *The Sherman Democrat*, and then it was on to *The Galveston Daily News*. Although some of his colleagues in the newspaper business predicted that specialty magazines would never last, Jacobs did an exceptional job as the editor at *Aggies Illustrated* for roughly four years, and he was the logical choice to start *12th Man Magazine* when the 12th Man Foundation decided to go to a magazine format.

12th Man Magazine is an award-winning publication that is mailed to donors of the 12th Man Foundation 20 times a year. It delivers in-depth features of A&M student-athletes and coaches, along with behind-the-scenes content and insider columns from Jacobs. It has been voted by the donors as the No. 2 benefit of membership in the 12th Man Foundation, behind only tickets to athletic events.

Jacobs, also the author of two A&M-themed books, is at his best when the Aggies are winning, as the magazine specializes in feel-good stories and positive public relations pieces. But he's also mastered what he refers to as "happy columns" when things are not so rosy. For example, Jacobs still wrote positive columns throughout the 2003 season when the Aggies went 4–8 and lost to Oklahoma, 77–0.

"It's so much easier when the Aggies are winning," said Jacobs, who finished his 16th football season with *12th Man Magazine* in 2012. "With our magazine mailing 20 times a year, I've written more than 320 'Inside the Aggies' columns from 1996 through 2013. Those columns can be really fun when things are going well like the 2011 women's basketball national championship or the 2012 football season with Johnny Manziel winning the Heisman. On the other hand, it's challenging when things are not so great on the fields and courts. But I always, always remind myself how lucky I am to work in an office at Kyle Field and cover the Aggies for a living. Even in the toughest times, I know I'm lucky to be in Aggieland."

And not still in Galveston, paying his way to college football games.

Gabe Bock

After graduating from Texas A&M with a journalism degree in 2004, Gabe Bock landed an internship, part-time job, or full-time role with practically every media outlet that covers the Aggies in the Bryan–College Station area, bouncing from small roles with KBTX-TV and *Chip Howard's Sports Talk Show* to larger reporter roles with Bryan Broadcasting and TexAgs.com.

The hard-working, quick-witted Bock knew practically everyone who covered A&M. He was also a multimedia machine, dabbling in virtually every electronic or print medium that existed at the time.

Until the summer of 2011, Bock might have been best described as Bryan–College Station's media "Jack of all trades, master of none." He was good at everything; he was diligent and determined; he was well-liked and well-received, but he simply hadn't found his professional niche—until August 22, 2011. That's the day that "Vaga-Bock" found a home. On the same day in sports history that one of Bock's all-time heroes, Nolan Ryan, recorded his 5,000[th] strikeout in 1989, Bock struck a chord with Aggie fans everywhere as he began hosting a daily, two-hour, Aggie-focused sports talk show on TexAgs Radio.

It was broadcast locally in Brazos County on KZNE-AM 1150, and it was available in an audio and video format to Aggie fans throughout Texas and across the country via the Internet. But the availability was only part of the overall allure of the show. The biggest reason for the show's immediate and continued success is the perpetually upbeat and consistently engaging Bock.

He was good at many other previous media roles, but he is a great radio host, giving Aggie sports fans a high-quality, entertaining, and intriguing radio/video show that was so popular in its first year and a half that it moved to three hours on weekday mornings beginning on January 28, 2013.

"I thought Gabe would be good when we first hired him in 2008 as a writer and reporter, and he was really good at that," said TexAgs co-owner and lead writer Billy Liucci. "But he has turned out to be even better than I could have imagined, especially in the role he now has on TexAgs Radio. I can't tell you how many compliments I regularly receive about Gabe."

On the one hand, Bock is a natural. He's comfortable, well-spoken, and extremely knowledgeable about A&M's past, present, and future potential in all sports. Depending on the situation, he can be condescending or compassionate, sarcastic or sincere.

Bock possesses an effortless on-air delivery, an easygoing demeanor, a strong radio voice, a keen sense of humor, and a tremendous knack for smooth transitions from one story to another and from delivering the news to making an advertising pitch.

On top of all that, Bock is relentless and fearless in his approach to booking guests. Some outsiders may have initially viewed the show as a regional, small-market production, but right from the start, Bock has sought and landed the biggest names in college sports, especially during football season.

Leading up to the 2012 Heisman Trophy presentation, for example, Bock booked former Heisman winner John David Crow from Texas A&M, which was a natural fit. But he also landed former Heisman winners such as Doug Flutie, Archie Griffin, and Gino Torretta. And in the final weeks of the '12 football season, Dan Rather, Spencer Tillman, Archie Manning, Joe Namath, Bart Starr, and Verne Lundquist appeared on the show.

"I've always taken the approach of shooting for the stars in terms of lining up guests," said Bock, who grew up in Denison and was a two-year varsity baseball letterman in high school. "The worst they can say is, 'no,' and more times than not, if you work enough contacts, you will end up with some big-time guests. It's one of those deals where you might as well start off by asking the prettiest girl in the bar to dance, and you can work your way down from there until somebody finally accepts. I'd rather start on that end of the line than the other."

Bock's a smooth operator once he lands a guest, as he is a tremendous interviewer. One of his most endearing qualities as a radio host is that he truly allows guests to be the star of the moment. Unlike so many other radio hosts, Bock does not feel the need to interrupt or hear himself speak.

On the contrary, he is often hilariously self-deprecating, regularly poking fun of himself and gladly making a fool of himself in the name of entertainment. In February 2013, for example, Bock went on the air with Liucci and former ESPN sideline reporter Jenn Brown while wearing a robe and wide receiver's gloves to advertise products for an Aggie-owned retailer. Bock modeled the robe by playfully showing off his boxers, which was a big hit with Brown.

"I vow to never take myself too seriously," said Bock, whose first job in the media was a 2003 internship with KBTX-TV's Darryl Bruffett, who allowed Bock to work through the fall of '03 as a part-time writer, photographer, and editor. "I take my job seriously, but never myself. This is a fun job and I always, always try to have fun with it. I am very thankful to be doing what I am doing."

Most of all, he's thankful for his family, and the only thing he follows more thoroughly than the Aggies is his "home team." Bock married way up to the former Megan Gerken in December 2004, and the couple has two children, daughter Ella (born in 2009) and son Easton (born in 2012 and named after the baseball equipment company).

85 Randy Bullock

After being drafted in April 2012 by his hometown team, the Houston Texans, Randy Bullock endured a serious muscle tear in his kicking leg during the 2012 preseason. Unfortunately, Bullock was done for the year before he ever officially began his rookie season.

"I've been through plenty of adversity in my life, so I am tackling this situation the same way I have approached so many other things," the soft-spoken Bullock said while rehabbing in the fall of 2012. "I will use this situation to come back stronger than before."

Bullock was so confident in his future because he'd already traversed some extremely difficult roads.

He became one of the most dependable kickers in the history of Aggie football, using his own emotional scars as motivation to propel him to seemingly unimaginable heights. In 2011, Bullock shattered the second-oldest record in A&M history by scoring 142 points—14 more than Joel Hunt accounted for 84 years earlier in 1927.

In the process, Bullock earned consensus All-America honors and claimed the 2011 Lou Groza Award, which is presented annually to the nation's top placekicker. Bullock may have been the only person in the country—aside from his own family members—who was not surprised by his Herculean efforts in 2011 when he led the nation by converting 29-of-33 field goals. When he walked on at A&M prior to the 2008 season, he wrote a goal sheet that included his desire to be an All-American and to win the Groza Award.

"How realistic those goals were at the time, I really didn't know," Bullock said. "But I wanted to set my goals very high. I definitely had my father in mind when I wrote those goals. I will always carry his memory with me and try to honor him with what I do."

In 2004, Bullock and his older brother, Rhett, went on a hunting trip with their father, Richard. On the final day of that trip—December 23—Randy and Rhett found their then-53-year-old father after Richard had suffered a heart attack.

Cathy Capps: Winning Over the Winners of A&M Athletics

Cathy Capps has one of the most enviable jobs on the Texas A&M campus—she works closely with many of the biggest stars in the history of the Texas A&M athletics department in her role as the director of the Lettermen's Association. On the other hand, it's also one of the most difficult and demanding jobs on the A&M campus, as Capps must manage the egos of some of the biggest stars in A&M's athletic past when they are disappointed about not receiving the recognition they think they deserve or have complaints about practically anything under the sun.

When former players are upset about anything, they usually start by calling Capps, the level-headed, mild-mannered, and highly personable manager of everything pertaining to former players in all sports.

Capps is part administrator, part psychologist, part cheerleader, part therapist, part event planner, part ticket manger—and she's well-rounded enough to handle it all. She is truly one of the absolute gems of the entire athletic department and a tremendous ambassador for Texas A&M.

Capps, who joined the Texas A&M athletic department staff in 1995, is an assistant athletic director. Her responsibilities include oversight of the Texas A&M Lettermen's Association and the Texas A&M Sports Museum in the north end of Kyle Field. She organizes all the volunteers who work in the museum and ultimately manages the displays in the facility.

A native of Laramie, Wyoming, Capps earned her bachelor's degree from Texas A&M University in 1995. She has two grown children, Nikki (A&M Class of '04) and Jonathan (A&M Class of '06).

It was too late to save him. The boys were devastated by their father's death, but they were both determined to honor his memory by attending the university he grew to love. Richard Bullock graduated from Ohio State, but the petroleum engineer had relocated to Houston and met so many Aggies in his business field that he became a big fan.

Rhett graduated from A&M with a degree in mechanical engineering, and Randy followed in his older brother's footsteps, even though he didn't initially have a scholarship offer. Because of his longtime desire to be an Aggie and the proximity of the A&M campus to his mother's home in Houston, Bullock chose to walk-on in the 2008 fall semester. By the midway point of that season, he earned the starting placekicking position. He made six of his seven field-goal attempts throughout the second half of the season and was one of the few bright spots of an otherwise bleak 4–8 season.

The next year, Bullock was 12-for-19 in field-goal attempts and was 51-for-51 in converting extra points. As a junior in 2010, he earned honorable mention All-Big 12 accolades by making 16-of-21 field-goal attempts and all 50 extra point tries. Still, Bullock was certainly not on anyone's national radar entering his senior year. But he resolved to make his last season his best in hopes of truly honoring his father's name.

"I think the most proud moment for me personally [in 2011] was when I had the opportunity to go to the College Football Performance Awards and to accept the [Groza Award] on behalf of my family, teammates, coaches, and Texas A&M," he said. "On that night, I was optimistic about my chances of winning, but it was a complete surprise to actually hear my name called."

Even with all the awards and accomplishments during his senior season, it was uncertain whether Bullock would be drafted or not. During interviews at the NFL Scouting Combine, Texans special teams coach Joe Marciano asked Bullock how he would handle his first adverse situation in the NFL.

Without hesitation, Bullock replied, "Coach, my dad died when I was 15. How much more adversity is there?"

The Texans obviously liked his attitude and his abilities, taking Bullock in the fifth round (161st selection overall). And even in the aftermath of the injury, the team still had plenty of faith in his future.

86 Forget the Fran Era

The 2003 Texas A&M media guide featured a beautiful cover photo of Kyle Field with the sun rising in the distance. It also included a picture of first-year head coach Dennis Franchione next to the cover caption that read, "Dawn of a new era."

It would have been more appropriate if the cover had read, "Dawn of a new error."

While Franchione had been a good fit for three years at TCU (1998–2000) and two years at Alabama (2001–02) before arriving in Aggieland, the "Fran Plan"—he loved to refer to himself as "Fran" and enjoyed rhymes like "Fran the Man"—was a failure in College Station.

In a matter of months after taking over the job on December 5, 2002—a day that will live in infamy at A&M—Franchione infuriated current players and alienated former players. He also made curious personnel decisions, like hiring a head football strength and conditioning coach (Rick LaFavers) who'd never previously been a strength and conditioning coach, and bringing in a public relations specialist (Mike McKenzie) who penned secret newsletters that eventually played a major role in the "ban of Fran in Aggieland."

And some of the new traditions he brought with him—like the Night of Champions weight-lifting exhibition—seemed completely counterproductive. School records were shattered at the exhibition, but that's because spotters in the bench press, squat, and other lifts often assisted players with the lifts.

"The weight room philosophy was a joke, which was probably the first indication that we, as players, had that the new regime was not going to be good for A&M," said Brandon Leone, a redshirt freshman running back/defensive back in 2002, R.C. Slocum's final year as head coach at A&M. "Fran wanted everybody to bench press 400 pounds and squat 500, and he didn't care if you ran a 4.38 40 or if you could leap out of the gym with your vertical jump. With Fran, if you couldn't bench 400, you weren't working hard enough. That went for kickers, too.

"Then as we went into spring, it became evident that Fran was mostly about promoting Fran. The way he treated assistant coaches and players was not good. There were many times when the players looked around at each other and were like, 'This is not what we signed up for.'"

That was before the on-the-field embarrassments began. After a 2–2 start to the 2003 season, A&M went to Lubbock to open Big 12 play and lost to the Red Raiders...by 31 points. Two weeks later, Nebraska beat A&M by 36, and on November 8 in Norman, Oklahoma, the Sooners built a 77–0 lead at the end of the third quarter.

OU literally tried not to score in the fourth quarter. It was awful. And it could have been so much worse.

A&M lost six games in 2003 by at least 23 points or more and opened the 2004 season with a 20-point loss at Utah. The Aggies improved enough to win seven games after the opening flop in '04, but there were still embarrassing moments, like losing to Baylor

The 2006 season, highlighted by the Aggies' win in Austin, was one of the few high points of the Dennis Franchione era. (Photo courtesy of Texas A&M SID)

for the first time in 19 seasons and falling behind Tennessee in the Cotton Bowl, 38–0.

Fran also misused the talents of quarterback Reggie McNeal, who had considered transferring right after Slocum had been fired. McNeal was worried that Franchione might return to the option-style football he had utilized at TCU, Alabama, and other previous stops.

"I knew the type of offense Coach Fran ran because he recruited me at Alabama, and I didn't go there because I didn't want to be part of that system," McNeal said. "But I ultimately decided to stay because Coach Fran said he was going to open the offense up and let me throw. In hindsight, that wasn't the case, and that '03 season was worse than anyone could have imagined. There were a lot of reasons for that, but I never felt like I was a good fit in Fran's system."

Neither was Stephen McGee, who arrived at A&M as a heralded passer. After starting the first game of his career at the end of the dismal 2005 season (5–6 overall, 3–5 in the Big 12), McGee was sensational for much of 2006, accounting for 2,295 passing yards and 12 touchdowns. McGee completed 62 percent of his passes and tossed just two interceptions in 313 attempts.

Most Aggie fans figured that the '06 season would serve as the springboard to bigger things for the Aggies and McGee. They were wrong.

The signature moment of the 2006 season for A&M was the 12–7 win over Texas in Austin. Trailing 7–6, the Aggies took possession at their own 12 in the fourth quarter. Sixteen plays later, McGee bolted through an opening in the No. 1 rushing defense in the country for an eight-yard touchdown that gave the Aggies their biggest victory of the season.

But Fran didn't even use that to his advantage, as he became enamored with the generic offense A&M used to beat UT. The 2007 Aggies took significant steps backward on and off the field. There was the secret newsletter scandal; there were lopsided losses at Miami, Texas Tech, and Oklahoma; and there was the step back in time in offensive philosophy as the Aggies became a zone read/option offense that more closely resembled the Old West than the new millennium.

Fortunately, it all resulted in Fran being fired. In five years, he compiled an overall record of 32–29 with 14 of those losses coming by 20 points or more. But let's not dwell on that anymore. It's far better to just forget about the entire era.

87 Beating No. 1 Oklahoma in 2002

Prior to November 9, 2002, Texas A&M had never beaten a top-ranked team in the Associated Press poll. And quite frankly, it didn't seem likely that it would happen on that day, either.

The Aggies had lost the week before at Oklahoma State, and A&M had dropped three of its previous four home games as the No. 1-ranked and unbeaten Oklahoma Sooners (8–0) cruised into College Station. OU also took a 10–0 lead early in the second quarter as 84,036 fans watched the Aggies' offense struggle behind starting quarterback Dustin Long who was 3-of-9 for 28 yards and an interception in the early going.

Hoping to ignite a spark, A&M head coach R.C. Slocum and then offensive coordinator Kevin Sumlin inserted backup quarterback Reggie McNeal into the game. McNeal quickly lived up to his "Real Deal" nickname, hitting Terrence Murphy for a 61-yard TD pass midway through the second quarter and finding Greg Porter in the back of the end zone just before the half. Porter's fingertip catch in front of the Aggie Band that had lined up just behind the north end zone gave A&M a boost of momentum and tied the game at 13–13 heading into the locker room.

McNeal then delivered two more scoring passes in the third quarter—a 17-yard strike to Bethel Johnson and a 40-yarder to Murphy—to give the Aggies a lead they would never relinquish.

The A&M defense made a couple of big plays in the final quarter, and the late Terrence Kiel sealed the 30–26 win with an interception with 1:12 left in the game.

"It was magical," fifth-year senior linebacker Brian Gamble said at the time. "This one ranks way, way up there on my all-time list.

255

It's tough to compare to the '99 Bonfire game. I think that game is in a category of its own. But this is the biggest 'normal' game I've been a part of. This was just a complete victory that I will never forget."

Overall, McNeal was 8-of-13 for 191 yards and four touchdowns in relief of Long. McNeal also gave the Sooners fits with his scrambling, producing 280 yards of total offense.

"It was an incredible day for me and our team," McNeal recalled many years later. "To be able to lead our team to a victory over the No. 1 team in the nation before 80,000 screaming fans was something I will never forget, and it's something that people still talk about whenever I am on campus. We all hoped that would be the start of something really big."

Unfortunately, it was not. In the aftermath of that glowing performance, McNeal appeared on the front page of *The New York Times* and was quite literally the national media darling in college football. At least for one week.

But the victory over OU turned out to be the most memorable mountaintop moment of McNeal's collegiate career, and it was immediately followed by a deep dive into the valley. One week after the euphoria of the OU triumph, McNeal started the first game of his collegiate career but didn't complete it. He injured his ankle against a mediocre Missouri team, and the Aggies lost in double overtime. A&M then lost to Texas 50–20 to finish the regular season at 6–6.

R.C. Slocum was fired at the conclusion of that season, and Dennis Franchione's offense was never the right fit for McNeal.

88 Brent Zwerneman

In 1991, as a freshman on Sam Houston State's baseball team, pitcher Brent Zwerneman stood in front of Olsen Field's first-base dugout, soaking up the atmosphere, when a "Raggie" from the second deck of the two-tiered stadium screamed, "Hey No. 11, what do you do with a degree from Sam Houston State?"

Four years later, Zwerneman had the answer: "Cover Texas A&M," he said with a laugh.

Zwerneman, a 1994 graduate of Sam Houston, doesn't merely cover Texas A&M athletics; he covers the Aggies thoroughly and exceptionally. In fact, he does such an outstanding job that Zwerneman is the A&M beat writer for two major daily newspapers in the Lone Star State, the *San Antonio Express-News* and the *Houston Chronicle*.

While that is partly an indication of the dire financial circumstances that exist in today's newspaper industry in an era of instant communications, Zwerneman is truly one of the best and hardest-working beat writers to ever cover Texas A&M.

Some great print reporters have covered the Aggies through the years, including men and women such as Denne Freeman, Al Carter, Larry Bowen, Randy Riggs, Neil Hohlfeld, Rachel Cohen, Charean Williams, Olin Buchanan, Kate Hairopoulos, John Lopez, and many more. Like those aforementioned journalists, Zwerneman combines an outstanding ability to write with strong reporting skills. Zwerneman has also evolved with the times, becoming a multimedia/social-media specialist with his Tweeting, videoing, and more.

In 2012, longtime A&M athletics staffer Billy Pickard, who may have first arrived in Aggieland in a covered wagon, paid

Zwerneman a tremendous compliment when he compared him to legendary Houston-based reporter/columnist Mickey Herskowitz, who covered A&M during the Bear Bryant era. And that comparison was not made solely because of the similar lengths of their last names.

Zwerneman, the first Division I baseball product from Conroe's Oak Ridge High School, loves what he does and often goes the extra mile while covering the Aggies, just like Herskowitz did for so many years. Zwerneman, the youngest of six kids, earned his start in the newspaper business as a copy editor at *The Bryan–College Station Eagle*. His primary writing responsibility in the early days was obituaries. But it certainly wasn't a death sentence to his career.

"I was thrilled to 'pay my dues' because I was getting to write," said Zwerneman, a fifth-generation Texan and fourth-generation Houstonian. "I couldn't believe I was getting paid to write, even for $14K a year. Within a few months, I was promoted to assistant city editor and Bryan–College Station city halls reporter. I would just go to A&M games in all sports for fun then, and I still couldn't believe I was getting paid to write.

"A year later, at the urging of mentor Larry Bowen, I moved over to cover A&M athletics in the summer of 1995 when Olin Buchanan left to work for the *Austin American-Statesman*."

It was a great move for Zwerneman and A&M fans who followed his work. Zwerneman covered the Aggies from 1995–99 for *The Eagle*, and then covered the San Antonio Spurs and Dallas Cowboys for the *Express-News*. He moved back to the A&M beat for the *Express-News* just prior to the Red, White, and Blue-Out game in the aftermath of the September 11, 2001 terrorists attacks.

"I am still in awe of that Red, White, and Blue-Out," said Zwerneman, who has authored four A&M-related books. "By far my favorite thing to cover is college sports, especially college football. Nothing beats a fall Saturday at Kyle Field."

Zwerneman, who broke the Dennis Franchione "secret newsletter" story in 2007, won five national writing awards from 2007–12, including four national top 10s from the prestigious Associated Press Sports Editors (APSE). But his biggest "win" was the heart of KBTX-TV anchor Crystal Galny, whom Zwerneman met at the Dixie Chicken the night before Texas Tech played at A&M in 2002. The couple has two children, Will (born in June 2009) and Zoe (April 2011).

89 Antonio Armstrong

As a standout linebacker at Houston's Kashmere High School, Antonio Armstrong once had visions of becoming the next Lawrence Taylor. Armstrong, who was born to a 15-year-old mother and fathered by a 16-year-old boy, found refuge on the football field and emerged as a star player in the Houston area.

But just as he began to rise to new heights, Armstrong's health sunk to its lowest depths. As a senior, he was diagnosed with a brain aneurysm. The doctors didn't know if he was going to live or die.

"They said if I did come out of it, I would never play football again," Armstrong recalled. "Thankfully, I had a praying mother, and she wouldn't stop praying."

Her prayers were answered. Armstrong underwent a miraculous recovery that doctors could not explain. However, after his recovery and losing a significant amount of weight while in the hospital, most of the schools that had shown interest in him before the aneurysm—Oklahoma, Colorado, and UCLA, to name a few—no longer wanted him. But A&M continued to express interest, so he signed with the Aggies in 1991.

"After losing so much weight, however, I was in for a rude awakening when I arrived on campus," Armstrong said. "I was so undersized during the early part of my freshman season that the A&M video staff—at the direction of defensive coordinator Bob Davie—made me the star of a mock 'crash dummy' tape, showing footage of tight ends Greg Schorp, James McKeehan, and Jason Matthews driving me 10-to-20 yards off the line of scrimmage. I was probably close to 190 pounds on the day I first stepped foot on campus. But I familiarized myself with the weight room and worked hard. I was always asking our strength and conditioning coach, Mike Clark, 'What do you want me to do next?'"

Armstrong primarily played on special teams as a freshman, but he worked so hard in the off-season and increased his strength so dramatically that Clark had him tested for steroids. But he was as clean as a rated-G movie, and as a sophomore in 1992, Armstrong backed up the great Marcus Buckley as the Aggies won their second straight SWC championship. By 1993, Armstrong weighed 225 pounds and earned All-SWC outside linebacker honors with 73 tackles and 8.5 sacks.

Until that point in his life, the name on the back of his jersey was "Shorter," as his mother's name was Kay Shorter Specks. But prior to his senior year at A&M, he decided to honor the father he never really knew by changing his last name from Shorter to Armstrong. Armstrong's father dropped out of high school to find a job when his son was born, and the streets consumed him. He died the month before his son went to A&M.

"The name change allowed me to gain a sense of peace regarding his shortcomings and death," Armstrong said. "I also dedicated my senior year to my father. It was a memorable season, to say the least."

The '94 Aggies completed just the ninth unbeaten season in A&M history (10–0–1) and the first since 1956. Armstrong recorded 62 tackles, including 17 behind the line of scrimmage, to earn All-American honors.

"What makes me most proud about my accomplishments as a senior was that I did those things with a debilitating injury," he said. "Prior to the season, I was diagnosed with a rare and painful condition called osteitis pubis, in which I was constantly tearing the abdominal muscles from my pelvic bone. Today it would be called a sports hernia. I struggled with pain every day, but I battled through it because I wanted to be part of that unbeaten year."

Because of the injury, Armstrong slipped into the sixth round of the NFL draft before the 49ers took him. He played well in training camp, but he fractured his right leg, and on his 22nd birthday, the 49ers released Armstrong.

He tried out for a couple more NFL teams and eventually made a name for himself in the CFL until he broke his leg again on October 15, 2000—his birthday. His leg didn't heal correctly, but Armstrong returned to action and helped lead the Blue Bombers to the Grey Cup the following season.

He never played again, but Armstrong is still in great shape and is still as competitive as ever. The devoted husband and father of three is the owner of 1st Class Personal Training Studios, which has three facilities in the Houston area.

"I try to honor God each day by leading my family in a manner which reflects His glory," Armstrong said. "We first serve the Lord in our house, and everything else falls into place. We attempt to instill biblical values, and we are determined to raise our kids to become men and a woman of character and integrity. We want them to be beacons of God's light at school, just as we—as their parents—attempt to be the same in the work place, in our community, and beyond. In today's world, that can be very challenging. Fortunately, God prepared me for the challenges by testing me, molding me, and strengthening me in the past. My life is a testament to the fact that faith can move mountains and that the best way to start attacking any problems is through prayer. I've been through a lot, and I now can clearly see that God used those struggles and hardships to develop my character, my resolve, and my faith."

Dan Campbell

With his white uniform covered in a mixture of grass stains, mud, and blood, and his eyes filling with tears of frustration, sophomore tight end Dan Campbell glanced toward the agonizing numbers on the Memorial Stadium scoreboard and looked back at his own sideline.

At that moment in late November 1996, it was difficult for Campbell to determine which was more sickening—the score of the game (Texas 51, Texas A&M 15) or the attitude along the Aggies' sideline.

"We were getting our ever lovin' [butts] kicked by our biggest rivals, and I saw people on our sidelines laughing, cutting up, and not even caring," Campbell recalled years later. "I knew right then, right there, that something was going to have to change. I didn't care if I was an underclassman. I wasn't going to let this happen again. It was time for a leader to emerge, and I wasn't about to wait to see if anybody else was willing to do it. As far as I'm concerned, the [1998] Big 12 championship really began on that day in Austin in '96. A couple of guys, including myself, said this [crap] ain't gonna happen again."

A big-time leader was born amid the A&M embarrassment on that afternoon in Austin. Campbell took the reins of the Aggies that day and didn't relinquish them until A&M had won the '98 league title and played in the 1999 Sugar Bowl.

During his entire career at A&M, Campbell caught only 27 passes for 314 yards and three touchdowns. But to this day, he remains one of the most respected and revered leaders in the recent history of A&M football.

There were certainly other leaders who contributed to the Aggies' rise from '96 humiliation to '98 exhilaration—Steve McKinney, Dat Nguyen, Rich Coady, and Warrick Holdman, to name a few. But without much of a doubt, it was Campbell who was the driving force and vocal leader of the 1998 Aggies.

It was Campbell who scoffed at the notion of a "moral victory" following the close loss to Florida State in the 1998 season opener. It was Campbell who often dragged tacklers with him, igniting fans and teammates. It was Campbell who teammates both admired and feared. And it was Campbell, the 1998 Aggie Heart Award winner, who vowed following the close loss to Texas at the end of the '98 season to rally the troops in time for the Big 12 championship game against Kansas State.

"Dan was the heart and the voice of that team," recalled Nguyen, the Lombardi winner and first-team All-American in 1998. "Dan set the tone with practically everything he said. Not everyone loved Dan, but they respected him."

Most certainly, there was a fear factor involved in Campbell's leadership style. At 6'5", 255 lbs., Campbell's mere presence commanded respect. While Campbell possessed an entertaining sense of humor, his intense glare could be intimidating to friends and foes alike.

When the pads were on, Campbell had no problem reminding teammates it was time to focus and take care of business. But off the field and away from campus, Campbell went out of his way to make certain that team unity was constantly being built.

"I got made fun of so much, but I had so many parties on weekends I couldn't even begin to recall how many there were," Campbell said. "I would invite everybody on the team practically every weekend. And that was our time to bond. It didn't matter what class you were or what skin color you were. We would get together and just bond as a team.

"I think there was a unity that developed from those weekends together that you can't really get just by being together for practices, workouts, meetings, and so forth. You know, the coaches can only do so much. The team has to have a bond to carry you through those difficult times. We got behind in a lot of games [in 1998], but we were all on the same page, and we all knew each other personally, not just as football players but as friends. You can't underestimate what that did for us. Chemistry is invaluable."

Campbell is still studying and developing chemistry within the football locker room.

In 2012, he completed his second year as a tight ends coach with the Miami Dolphins. He originally joined Tony Sparano's staff prior to the 2010 season, serving as a coaching intern/ offense. Campbell joined the Dolphins after 11 years of playing experience with the Giants (1999–2002), Cowboys (2003–05), Lions (2006–08), and Saints (2009).

And those who know him well predict even bigger things for his future.

"There's no doubt in my mind that he will eventually be a head coach," former A&M star Hunter Goodwin said of Campbell. "He not only understands the game, he also knows how to punch all the right motivational buttons. I think he will make a great head coach."

91 The McKinney Brothers

For as long as they live, Mike and Lou Ann McKinney will always have emblazoned on their minds the memory of their awestruck little boys standing in the south end zone at Kyle Field and gazing at the size of the Texas A&M football players as they entered the field. Steve McKinney, the oldest boy in the family, was probably seven or eight, while his brother, Seth, was four years younger.

Both McKinney boys were mesmerized by the aura of Kyle Field, the pageantry of game days in College Station, and the enormity of the A&M players.

"Seth used to tell me, 'I wish I could be that big,'" recalled Mike McKinney, who served as chancellor of the Texas A&M University System from 2006–11. "I said, 'Well, I hate to tell you this, but you probably won't be.'"

Mike was wrong. Both Steve and Seth had their big wishes granted. Both boys grew to be monstrous young men, and they both played huge roles in A&M's success for many years. From 1995 to 2001, the A&M football program underwent many changes. The Aggies switched conferences, dramatically altered the capacity of Kyle Field with the north end zone facility, and began fundraising efforts for an overhaul of other football-related athletic facilities.

Through all the changes, however, one of the constant components of Aggie football during that era was that a McKinney was always one of the anchors of the offensive line.

Steve McKinney earned high school All-American honors as a tight end and defensive end at Clear Lake. He arrived at A&M in 1994 and played along the defensive front. But as a sophomore in '95, McKinney switched to the offensive line where he started the final nine games of the year. McKinney started every game throughout the rest of his collegiate career, earning first-team All-Big 12 honors as a senior in '97.

Steve was also particularly influential in helping the Aggies bounce back from a 6–6 season in 1996, the first year of the Big 12, to win the school's first Big 12 South Division title in '97. The hard-nosed, outspoken, and fiery McKinney was nasty...in a really good way. Many teammates feared McKinney, but they all respected his work ethic, toughness, and tenacity on the field.

Steve, who now owns several McDonald's restaurants among his business endeavors, was chosen in the fourth round of the 1998 NFL Draft by the Indianapolis Colts, and he later played with the Texans, Dolphins, and Seahawks before retiring in 2008.

Seth McKinney never played with his older brother at A&M, but there was never much of a doubt that he would follow Steve's footsteps to Aggieland. Seth played in high school at Austin Westlake with Drew Brees, and the duo led the Chaparrals to the 1996 state championship. Long before that, Seth announced his intention to attend A&M, and he did it right after the Aggies lost the opener of the '96 season to BYU.

"I wanted to prove my allegiance to A&M even after a tough loss," recalled Seth, who had a much more low-key demeanor as a college student than Steve. "I guess I briefly considered some other schools, but I knew all along that I wanted to be an Aggie. I remember back in the early 1990s getting autographs from Greg Hill, Antonio Shorter, and Bucky Richardson. I would always wear my 12th Man jersey and dream about playing for the Aggies."

He did much more than merely play; he often dominated opponents.

Seth redshirted during Steve's senior season and started as a freshman in 1998, playing center on the only A&M team to ever win a Big 12 title. While Seth wasn't as outspoken as Steve, he was often more overpowering as a blocker. Seth was a two-time All-Big 12 selection in 2000 and '01, and he was a third-round pick of the Dolphins in 2002. He also played with the Browns and Bills before moving back to College Station with his wife, Paige, and the couple's three daughters. In 2013, the couple opened a business together called Crossfit Aggieland.

Ty Warren

On Monday, September 23, 2002, Texas A&M senior defensive lineman Ty Warren awoke before dawn, began his weight workout at 6:00 AM, attended classes from 8:00 to 11:00, went to two tutoring sessions, spoke at the football press conference in the afternoon regarding being named the Big 12 Defensive Player of the Week for his efforts in the Virginia Tech game two days earlier, spent much of the afternoon watching video tape of Louisiana Tech—the upcoming opponent on the A&M schedule—and made it home in time to change for his wedding.

Yes, his wedding. At about 4:30 that afternoon, Warren was married to the former Kesha Drayton, whom he first met back in their days at the Bryan Boys and Girls Club.

"That was a long day," acknowledged the big-hearted Warren. "But it was also a very meaningful day I will never forget. We thought about waiting to get married [until he was drafted in April 2003], but it was important to us to do it then."

It's always been important to Warren to do the right thing. While waiting for the wedding would have probably made financial sense, it did not seem like the right thing to do. Warren's first daughter, Brionna Michelle, was born on July 24, 2002, and each time Warren gazed into his infant daughter's eyes, he felt more certain about not waiting for a big wedding ceremony.

More than 10 years later, Brionna is now the oldest of four kids, and her father has won two Super Bowls with the New England Patriots and compiled 374 career tackles and 20.5 sacks in nine NFL seasons (through 2012). But through all the lifestyle changes and years, Ty Warren remains completely committed to always doing the right thing and serving as a role model to his kids.

Warren, who turned 32 in February 2013, has suffered a rash of injuries since 2009. He missed all of 2010 with a severe hip injury, and after signing with the Broncos in August 2011, he missed the '11 season and played just one game in '12 due to severe triceps injuries. He may have played his final game, but what a legacy he has built in the NFL.

Warren was a fan favorite in New England for many years after the Patriots selected him in the first round of the '03 draft. His teammates selected him as a captain in '07, and prior to Super Bowl XLII in February 2008, Patriots head coach Bill Belichick praised Warren's work ethic, attitude, and leadership. Warren was a warrior on the field, and he has consistently been a hero in the community.

For many years, Warren and Kesha, through their First and Goal Foundation, have bought Thanksgiving meals for underprivileged families and helped other needy families shop for Christmas gifts for their kids. Warren's heart is even bigger than his 6'5", 300-lb. frame.

"I've been on the other end of the spectrum, being raised in a single-family home where what we earned wasn't enough to provide for me and my two siblings," said Warren, who was raised by his single mother and maternal grandparents in Bryan. "I've always wanted to do what I could to help others."

He's done that ever since his rookie season in '03. He's made a huge difference annually in communities from Boston to Bryan, donating funds, time, and compassion to thousands of people in need.

Ty Warren was a run-stopping force in the middle of A&M's defense from 1999–2002. (Photo courtesy of 12th Man Magazine)

Warren, who is the nephew of former A&M star running back Curtis Dickey, accounted for 144 tackles and 13 sacks during his career at A&M (1999–2002). He was an All-Big 12 pick in '02, and he probably would have been an All-American as a senior if not for an injury late in the year. But he says he left A&M with unfinished business.

In 2010, Warren made national headlines by forgoing his $250,000 off-season workout bonus so that he could instead return to A&M to finish his degree, which he earned in 2011.

"I try to put my kids in the best educational system possible, and I think there is something to be said for their father, who has been blessed to play in the NFL and do something he's loved to do, going back and finishing what he started," said Warren, one of the most widely popular and respected A&M players to ever play in Aggieland. "In the big picture, I think it was important for me to do the right thing."

That's always been Warren's lifetime motto, and there's probably no better role model to ever come out of A&M.

John Roper

In a preseason 1988 interview with a writer from *Sports Illustrated*, Texas A&M outside linebacker John Roper simply couldn't contain himself. The reporter purposely asked the question, and Roper, the Aggies' intimidating, bloodthirsty, seek-and-destroy outside linebacker, answered it honestly.

Maybe a bit too honestly.

"I don't just like to sack a quarterback," Roper said. "I like to hear the air come out of the quarterbacks when I hit them."

Yikes. Even when Roper was just talking, he had a way of putting the fear factor into opposing QBs.

Roper came to A&M from Houston Yates High School where he enjoyed a stellar prep career and was the 1983 Touchdown Club of Houston Defensive Player of the Year. He redshirted in '84 and became a key component of three straight Southwest Conference championships from 1985–87.

He was good in a reserve role early in his career, but he was practically unstoppable on the edge in R.C. Slocum's attacking defensive style in his junior and senior seasons. As a junior in '87, Roper led the Southwest Conference with 15 sacks, recorded a team-high 104 tackles, caused two fumbles, and broke up three passes. He was named the SWC Defensive Player of the Year and a first-team All-American.

Along with fellow outside linebacker Aaron Wallace on the other side, Roper fully embraced the "Blitz Brothers" nickname that became well-known regionally and even nationally.

"We couldn't wait until third down," Roper said in 2009 when he was inducted into the Texas A&M Letterman's Association Hall of Fame at the annual Burgess Banquet, "because we knew what Coach Slocum was going to call."

Slocum, then the defensive coordinator for the Aggies, called on Roper and Wallace often. Roper's 15 sacks in 1987 tied Ray Childress for the second-best single-season total in Texas A&M history.

As a testament to his consistency, Roper matched that total as a senior in 1988 when he entered the year as one of the leading candidates for the Butkus Award and appeared on the cover of *Dave Campbell's Texas Football* with the Texas Longhorns' Eric Metcalf.

Unfortunately, the '88 season was a disappointment for the Aggies as A&M went 7–5 in Jackie Sherrill's last season in Aggieland. That's one of the primary reasons that Roper did not figure prominently in the national awards that season, as Alabama's Derrick

Yale Lary's Second Choice Worked Out Well

From 1894–2012, Texas A&M produced plenty of college superstars, All-Americans, and NFL standouts. But at the time of this writing (prior to the 2013 season), only one Aggie had ever been inducted into the Pro Football Hall of Fame in Canton, Ohio.

It's not the name most average fans would easily guess.

Robert Yale Lary was a three-sport star at Northside High School in Fort Worth, but the 5'11", multitalented athlete loved baseball far more than he liked football or track. As a high school senior in 1949, he won a city-wide baseball competition that provided him with the opportunity to travel around the Texas League, taking batting practice with each team in hopes of landing a pro contract.

While his hitting skills were impressive, his fielding abilities were not yet at a professional level, so Lary somewhat reluctantly accepted a scholarship to play football and baseball at Texas A&M University.

He was very good on both fields, earning first-team All-SWC honors as a defensive back in 1951 and as an outfielder in '51, as well. Most A&M fans who watched him play expected Lary to receive a chance to play professionally in one sport or the other, but no one—including Lary—could have anticipated that he would enjoy a Hall of Fame football career.

Lary was selected by the Detroit Lions in the third round of the 1952 NFL Draft, and he blossomed as a defensive back with the Lions. He had a nose for the ball, breaking his nose five times during his career and making 50 career interceptions. He anchored Detroit's fearsome defense of the 1950s.

His professional career was interrupted by two years of army service (1954–55) at Fort Benning, Georgia. After returning to Detroit, Lary became one of the best punters to ever play the game. He won NFL punting titles in 1959, 1961, and 1963, and he missed another one in 1962 by only 3.6". In 1960, Detroit's opponents averaged less than one yard per return on his punts.

Lary was named All-Pro four times and played in nine Pro Bowls, including his last game as a professional in 1965. He was inducted into the Pro Football Hall of Fame in 1979.

Thomas won the '88 Butkus, and Auburn's Tracy Rocker won the Lombardi.

But Roper was tremendous once again, and he finished his tenure at A&M with the second-most career sacks (36) in school history, one behind Jacob Green. One year later, Wallace surged past both Green and Wallace to take the all-time lead with 42 career sacks.

Roper was considered a possible first-round draft pick in 1989, but he instead fell to the second round and the Chicago Bears. Roper played four years with the Bears, displaying flashes of greatness, but he also battled injuries. He was traded to the Cowboys prior to the 1993 season and played well early in the season for the '93 Cowboys, who went 12–4 and won the Super Bowl.

But in October 1993, Roper was cut by head coach Jimmy Johnson after the coach discovered that Roper was taking a nap during film sessions.

"John didn't fit in," Johnson said. "He's a good football player and has the ability to make plays, but we expect certain things from our players."

94 Jerrod Johnson

Following a 2010 spring practice, Von Miller was asked whether he believed teammate Jerrod Johnson was a legitimate first-team All-Big 12 candidate. Miller practically leapt onto his soap box, answering quickly and convincingly.

"Jerrod Johnson is a stud," said Miller, who earned All-American honors in the 2010 season. "He is my kind of quarterback. I don't just think he is an All-Big 12 candidate—I think he's a Heisman Trophy candidate. He's that good."

Perhaps Johnson could have been that good in 2010…if only he'd been healthy.

Johnson emerged as the starting quarterback in the third game of the 2008 season after taking over for an injured Stephen McGee. Then in 2009, Johnson shattered numerous school records, including throwing for 30 touchdowns and registering six 300-yard passing games. He became the first player in A&M history to surpass 3,000 yards through the air, and he directed the first A&M offense to generate more than 6,000 yards in a season.

But the Aggies went 4–8 in '08 and 6–7 in '09, so Johnson did not receive the national recognition that he would have garnered if he'd been playing on a better team. As A&M prepared for the 2010 season, however, the Aggies believed they were on the verge of a breakout year partly because of how well Johnson had played.

In the 2009 regular season finale against No. 3 Texas, for example, Johnson passed for 342 yards and four touchdowns while adding 97 rushing yards. He was every bit as impressive as Davey O'Brien winner Colt McCoy in the game, but unfortunately, he also injured his shoulder against the Horns.

The shoulder injury bothered him in the Independence Bowl and required off-season arthroscopic surgery that caused him to miss spring practices. Regrettably, the shoulder wasn't right in 2010, either. Johnson struggled with his throwing motion early in the season and was ultimately replaced midway through the year by Ryan Tannehill.

Despite not finishing the year as a starter, Johnson ended his career as the leading passer in A&M history with 8,011 yards. No other Aggie has thrown for as many as 7,000 yards in his career. Johnson also holds school records for career completions (650), attempts (1,109), and career TD passes (67), among others.

Beyond the numbers, Johnson will forever be appreciated by A&M fans because of his love for the university and the way he responded after being replaced by Tannehill. Even though he was no longer the starting QB in the second half of the 2010 season, he remained a strong leader and played an emotional role in the six-game winning streak that ended the season.

He loved A&M too much to act any other way. Johnson's late father was former Texas A&M wide receiver Larry Johnson, who passed along his love for Aggieland to his son. The younger Johnson, a multiple sports star at Humble High, first committed to A&M basketball coach Billy Gillispie.

Johnson was a scout team quarterback on the '06 team that went to the Holiday Bowl, then he tried to play basketball immediately afterward.

"When I got to basketball, we were a top team in the country, one game away from conference play," said the articulate and engaging Johnson. "That was Acie [Law's] senior year, and being around him was special. But just before we went to the NCAA Tournament that year, I knew I needed to make a decision."

He decided to quit basketball and focus entirely on football. Johnson saw action in five games in '07 as McGee's backup and led the offense to touchdowns on six of the eight drives in which he played under center. His future looked incredibly bright...and it undoubtedly would have been so much better if not for the shoulder injury.

95 Corey Pullig

Corey Pullig is not the most dynamic or memorable quarterback in Texas A&M history. He didn't throw the prettiest passes or juke defenders in the open field with his speed or elusiveness. And he wasn't particularly outspoken in the media.

But from 1992–95, Pullig embodied the lyrics from the popular DJ Khaled song that debuted in 2010, 15 years after Pullig last played for the Aggies: "All I do is win."

It's the name of a song. It was also the name of Pullig's game, as the Deer Park native started 33 career victories at A&M, which was only matched during that span only by Nebraska's Tommie Frazier.

Based on career yards, Pullig also left Aggieland as the most proficient passer in A&M history, throwing for 6,846 yards in an era when the Aggies sometimes viewed "pass" as a four-letter word.

Yet for all he accomplished, Pullig may be the most under-appreciated quarterback in A&M history. In the age of Internet message boards, Pullig is rarely mentioned in the same breath—or paragraph—as Johnny Manziel, Ryan Tannehill, Jerrod Johnson, Kevin Murray, Bucky Richardson, or Edd Hargett.

That probably has everything to do with timing. Murray, Richardson, and Hargett each captivated Aggieland by leading A&M to SWC titles, while Manziel won college football's ultimate prize, Johnson shattered the school's passing records, and Tannehill became the first Aggie QB to ever be selected in the first round of the NFL draft.

But Pullig was rarely applauded for quarterbacking the Aggies to the 1993 and '94 Cotton Bowls and guiding A&M to an unde-feated record in '94. Instead, he received considerable criticism for A&M's struggles in 1995. The Aggies entered that season with national title aspirations, but those dreams died in the Rocky Mountains. The No. 3 Aggies lost to No. 7 Colorado on September 23, 1995, and A&M never fully recovered from the frustrating loss to the Buffs.

Meanwhile, Pullig was labeled by some as a quarterback who couldn't win the big one.

In reality, though, Pullig played well enough to win most of the big ones, including that one. It was his supporting cast that literally dropped the ball. One receiver dropped a potential touchdown pass and another A&M wideout let a pass slip through his hands, resulting in Pullig's lone interception of the day and a CU touchdown in the Buffs' 29–21 win.

"It bothered me at the time, but I don't hold grudges," Pullig said of the negative press and harsh labels. "Looking back, I wouldn't have traded my time at A&M for anything. I don't think it ever came out publicly at the time, but I thought about transferring after my sophomore season when Bob Toledo was fired. He and I were really close, and I really respected him as a person. But I'm glad I stayed, and I'm glad I graduated from Texas A&M."

So were his teammates. What often goes overlooked about Pullig was his presence on the field. He wasn't a rah-rah, boisterous leader in the locker room. Nor was he an animated press conference speaker. But he definitely commanded the respect of his teammates.

"Corey Pullig was a great performer on the field and a great role model off the field, as he is today," said former Minnesota Vikings tight end Hunter Goodwin, Pullig's college roommate. "In my opinion, he is probably one of the most underappreciated athletes in the history of A&M. All he did as a quarterback for us was win, win, and win. I think maybe our fans were spoiled by how many wins we were getting at that time. I know that as a player who played with him for several years, he had the utmost respect of his peers. His leadership in the huddle and off the field is something that we looked up to and admired. He was the field general."

Pullig still holds an impressive rank and is still a leader of men. In 2012, Captain Pullig celebrated his 10th year in the Marine Corps, serving as the Military Justice Officer of the 3rd Marine Aircraft Wing at Marine Corps Air Station Miramar. In 2007, he was deployed in support of Operation Iraqi Freedom.

After deploying, he and his family were stationed in Houston where he was the Executive Officer in Charge of Recruiting. During that time, his wife, Lisa, gave birth to son Owen Patrick Pullig while Corey was still in Iraq. Soon after Pullig returned home, Lisa gave birth to the couple's second child, Luke Thomas Pullig.

96 Charlie Moran

The first official game matching the Texas A&MC Farmers against the University of Texas—known at the time as "Varsity"—came in 1894 at Austin's Hyde Park where a playing area was roped off and fans were charged $1 for admission. In that first game, A&MC won the coin toss. That was the Farmers' highlight of the day.

A&MC fumbled the opening kickoff, and Texas rolled to a 38–0 win. It was a sign of things to come.

By the end of the 1901 season, the Farmers had gone through six different coaches and had produced an overall record of 15–13–2. But against Texas, A&MC was 0–7 and had been outscored 157–0. The Farmers finally beat Texas on November 27, 1902, but by the end of the 1908 season, Texas had run its all-time record against the Farmers to 14–1–2, so the cadets ran head coach N.A. Merriam out of town during the 1909 season.

Enter Charles B. Moran, the first coach to truly captivate the Corps of Cadets. Moran, who had come to A&M as an assistant under Merriam, was also the first coach to whip Varsity on more than one occasion, giving the cadets a reason to rejoice.

After taking over following the second game of the 1909 season, Moran guided the Farmers to wins over Haskell Institute and Baylor, setting up a showdown with Texas in Houston. The '09 Farmers went to Houston filled with Moran's confidence and command. And A&MC whipped Texas, 23–0. The Farmers followed up that milestone victory by manhandling Trinity, beating Oklahoma, and beating Texas again.

In one season, Moran had delivered two wins over Varsity— one more than the previous 15 years combined.

"[Moran] led in the fashion of certain Marine Corps officers," Caesar "Dutch" Hohn wrote in his 1963 book, *Dutchman on the Brazos*. "Moran wouldn't order you, he'd show you, leading the way. He came to football practice in full regalia himself, ready to play. He brought hard-nosed football to Texas A&M."

In his first two years at A&MC, Moran went 15–1–1, including three consecutive wins over Texas. But Moran was accused by many opponents, including the lawmakers in Austin and Texas Exes, of cheating…or at least stretching the rules of the era.

Moran, who had once umpired baseball in the National League, was accused of bringing in "ringers" (professional players posing as students). He was also accused of recruiting ringers from the Haskell Indian Institute near Abilene, Texas. Taking advantage of a state rule that allowed a player to suit up for a team if he'd gone to classes on campus for just one day, the Indian players would routinely arrive on campus on Thursday night, attend classes on Friday, and play on Saturday.

Technically, it wasn't illegal, but the fact that the Farmers were suddenly beating Varsity—and virtually everyone else—rankled the folks in Austin. Following the 1911 season, Texas took a firm stance and refused to play A&MC. Texas broke off relations with A&MC from 1912–14, although the Farmers continued to win under Moran. In his first four years, Moran's teams went 29–3–1, and his six-year record of 38–8–4 gave him a career winning percentage at A&MC of .800, the best of any coach in school history who stayed at least three years.

Unfortunately for Moran and the Farmers, not playing Texas for three years took its toll on the A&MC budget. Hohn wrote that the break in competition "all but sent the [A&MC] athletic department into bankruptcy."

Reluctantly, A&MC and Moran parted ways following the 1914 season. His legacy, however, was far from over. In 1915, the first year of the Southwest Conference, Texas and A&MC resumed football competition with the Farmers under the direction of E.H. Harlan. From his home in Kentucky, Moran wrote to the A&MC players, encouraging them to "beat those people from Austin. If you still love me and think anything of me, then beat Texas."

The Farmers did just that, forcing 12 Varsity fumbles in the Farmers' 13–0 win. It was A&MC's fourth win over Texas in the last five meetings, and that score would literally be branded into the minds of both schools.

In the 1916 A&MC-Texas game in Austin, Texas paraded its first steer mascot around the stadium. The Longhorns won 21–7, and the victory over A&MC meant so much to Texas fans that the following spring, in observance of an annual March meeting of Texas Exes, UT officials decided to brand the mascot with the final score of that game.

News of that decision traveled quickly to Aggieland where six A&MC students decided to beat the Texas Exes to the branding

The State Fair Shocker of 1914

State fairs have long been known for their bizarre sideshows and supernatural sights. But most often, the snake charmers, the sword swallowers, the two-headed animals, the world's largest or smallest humans, and other oddities are confined to controlled, enclosed stages and booths.

But one of the most bizarre events in the history of the Texas State Fair was not predicted, advertised, or expected. On October 31, 1914, head coach Charlie Moran, in his final season as head coach at Texas A&M, took the Aggies to Dallas to play LSU.

In the afternoon of Halloween, LSU took a 9–7 lead over the Aggies into the locker room at halftime. But Moran's boys produced perhaps the most incredible second half of football in Aggie history after the intermission.

A&M's Dudley Everett returned the opening kickoff of the third quarter for a touchdown. "After that, everything we tried turned out right," recalled Dough Rollins, a player on that team and a future coach at A&M.

Indeed, A&M could do no wrong the rest of the way. Everett ran for three more touchdowns and passed for another, while Rollins scored on a 65-yard run and an interception return while also kicking a field goal. When it was all said and done, the Aggies had scored 56 unanswered points en route to a 63–9 win.

It was such a bizarre second half that the game was eventually featured on *Ripley's Believe It or Not!*

iron. According to the 1974 book, *The Twelfth Man*, six A&MC students gathered in Waco and drove to Austin to meet with Abe Bull, who had been a student manager on the 1915 A&M team. Bull led the group to an Austin stall, where the mascot was kept. The seven Aggies wrestled the steer to the ground and branded "13–0" in its side…the score of the Aggies' 1915 win over Texas.

Texas officials later made the best of the situation, changing the "13" into a "B." The dash was shaped into an "E," and a "V" was inserted in front of the 0. The mascot became known as "Bevo," which was also the name of a near beer at that time.

97 Stealing Tim Brown's Towel

In 2008, Warren Barhorst authored the book, *Game Plan: The Definitive Playbook for Starting or Growing Your Business*, which provides a step-by-step blueprint for entrepreneurs seeking to start or grow a business. Barhorst begins by stressing the importance of goals, pointing out that ordinary men and women can accomplish extraordinary things if their dreams are big enough.

Barhorst considers himself an expert on that subject, as he's built an entrepreneurial empire called "Iscential," starting with one insurance office in the Houston area and expanding to a group that, as of 2013, included more than 40 offices throughout Texas, 100 associates, and in excess of $50 million in sales.

His business has been a storybook success. But his career wasn't the first time he achieved seemingly far-fetched goals. Long before he began building his brand, Barhorst realized the power of dreams on the football field at Texas A&M, going from an unknown, unheralded walk-on to national headliner overnight.

He even stole the spotlight from Heisman Trophy winner Tim Brown in the 1988 Cotton Bowl as well as part of Brown's uniform.

Barhorst began his collegiate career at Stephen F. Austin in Nacogdoches, and he didn't even believe he was good enough at the time to play football for the Division I-AA Lumberjacks.

"When I came out of high school, I weighed about 180 pounds, and I was scared to even give it a shot at Stephen F. Austin," Barhorst said. "I had spent much of my life dreaming about playing college football, and I'd spent countless hours envisioning myself at A&M. I even had two older brothers and a sister who had preceded me at A&M. But fear stopped me in my tracks.

After two years at SFA, I had gained about 30 pounds and a little courage. At the urging of my older brother, Alan, who'd come back to A&M to work on his master's degree in mechanical engineering, I transferred to A&M and also decided to try out for the 12th Man Kickoff Team."

That team, consisting of 10 walk-on players and one scholarship kicker, had gained national recognition under head coach Jackie Sherrill, and approximately 350 A&M students tried out for it the same year Barhorst did (1986). Barhorst made the squad, but he was unable to participate in any games because of the transfer rules. In 1987, however, he was a key contributor on the kickoff team as A&M rolled toward a third consecutive SWC title.

One of the interesting angles of the 1988 Cotton Bowl was the matchup between the 12th Man Kickoff Team and Brown, who had established a Notre Dame school record for the most career kickoff return yards.

"We looked at it as a real challenge to keep him under control," Barhorst said of Brown. "He was from Dallas, and he had played high school ball against one of our defensive backs, Chet Brooks. Before the game, Brooks told the 12th Man Kickoff Team guys that if we had the opportunity, we should steal Brown's belt towel. They had played each other in high school, and Brooks told us that stealing his towel would drive Tim crazy. After we had taken a 28–10 lead in the fourth quarter, I got my chance."

Brown nearly broke the kickoff for a big gain, but Barhorst made the tackle and acted on Chet's idea. Barhorst swiped the towel and started running off the field while trying to stuff the towel in his pants. Before he made it to the A&M bench, Brown jumped on his back, tackling him and grabbing back his towel.

The infuriated Brown was flagged for a 15-yard unsportsman-like conduct penalty, and the Aggies went on to win the game 35–10. On the following day, newspapers across the country featured pictures, headlines, and stories with Barhorst's name prominently in print. Years later, in a survey conducted by the A&M Lettermen's Association, Barhorst's thievery was voted as one of the most memorable moments in Aggie sports history.

"Here's the lesson to be learned," Barhorst said. "Stealing someone else's ideas and then implementing those strategies on your own can propel you into the spotlight beyond your wildest imagination. I'm living proof of that. And not just in the sports arena. I've been stealing ideas from other successful business people for many years, [and] I built my insurance agency from the ground up.

"On average, I still receive about four or five reminders per week that many Aggies still remember me taking Brown's towel. During December 2009, Houston sports radio talk show host John Lopez had me on his show and—as a total surprise to me—he also had Tim Brown on the air. It was a great interview, and Tim was awesome. He's long forgiven me for taking that towel, and I hope that I can now consider him a friend."

 **Reveille**

Texas A&M is not unique in possessing a canine mascot. The University of Georgia, Washington, Mississippi State, Fresno State, Louisiana Tech, Tennessee, and various other universities feature dog mascots that appear on the sidelines of football games or courtside at basketball games.

By and large, though, the stories of how they came to be the mascots of their particular schools are not extraordinary. At Tennessee, for example, the students in 1953 simply decided they wanted a live mascot. They conducted a poll, and at halftime of a football game, Smokey, a blue tick hound dog, was selected from the other hounds as Tennessee's mascot by the ovation level of the crowd.

The original Reveille, on the other hand, earned her way into the hearts of Aggieland. Besides, Reveille has always played an integral role in the day-to-day life of the student body she represents. She is a visible part of university life throughout the year. She doesn't simply show up at a stadium on game days or appear only at school fund-raising functions.

Reveille doesn't live on campus in a cage; she resides inside the dorm. Reveille attends classes with the students every day of the week, jogs with Company E–2, is the highest-ranking member of the Corps of Cadets, and is welcomed into campus dining halls and restaurants throughout the community.

In Aggieland, Reveille is to the doggie domain what Lady Diana or Jacqueline Bouvier Kennedy were to femininity in their time icons of class, grace, charm, style, beauty, and nobility.

Of course, the Reveille of today—a regal, pure-bred collie—is much different than the original mutt who earned her way on campus. The most popular and widely accepted version of how the first Reveille arrived in Aggieland recounts how several Aggies returned from a Navasota bar late one night in 1931 and accidentally hit a small puppy with their Model T. The cadets backtracked and found the dog wounded but wagging her tail. According to legend, they put the dog in the car and smuggled her back into the dorm, violating university policies regarding pets in the rooms.

As the story goes, the cadets bandaged the pup that night, and the dog awoke to the sound of the bugler blasting "Reveille" the next morning, barking enthusiastically at the music. Her reaction to the song inspired the cadets to begin calling her Reveille.

That's the neat, tidy tale that has been told, printed in official university publications, and immortalized throughout the

Reveille VII poses in front of stuffed Reveille dolls at the MSC Bookstore.
(Rusty Burson photo)

years. But dying men literally went to their graves willing to take a lie detector test to prove that they either knew or participated in other origins of Reveille. Files in the Texas A&M University Archives contain dozens of versions crediting at least 10 different sources with bringing Reveille to campus. Through University Archives and other published reports, at least 36 people publicly claimed to have been involved in bringing the first Reveille to campus.

Regardless of how she actually arrived, it's clear Reveille, who was 40-something pounds of pure compassion, warmth, and unconditional love, was definitely not an ordinary dog. After being initially smuggled into the dorms and being fed with table scraps from the mess hall, Reveille, for all intents and purposes, was turned loose. But instead of wandering away, she watched and learned. She roamed the 4,000 acres of the A&M campus at will and quickly learned that anyone in a khaki uniform was her friend, while those in civilian clothes should be viewed in a less trusting light. She also learned when and where to appear for "mess formation," marching with the cadets into mess hall for meals.

In the public eye, perhaps the first Reveille's No. 1 legacy was established at a football game during the fall of 1932 when she made the first formation with the Aggie Band on Kyle Field, prancing in front of the drum major to the roar of the crowd. Reveille seemed to feed off the energy of the band and frolicked to the approval of the crowd. It was an impromptu move by the dog, but it was also the moment that officially earned her the designation as the school's mascot.

On January 18, 1944, Reveille breathed her last breath. The lovable mutt, who seemed to sense that she had a higher purpose to serve than most other dogs, died in the A&M Veterinary Hospital. On the following day, the entire Corps of Cadets, several hundred former students who were back at A&M for military training, and numerous residents in the Bryan–College Station area poured into Kyle Field for a full military funeral for Aggieland's little lady.

She was laid to rest in an infant's casket just outside the north end zone of the stadium. Her death and funeral made international news, reaching servicemen around the world and generating a flood of consoling telegrams, letters, and flowers. Since that time, every other Reveille has been buried outside the north end zone of Kyle Field.

Other Reveilles have also made their mark on football game days. Reveille II, a Shetland shepherd, practically guarded the field during the Aggie Band's halftime performances. And today, Reveille continues to be one of the must-see attractions, especially for young fans visiting College Station on game day.

"She's one of the great ambassadors of Texas A&M," said 1997–98 mascot corporal Jeff Bailey. "There's no telling how many kids first fell in love with Reveille before they knew anything else about Texas A&M."

99 The Hurricane Game of 1956

As he entered the Kyle Field locker room following pregame warm-ups, senior linebacker Jack Pardee grabbed a towel, wiped the sweat from his crimson-colored cheeks, looked down at his drenched jersey, and wondered how many pounds he might lose during an unseasonably hot and unmercifully humid afternoon.

"It was miserable heat and humidity," Pardee later recalled. "We were playing TCU, which was a really good team led by [Heisman Trophy hopeful] Jim Swink. Kyle Field was sold out, and since we were on probation, we looked at the TCU game as our bowl game. But after we took the field for warm-ups, all anyone could think about was how darned hot it was out there. We had no idea that the weather was going to change so dramatically."

Mother Nature soon stole the spotlight of a showdown that matched defending SWC champion and No. 4 TCU against Bear Bryant's No. 14 Aggies (3–0–1 at the time). The game started innocently as TCU appeared to take the early lead under clear skies when Swink dove into the end zone. But a penalty nullified the score, prompting a roar from the crowd.

The next roar came from the clouds, not the crowd. In an instant, the heavens opened up and the weather turned from scorching to scary.

"And all hell broke loose," said A&M running back John David Crow.

The force of the storm was so violent that the contest became known as the Hurricane Game. The wind whipped so hard that flags were shredded, light standards swayed, and approximately 150 planes at nearby Easterwood Airport were damaged. Sheets of rain were so thick that it was difficult to see across the field. Officials had to hold the ball in place on the ground after marking it because it would float away if not secured.

Yet, the game played on. The Aggies fumbled deep in Horned Frogs territory late in the first half, and TCU took over at the A&M 8. That set up one of the most debated series in SWC history.

Swink carried on three of the next four plays. Twice, it appeared to TCU players that Swink scored, but officials ruled differently and the half ended in a scoreless tie. In the days and weeks following the game, numerous articles were written about whether Swink scored or not. The TCU players and coaches swore that he did.

"But he didn't," Crow said. "I was right there, and I saw it all. He did not score."

At the half, Bryant shouted for assistant coach Elmer Smith, but there was no reply. After a few puzzling moments, Bryant realized Smith had been left to weather the violent storm on a platform in the end zone. The phone lines between the field and the press box had been knocked out by the storm. While looking for an edge, Bryant instructed Smith to climb onto a tiny platform at the end of the stadium so he could chart TCU's line splits.

"Elmer took a student manager with him and climbed on top of the platform," said former Houston sportswriter Mickey Herskowitz. "Even during the storm, he would chart plays on a piece of paper, stick the paper in a sock with a rock in the bottom of it, and drop it to the student manager who would run it over to Coach Bryant. It was almost as dark as night, but Elmer stayed up there, clinging to the pole as the wind howled. At some point, in the excitement of the goal-line stands, the student manager stopped running back and forth and the ladder was blown over. It wasn't until about 10 minutes into halftime that Bryant realized Elmer was still out there, hanging on for dear life."

Smith was rescued, and the storm blew through the second half. TCU converted an A&M fumble into a touchdown, but the Frogs missed the extra point, leaving the door open for the Aggies. Following a Don Watson interception in the end zone, the Aggies took full advantage of the opening.

Late in the game, Watson took a pitchout, pulled up short of the line of scrimmage, and hit Crow in the end zone for a seven-yard score. A&M's Loyd Taylor converted the extra point, giving the Aggies a 7–6 victory that propelled A&M to the '56 SWC title. Afterward, a reporter asked Bryant if the game had gone according to plan. He replied, "It went according to prayer."

Billy Pickard

According to most honest assessments, Billy Pickard has essentially been a cantankerous old man since he was a young man. But even though he has often been volatile through the years, Pickard's heart is filled with pure love for Texas A&M and Kyle Field.

He began his love affair with Kyle Field in 1952 when he first stepped on campus as a freshman student. He has basically been working in and around Kyle Field ever since. His responsibilities have changed since his student trainer days under Bear Bryant in the mid-1950s, and Pickard has held various titles through the decades. He's been A&M's Director of Athletic Facilities, and he's been officially retired for several years [as of 2013], but he's still around, still showing up at 6:00 AM on most days, and still considered the "caretaker of Kyle Field."

"I've always considered myself a company man," Pickard told *12th Man Magazine*'s Homer Jacobs. "You either do what the company wants or get the hell out. I'm no damned legend. How lucky can you be to be in one place for all these years, especially in athletics, and keep your health, too?"

Pickard has stayed healthy by maintaining a remarkable routine. He runs 3.82 miles along the same campus route every day and takes an office power nap—sitting up in his chair—each day, as well. He still shows up at 7:00 AM on each home game day, barking out instructions and overseeing the operations of many aspects of the game-day routine.

Pickard has worked under the leadership of A&M football coaches such as Bryant, Gene Stallings, Emory Bellard, Tom Wilson, Jackie Sherrill, R.C. Slocum, Dennis Franchione, Mike Sherman, and Kevin Sumlin.

During that time, he has seen more at Kyle Field than most Aggies could ever imagine…and not just memorable games.

Pickard has witnessed the spreading of ashes at Kyle Field numerous times. The AstroTurf in the 1970s to mid-'90s was not a deterrent. "The strangest funeral we ever had was a family that scattered the guy's ashes from one goal post to the other," Pickard said. "When we went to practice, [former defensive coordinator] Bob Davie said, 'Billy, what's this stuff?' I told him those were ashes. He said, 'What? That's a human being?' I said, 'What's left of him.' He turned and ran into the tunnel and said he wasn't coming back until I vacuumed."

Pickard has also encountered many couples who have attempted to join the "50-yard-line club" or who tried to "score" where the Aggies score. "It was Jackie Sherrill's first spring practice, and we had AstroTurf," Pickard said. "In the middle of the field is a wine glass and some 'leftovers.' Jackie says, 'What the hell is this?' I asked him what it looked like. He said, 'You mean, they do that out here? What are we going to do about it?' I told him it happened all the time. But since we have gone to grass, it doesn't happen quite as often. We don't arrest the kids, but we threaten them and take their names down."

Pickard has certainly seen it all while watching Kyle Field expand from a single deck to a stadium that packed in more than 90,000 fans for a game in 2010. He will probably also be around when the construction begins on the renovation of Kyle Field.

"I feel very fortunate," Pickard said. "I have never taken anything for granted. If you are going to get paid to do a damn job, get your ass out of bed and do the job. If it comes time when you can't do it or don't want to do it, go find something else to do."

Sources

Books

Bucek, Roy, and Rusty Burson. *Roy Story*. Bloomington, IN: AuthorHouse, 2012.

Burson, Rusty. *Texas A&M Football Vault*. Park Ridge, IL: Whitman Publishing, July 15, 2009.

Burson, Rusty, and Cathy Capps. *What it Means To Be an Aggie*. Chicago, IL: Triumph Books, 2010.

Burson, Rusty. *Texas A&M: Where Have You Gone?* Champaign, IL: Sports Publishing L.L.C., 2004.

Dent, Jim. *The Junction Boys*. New York: Thomas Dunne Books, 1999.

Evans, Wilbur, and H.B. McElroy. *The Twelfth Man: A Story of Texas A&M Football*. Huntsville, AL: The Strode Publishers, 1974.

Jacobs, Homer, and Rusty Burson. *Standing Together: The Spirit of Kyle Field*. Nashville, TN: The Booksmith Group, 2008.

Jacobs, Homer. *The Pride of Aggieland*. New York: Silver Lining Books, 2002.

Nguyen, Dat, and Rusty Burson. *Dat: Tackling Life and the NFL*. College Station, TX: Texas A&M University Press, 2005.

Walker, Doug. *Aggies: A Century of Football Tradition*. New York: Professional Sports Publications, 1994.

Zwerneman, Brent. *Game of My Life: 25 Stories of Aggies Football*. Champaign, IL: Sports Publishing L.L.C., 2003.

Magazines

Burson, Rusty. *12th Man Magazine*. Volumes 1–18. 1996–2013.

Jacobs, Homer. *12th Man Magazine*. Volumes 1–18. 1996–2013.

Moses, Sam. *Sports Illustrated.* November 19, 1979. "The Dickey Dilemma: Texas A&M Running Back–Sprinter Curtis Dickey must decide between signing with the pros and training for the Olympics."

Looney, Douglas and Carlton Stowers. *Sports Illustrated.* September 27, 1982. "Whatever Happened To The Sugar Land Express?"

Newman, Bruce. *Sports Illustrated.* September 5, 1988. "The Top 20."

Newspapers

Keyho, Megan. *The Battalion.* January 22, 2009. "Boys and Girls Clubs receive pennies from Sul Ross statue."

Schmitt, Mary. *The Milwaukee Journal.* December 11, 1987. "Legend of Johnny Holland."

The Associated Press. *Los Angeles Times.* October 19, 1993. "Cutting-Room Floor: Roper Released After Snoozing During Film."

Glauber, Bob. *Newsday.* September 8, 1992. "Huge settlement didn't ease pain for Krueger."

Websites

Mandel, Stewart. SI.com. November 11, 2012. Texas A&M's upset win at Alabama could have far-reaching SEC impact.

Aschoff, Edward. ESPN.com SEC Blog. November 10, 2012. Aggies run over Tide to prove they belong.

Drehs, Wayne. ESPN.com. November 26, 2003. Follow the yell leaders.

Texas A&M University. Remembering Bonfire.

About the Author

Rusty Burson is currently the associate editor of *12ᵗʰ Man Magazine* and vice president with the 12ᵗʰ Man Foundation. Burson, a 1990 graduate of Sam Houston State, began his professional career as a newspaper sports reporter, columnist, and editor at *The Galveston Daily News* and later joined the staff of the *Fort Worth Star-Telegram*, where his "general assignments" title also earned him the right to cut and paste together the agate page in the wee hours of the morning.

After leaving the newspaper industry, Burson took a role in municipal public relations and then became an editor for numerous business publications in the Dallas-Fort Worth area. Burson finally landed a job he loved in 1998 at the 12ᵗʰ Man Foundation, the fundraising organization for Texas A&M athletics. In that capacity,

From left, Payton, Rusty, Summer, Vannessa, and Kyleigh Burson in the spring of 2013. (Photo courtesy of the author)

he's spent the last 15 years in sports marketing, public relations, and journalism.

He lives in College Station with his wife, Vannessa, and the couple's three children—son, Payton, and daughters, Kyleigh and Summer. Burson has authored 13 previous books, mostly associated with Texas A&M athletics. But he has also written books associated with the Texas Rangers (the baseball team, not the law enforcement officers), the history of hockey in the Lone Star State (it's actually much longer than most people realize), and several business publications (thanks to some of the fabulously successful donors at the 12th Man Foundation).